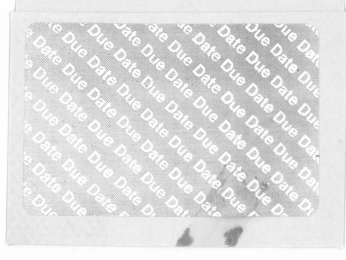

LAST ESSAYS
Mainly on Anglo-Irish Literature

'Out of Ireland have we come.
Great hatred, little room,
Maimed us at the start.

'Remorse for Intemperate Speech'

LAST ESSAYS

MAINLY ON ANGLO-IRISH LITERATURE

Thomas Rice Henn

BARNES & NOBLE
BOOKS
10 East 53d St. New York 10022
(a division of Harper & Row Publishers. Inc.)

Copyright © 1976 The Estate of T. R. Henn

Published in the U.S.A. 1976 by
HARPER & ROW PUBLISHERS, INC.
BARNES & NOBLE IMPORT DIVISION

ISBN 0-06-492819-5

Library of Congress Catalog Card Number 75-41582

Printed in Great Britain

PUBLISHER'S NOTE

I first met Tom in 1964 when I was at Trinity College Dublin. I was much helped by his enthusiasm and the support that he gave me in my work then and later. He remained a true friend after I left T.C.D. and went into publishing, and when I decided to enter the Irish Literary field by publishing the Coole Edition of Lady Gregory's writings, Tom did me the honour of becoming its joint editor with me. His advice and aid over the years have been invaluable: he was always able to improve an essay with apt quotations or some point from his vast knowledge.

Everyone in the field of Anglo-Irish literature and literature in general are in his debt and the world is poorer for his passing. I and many others have lost a mentor and close friend. How great my debt is, I cannot adequately put into words, for he influenced me more than he knew.

Colin Smythe

CONTENTS

FOREWORD

The theme of these essays is the complexity and the ambivalence of Anglo-Irish literature; itself a mirror-image, though a limited one, of the Irish situation, and beyond.

With a few exceptions none have been published before. Most of them arose out of the pattern of events from 1959-71; which included my time as Director of The Yeats International Summer School at Sligo, and two subsequent visits (by the courtesy of Professor Norman Jeffares, who succeeded me) in 1970 and 1971. Within that period there were the Yeats Centenary celebrations of 1965, the founding of IASAIL[1] in 1970, and the Synge Centenary of 1971. Each brought forth the appropriate volumes of critical essays and papers.

It seemed a suitable moment to make a selection from my own essays and lectures during this period. The provenance of these is noted in each instance, but they have been extensively revised and expanded beyond the limits, and perhaps the limitations, which were originally appropriate.

I must also acknowledge my debt to Professor L.C. Knights and the late Professor Ure, for the Memorial Lectures given at Bristol and Newcastle respectively in 1965, and from which certain materials and views have been embodied in the essay called 'The Centenary Yeats'.

At Sligo it became customary that I should give the opening and closing lectures of the School. Out of a score or so, I have chosen those that now seem to me to be relevant; and, in one instance, prophetic. But my debt is greatest to the company of scholars who came from all countries during those years, and who came (as I like to think) because they found the atmosphere congenial, and the surroundings well-fitted to friendship and the commerce of knowledge. The financial rewards were, at best, negligible; and that is why The Yeats Society did not, during those years, attempt to publish any collections of these lectures. There was thus no question of copyright; we expected and hoped that much of the material originally brought forward there would be incorporated in books and journals after the 'proving ground' of Sligo.

My main debt is to my friends who came there. Of these I name

1 The International Association for the Study of Anglo-Irish Literature.

no more than a few; Brendan Kennelly of Trinity College, Dublin: Denis Donoghue: Tom Parkinson of Berkeley: Jon Stallworthy: George Mills Harper: Francis Warner: Marion Witt: Curtis Bradford: Lawrence Lee: Graham Hough: Muriel Bradbrook (Mistress of Girton): Richard Ellmann: Robert Speaight: Oliver Gogarty: Kevin Nowlan: Francis Byrne: Roger McHugh: F.A.C. Wilson: Hiroko Ishibashi: Robert O'Driscoll: John Kelly: Ann Saddlemyer: Robin Skelton: Kathleen Raine: Edward Malins: Raymond Lister: D.E.S. Maxwell: Walter Starkie: Austin Clarke: Donald Davie: Northrop Frye: Norman Jeffares: Oliver MacDonagh: J. R. Mulryne: Oliver Edwards: Daphne Fullwood. Above all, I recall with admiration and affection the blind and saintly Father Bodkin with his unrivalled knowledge of the background of the period. Indeed, no Municipal Gallery would contain these portraits.

The first essay was never delivered as a lecture, and is not cast in that form; though the possibility, and relevance, of the title had been considered some years before. It was written against the background of increasing violence in the North, of bombs and murder carried — as on several previous occasions — into England. Again, the intention was to underline the theme of the ambivalence, throughout the century, of the attitude of, and to, the Anglo-Irish race to which I belong. I had, long ago, written of *'The Study of Hatred'* in a chapter of *The Lonely Tower*. What I said then has been strengthened by George Harper's penetrating essay called 'Intellectual hatred and intellectual nationalism'.[1] I am aware that it will cause, in certain quarters, some offence: but perhaps no greater than the accusations I have faced, long ago, over other matters that seemed wholly innocent. Nor, when 'my seventieth year has come and gone', is there cause to fear reprisals, since the threats of violence (and occasional attempts to practise it) were among the earlier memories of my childhood; and later, from Maoists and anarchists, in the peaceful context of Sligo. So one remembered:

> They must to keep their certainty accuse
> All that are different of a base intent;
> Pull down established honour; hawk for news
> Whatever their loose fantasy invent
> And murmur it with bated breath, as though
> The abounding gutter had been Helicon
> Or calumny a song . . . [2]

One may be forgiven at this time for remembering the hymn:

> Hora novissima, tempora pessima sunt:
> Vigilemus.

---

1   *Theatre and Nationalism in Twentieth Century Ireland*, ed. Robert O'Driscoll, (Toronto, 1971, and London.)

2   'The Leaders of the Crowd'.

ACKNOWLEDGEMENTS

I acknowledge with gratitude permission for the following: To Messrs. Macmillan for the quotations from W.B. Yeats's *Collected Poems, Collected Plays, Autobiographies, Essays and Introductions* and *Memoirs;* for the Essay "The Rhetoric of Yeats' from the selection *In Excited Reverie* (ed. A. Norman and K.W.G. Cross); for a quotation from *Last Poems* by Jon Stallworthy.

To The Oxford University Press for the quotations from Synge's Prose Writing.

To Rupert Hart-Davis for *The Letters of W.B. Yeats* (ed. Wade) and for Shaw's *The Matter with Ireland*.

To Messrs. Faber and Faber for *The Experiences of an Irish R.M.* and *The Senate Speeches of W.B. Yeats*.

To the Editor of *The New Yorker* and to Professor Denis Donoghue.

To the Editor of *The Illustrated London News* for a review of Iain Hamilton.

To Colin Smythe Ltd for quotations from Lady Gregory's works.

To The Dolmen Press for certain material in an essay in the Synge Centenary Papers, 1971.

To the British Academy for parts of The Warton Lecture, 1965.

To Trinity College, Dublin, and to the Editor of *Hermathena* for the Trinity Monday Discourse 1971.

I owe a particular debt to Captain Diarmuid MacManus for much information about political and military events; and Dr. Nicholas Grene who kindly read the book in its early stages, and who made many valuable suggestions. Among those who seem to me to have written wisely and profoundly on the politico - military aspects are Robert Kee *(The Green Flag)*, J. Bowyer Bell *(The Secret Army)*, and Edward Norman *(A History of Modern Ireland)*.

To others whose work or ideas I may have inadvertently used I offer my apologies.

I am indebted (as every teacher must be) to my own pupils from whom I have learnt over the years: among them Patric Dickinson, Peter Allt, F.A.C. Wilson, Edward Engelberg, Hiroko Ishibashi, Hilary Pyle, John Kelly, David Esterley, Nicholas Grene: most of all, perhaps to that little group — I. A. Richards, Eustace Tillyard, Leonard Potts, Paul Sinker who met in each other's rooms in the 1930s to read *'The Winding Stair', 'Words for Music Perhaps'* and *'Last Poems'* as they came out.

The publishers wish to thank John and Mary Andrew for all their work on the proofs, and their help in many other ways, since Tom Henn's death.

I
'THE PLACE OF SHELLS'
$i

I have taken the title of this lecture from the Irish form, *Sligeach*,[1]
which means 'the Place of Shells'. Most of us, on holiday at some
watering-place or wandering on the shingle of some lake-shore, are,
instinctively, beachcombers; we look down to see what may be found,
left by some ancient or modern tide. We may use them for decoration
or just collect; and we have been familiar from childhood with the
sea-roar which we can hear from the convoluted heart of certain larger
shells, which is no more than the echo of our own restless blood. The
heraldic emblem of Sligo is a shell, a scallop shell, which (as you will remember) is also the badge of the pilgrim to some great shrine, or to the
Holy Land. May I remind you of Sir Walter Raleigh's poem?

> Give me my scallop-shell of quiet,
>   My staff of faith to walk upon,
> My scrip of joy, immortal diet,
>   My bottle of salvation,
> My gown of glory, hope's true gage;
> And thus I'll take my pilgrimage.
>
> Blood must be my body's balmer;
>   No other balm will there be given:
> Whilst my soul, like quiet palmer,
>   Travelleth towards the land of heaven;
> Over the silver mountains,
> Where spring the nectar fountains;
>   There will I kiss
>   The bowl of bliss;
> And drink mine everlasting fill
> Upon every milken hill,
> My soul will be a-dry before;
> But after, it will thirst no more.

I would not press the thought that you and I are among the pilgrims
to this place, though, indeed, we may well have needed our 'staff of
faith' to journey here. My purpose this morning is to invite your attention to the historical energy and momentum that lie behind the centuries; to the turbulence of history that Yeats saw, and which he has
dramatized in his characteristic way to inflame his imagination; and to
offer some thoughts about the growth of a poet's mind — remembering Wordsworth's *Prelude* — in relation to the music of this countryside in his youth.

1. Sligo: The Opening Lecture, 1968.

§ii

If we stand on the summit of Knocknarea — and you must carry a stone with you on your climb to put on the Cairn, else you will have no luck afterwards — we can watch the scene and the centuries mirrored as in some kind of glass. First and perhaps simplest, consider the geographical features which have made Sligo a centre of supreme military importance. For it is a point of passage; like Thermopylae, or Marathon, or the Plain of Esdraelon in Palestine. It stands across one of the great highways between Connaught and Ulster. There are at most only two strategic points where an army can cross; one, at low tide only, just below the lower bridge, and a second just above the upper bridge, opposite the Imperial Hotel, and not far from the spot (so one account says) where the warrior Eoghan Bel has stood upright in his grave, holding his spear ready, throughout fourteen centuries. For a defending or invading force, the eastern flank is protected by Lough Gill, and, if you are a soldier, you will see that the road round the Lake is commanded by hills and wooded country eminently suitable for ambush. Westward, of course, you are protected by the Atlantic, moody and terrible; as the galleons of the Armada found when they were driven on the shores of Lissadell Bay. The estuaries, bays, sandbanks make it quite impracticable to outflank your enemy by naval power, as in the Elizabethan and Cromwellian combined operations on the coast of Cork. Between Sligo and Drumcliffe the great plain — where Yeats saw Constance Gore-Booth ride.

'Under Ben Bulben to the meet' —

is a perfect arena for war-chariots, and the set-piece battles of the heroic age. It was on the slopes of Ben Bulben that the Irish version of Venus and Adonis was enacted, the story of Diarmuid and Grania, and Diarmuid was slain by the enchanted ravaging boar. (That story and its symbols are as old as history.) You will see from Drumcliffe the cliffs that lie to the North-West of the Mountain, over which a troop of cavalry were driven to their death. And at least one whom I have spoken with has heard, on a foggy day on the plateau on the summit (you can reach it from the Waterfall at Glencar) the thunder of phantom hoofs, and seen the mountain grass spring up again, a few yards away, after the horsemen had passed. This, I think, stuck in Yeats's mind, for he mentions it twice:

> *What marches through the mountain pass?*
> *No, no, my son, not yet;*
> *This is an airy spot,*
> *And no man knows what treads the grass.*[1]

1. 'Three Marching Songs', II. Yeats notes that airy 'may be an old pronunciation of eerie'. But we also use it of 'high places', and of their numen.

It was a cavern in the side of Ben Bulben that the giant Dhoya, marooned by the Formorian galleys in the Bay of the Red Cataract (you can visit the great waterfall that plunges into the head of Ballisodare Bay, and remember that Kingsley's Tom the Water-Baby came down the Yorkshire hillside 'like a salmon over the Fall at Ballisodare') sought refuge in a cave beside Glencar, and for a time lived in great happiness with a mysterious daughter of the underworld.[1] And I fancy that it was on the Drumcliffe plain, on the edge of Lissadell, that the tiny, exquisite and difficult poem, 'The Death of the Hare' came to being:

> I have pointed out the yelling pack,
> The hare leap to the wood,
> And when I pass a compliment
> Rejoice as lover should
> At the drooping of an eye,
> At the mantling of the blood.
>
> Then suddenly my heart is wrung
> By her distracted air
> And I remember wildness lost,
> And after, swept from there,
> Am set down standing in the wood
> At the death of the hare.

You remember, too, Yeats's tribute to Constance Gore-Booth:

> What voice more sweet than hers
> When, young and beautiful,
> She rode to harriers?[2]

§iii

It is a wild history on which you can look from the great cairn — which will never, I think, be excavated, and we shall never know if Queen Maeve really lies there or, as some think, at Croghan — or perhaps from the tower of one of the churches. Let us glance at it for a moment. Sligo was invaded in A.D. 1235, and granted to Fitzgerald, an ancestor of the Earl of Kildare. He built a castle here in 1245, to serve as a base for his intended conquest of Tir Chonail; and founded the Dominican Priory, whose splendid ruins you can visit. Within half a century that castle was destroyed *four* times by either O'Connor or O'Donnell. In 1310 a new castle was built, and a new town laid out, by Richard de Burge, the Red Earl of Ulster. Five years later the castle in its turn was destroyed by O'Donnell. In 1414 town and friary were destroyed by fire, but were rebuilt about 1416 by Friar Brian Mac-Donagh. In 1470 Red Hugh O'Donnell took the castle once again from O'Connor: in 1595 the English, Leicester's forces, besieged the castle and destroyed the friary. In 1641 both town and friary were

1. See *John Sherman and Dhoya*, ed. R.S. Rinneran: (New York, 1969).
2. 'Easter, 1916'.

sacked by the Cromwellian general, Sir Frederick Hamilton. In 1645 the town, having presumably recovered from the sacking, was captured by Sir Charles Coote. In 1689 it was seized by the Williamites under Lord Kingstown, but was retaken by Patrick Sarsfield for King James. Then there seems to have been a period of the Pax Britannica, and of loyalty to the Hanoverian cause. At least we know that Sligo raised three whole regiments of militia — all with carefully designed and differentiated uniforms, for your soldier is a vain sort of animal — to repel the French invasion of 1798. I mention these odd fragments from the past only to suggest to you what a long and turbulent history this peaceful market town has had; that there are many buried dead about us; and that any place that has been much fought over seems to acquire (as we should expect) the character of being saturated with witnesses from the unseen world. It was Jack Yeats, the painter, who told me of an ancient piece of myth: that where a great mass of fresh water meets the sea by way of a short river as it does beside us here, a kind of magic is generated and spread upon the whole neighbourhood.

$iv

These may be some of the influences of place on a poet's mind, and on the kind of poetry he writes. Of this general effect, one accepts it, I think, unconsciously. That the Lake District should have fired so greatly Wordsworth's imagination, that Cowper's poetry and his hymns should be related to the placid and comfortable waters of the Ouse, that Crabbe's grim realism should spring from that 'bold surly savage race' that you still find round Aldeburgh — we take these for granted; just as we see the praise of rivers in the song of poet after poet: Spenser, Marvell, Joyce. We accept (but cannot prove) how much of Warwickshire moulded Shakespeare; or how generations of writers have found themselves and their art in Greece and Italy:

> . . . Whence turbulent Italy should draw
> Delight in Art whose end is peace,
> In logic and in natural law
> By sucking at the dugs of Greece.[1]

But there is a world of difference between reading of the genius of place and meeting that genius face to face with the words moving in our minds. When I first saw the Cave of the Cumaean Sybil, on the south of the little sandy bay where Aeneas landed from Troy, its many mouths were filled with German machine-guns sited to fire on the beach; and it took on a strange metaphysical dimension from them. To see the long-extinct volcano of Solfatera where the ground rings hollow like a drum, with its pools of boiling mud, and to realize that you are walking on one of the classic entrances to Hell, is to understand, suddenly, something of

1. 'To a Wealthy Man . . .'

Dante. So in the Bible, above all books. One does not, I think, begin to realize the complexity and energy of its poetry until one has studied a little the geography of the Holy Land; and begun to understand how the great images of its poetry spring naturally from the clash of the desert with the valleys that stand so thick with corn; of the importance of the springing well and the waters of comfort; of whirlwind and thunder; of sudden storms upon Galilee; of the imagery of the threshing-floor and of the scattering of nations like chaff before the wind; of Israel's fear of the sea and of its great beasts that take their pastime in it. These, and a thousand other images, even to the bulwarks that defend or break the nations, spring naturally out of the very inscape of place. "Perhaps, also, to understand fully these poems one needs to have been born and bred in one of the western Irish towns; to remember how it was the centre of your world, how the mountains and the river and the woods became a portion of your life forever; to have loved with a sense of possession even the roadside bushes where the cotters hung their clothes to dry. That sense of possession was the very centre of the matter. Elsewhere you are only a passer-by, for everything is owned by so many that it is owned by no one".[1]

But there is another strange feature of the Sligo setting which has not, I think, been mentioned before.

All poetry is built on rhythm. Rhythm is in its turn built on stress, tone, pitch. All poets savour the juice of living words upon the tongue, 'bursting joy's grape against his palate fine' in Keats's phrase. All poets have a stock of words which they taste and relish to a special degree. If we were to take any three or four of the many poets here this morning, and analyse their vocabularies, we should find that they had in common the same large stock of words, but that they were in fact differentiated by a small individual vocabulary, perhaps a hundred or so, of words peculiar to themselves; of which they had, as it were, taken personal possession. We recall immediately some that Yeats was fond of: *wild* (in the Anglo-Irish songs;) *arrogant; fanatic; ungovernable; murmuring* and *murmur; withered; ignorant; mummy (*and *mummy-dead); gear; magnanimity.* We should note the polysyllabic proper names that he tastes, rolls upon the tongue: 'the Great Smaragdine Tablet', 'the Mareotic Lake', 'Guidobaldo', 'Michelozzo', 'Rhadamanthus; as well as the place-names round about Coole recorded in the poems of *The Seven Woods.* The list could be much extended. So, too, the nonce-words, those that are only used once in the poet's vocabulary of 10,666 words. But it is of the place-names of Sligo that I want to speak now.

I suggest that he found here a great reservoir of words that sing,

1. From an essay by Yeats on William Allingham: quoted by Finneran. Preface to *John Sherman and Dhoya* (v. Supra). For Palestine, see T R Henn, *The Bible as Literature,* London, 1971).

as it were of themselves. When we start to write Greek and Latin verse
we are taught to keep note-books of phrases, proper names, synonyms,
embellishments of expansions, even clichés, that have once been part of
some ancient fabric of poetry, whether hexameters or elegiacs or
sapphics; and which may legitimately be used again in our 'imitations'.
To use these broken fragments of masonry with wit and precision, and
to take advantage of allusions and references in depth, was once the
mark of the scholar and of the poet who had served his apprenticeship
among the classics. But if, as I believe happens here, the 'names' contain
in themselves special rhythmical and musical qualities, if their complex
musical values include this tone, pitch, stress so that they sing of their
own accord, not only can the poetic craftsman weave them into his
verse, but they may even suggest a sort of running tune, strongly
remembered from childhood, out of which, or on which, the rhythm of
a poem may grow.

Let us glance at some examples:
> Saddle and ride, I heard a man say,
> Out of Ben Bulben and Knocknarea.
> *What says the Clock in the Great Clock Tower?*

Now *Knócknaréa* is, technically, the foot known as a cretic, common in
Irish place names because the unstressed syllable -na (of) (as in
Lugnagall) is a frequent link between two heavier stresses. *Bén Búlbên*
on the other hand is the foot that prosodists call a *bacchius,* a kind of
rhythmic foil to the *cretic,* sliding off on to a lighter stress after its two
explosive but level initial stresses: *Ben Bulben.* But to my ear the strong
n-sounds that follow the stresses give a kind of sinister weight, as of the
very mountain itself: and these *n*-sounds are echoed (but with a
different cadence, or resolution of the chord) in *Knocknarea.*

In the same way,
> The light of evening, Lissadell,
> Great windows open to the south . . .

Líssâdéll is again a *cretic,* but softened and the initial stress lightened,
smoothed down by the liquid l's and resolved in the chord by the
sibilants

Liss/a/déll

—where the drama (as it were) of the rhythm is held up for a moment
so that the final stress shall be heavier.

But in 'The Ballad of Father O'Hart' we may examine the last four
stanzas:
> And these were the words of John,
> When, weeping score by score,
> People came into Colooney;
> For he'd died at ninety-four.

> (a bad line, even with precedents from the *Lyrical Ballads)*

There was no human keening;
The birds from Knocknarea
And the world round Knocknashee
Came keening in that day.

The young birds and old birds
Came flying, heavy and sad;
Keening in from Tiraragh,
Keening from Ballinafad.

Keening from Inishmurray,
Nor stayed for a bite or sup;
This way were all reproved
Who dig all customs up.

Now I hold no brief for this poem, even if we are charitable to it as a ballad by a very young poet, whose words and rhymes do not yet 'obey his call'; but listen to the amazing variety of the place-names:

Côloónêy, technically an *amphibrach* (x/x, two short 'arms' on either side of the central stress): wholly different in sound as well as position from *Coolaney.*

Knocknarea, again,

Knócknâshée ('the hill of the faery folk') where we have lost I think something as contrasted with the sharper e-sound of *Knocknarea,* followed by

Tîrârâgh (an amphibrach like *Colooney)*

mated with the complex and lovely *Bâllînâfâd* which is almost a metrical phrase in itself, and which slides over the two light syllables in the middle, to the strong beat at the end. Or we have the more famous lines from 'The Fiddler of Dooney': where the rhythm of the names seems to prepare us for the dance-setting:

When I play on my fiddle in Dooney,
Folk dance like a wave of the sea;
My cousin is priest in Kilvarnet,
My brother in Mocharabuiee.

We may note several things: that Yeats has cribbed — quite justifiably — a famous line from Shakespeare's *A Winter's Tale,* where Florizel praises Perdita (note here too those singing names of the lovers)

When you do dance I wish you
A wave o' the sea . . .

Again, hear the 'names' (I am thinking of 'Longinus') lengthen downwards as it were to the end of the verse.

Doónêy — the ordinary reversed iambic foot, the trochee

Kîlvárnêt — which is a strongly marked amphibrach again.

Móchârâbúiee — so that we end up with a four-syllable beat:[1] and we remember that this, the rhyming of the monosyllable with a poly-

1. The pronunciation that Yeats gives in a footnote is not (in my experience) quite accurate.

syllable, is a most effective technical device in Donne and Marvell.

You will read and, better, hear many other examples:

Drómâhâire is a cretic, like *Knocknarea,* but the heavier stress on the last syllable gives it a different pitch —

He stood among a crowd at *Dromahaire.*

Inîsfrée, the 'isle of heather', is of this form, but with a light accent on the first syllable.which again gives a different effect: while in the line

Castle Dargan's ruin all lit,
Lovely ladies dancing in it.[1]

—the peculiar harshness of the open a's gives yet another effect to what is technically two trochaic feet of the order of / x | / x.

§vi

Now I do not think this is idle speculation. I believe that Yeats learnt, as so many poets have done, something of his word-music from Spenser. His essay on that poet, and the *Selection* he made from him, have received too little attention. Look where you will, you will find these singing names in *The Faerie Queene:* Phaedra, Acrasia, Scudamore, Britomart, Florimell, Cymoducê; and those of all the renaissance ghosts that jostle each other out of Ovid's *Metamorphoses.* We remember too Milton's great catalogue of the battles that saved Western civilization, as Satan reviews those superb troops of Hell:

And what resounds
In fable or romance of Uther's son
Begirt with British and Armoric knights;
And all who since, baptised or infidel,
Jousted in Aspramont, or Montalban,
Damasco, or Morocco, or Trebisond,
Or whom Biserta sent from Afric shore
When Charlemain with all his peerage fell
By Fontarabbia.

You will remember, too, Wordsworth's

To lie and listen to the mountain flood
Murmuring from Glaramara's inmost caves . . .

And I remember from my own boyhood days in Clare other mysterious and exciting names: Glenavarra, a long dark pool on a trout stream; Clondagad, with a ruined church and graveyard near it: Lough Lomáun, Thrummeragh, Clonderlaw, Gort Glas . . . Later in life Yeats fancied himself more in the Greek world, ready to

Choose Plato and Plotinus for a friend . . .

We have 'the great Smaragdine Tablet'; one can almost taste the name like a pistachio-nut; 'the many-headed foam of Salamis', the *Mareotic Lake;* all the names of poets, sculptors, painters that flit through the works: Guidobaldo, Michelozzo, Veronese, Mantegna. So *Michael Angelo,* out of which he extracts two wholly different rhythms (the second a kind of resolution of the chord)

---

1. *The King of the Great Clock Tower.* See also the Variorum Edition p. 733.

> Michael Angelo left a proof
> On the Sistine Chapel roof . . .

as against

> There on that scaffolding reclines
> Michael Angelo.

I do not think this fanciful, and your ears will note these subtle discriminations of sound: as they will have been trained to do by Shakespeare and Donne and Keats and Bridges. I suggest one caution only.

In Prosody, that ancient science, we can go just so far, and so far only. We may gesture towards stresses and accents, vowel and consonantal combinations, and sometimes profit by such exercises. Only by these devices can we explore, for instance, Milton's exquisite counterpointing, by a kind of secondary rhythm, the primary wavemotion of the iambic line. But in the last resort we have no valid language for the critical discussion of rhythm, either in verse or in the movements of a play, though we commonly speak of rhythm as an aspect of dramatic structure, of the advance and retreat of sympathy, or participation, or alienation. In poetry there is one test only: your own ear, and what it tells you of the energy, momentum, the finality of the line. And that is why part of our study should concern (as Jon Stallworthy has shown)[1] the fragments from Yeats's workshop, the perpetual testing of the music by the ear, so that we may, if we are lucky, know for ourselves that perfection and finality that we call great poetry.

$vii

And here I want to attempt to lay one heresy by the heel. Sometimes my young men come and say to me: 'O we aren't interested now in what the poem *sounds* like we're only interested in how it *looks* on the page'. Granted that interesting and perhaps valuable effects can be achieved by typography, that the angels' wings of the Seventeenth Century or the experiments of, say, E.E. Cummings, have their place, the poet has always traditionally been the singer as well as the maker, the seer, the visionary, the unacknowledged legislator of the world. And for all those the voice seems to me essential.

It is for this reason (which Yeats would have approved) that Sligo has insisted that poetry is, among much else, music; and that it should be read aloud, interpreted, discussed, in terms of the human voice. Here of course we are in a mysterious country, and a numinous one; the word or the Word, and its power, on Sinai or beside the Lake. And it may well be that we are in danger of losing our sense of the capacity of the voice to transmit meaning, and the subtle qualities of emotion that go with

---

1. *Between the Lines* (Oxford, 1963); *Yeats's Last Poems* (London, 1968).

this kind of meaning; as well as the modulations of which a most delicate instrument is, after due training, capable. We know that Yeats's own experiments with 'Speaking to the Psaltery' were not successful. Whenever I have heard attempts to read poetry against some kind of musical background I have nearly always been disappointed, even frustrated. I would even say that, with a few superb exceptions which we all know, poetry and music do not form too happy a union. A strong music allows you to get away with murder as regards the poetry itself, and this the Elizabethan song-writers knew and often exploited in those often vapid and embroidered verses for madrigals. To interpret by reading aloud has from the beginning been a feature of Sligo, not only in the public readings of Yeats, and by poets of distinction, but by the students themselves. It is the first path to understanding. And one who has helped us so greatly is Mary Watson, the best reader of poetry whom I have heard.

You see, many people come to Sligo with, as it were, empty hands, saying in effect:

'I don't know much about Ireland, or Yeats, or indeed poetry. But I want to learn about these things'.

And Sligo has always held such people to be immensely important. We have not yet had to impose any entrance test for registration. We have instead provided seminars, centres of discussion, where we can learn. It would have been only too easy to have pitched the standard at a level where we had only professors, university teachers, advanced students; and many Summer Schools and Conferences do just that. It seems to me entirely fitting that a proportion here are not, and do not want to become, professional students of literature or 'to cough in ink'; but have come to get to know Ireland, and Sligo, and poetry. How many is, I believe, irrelevant. No teacher ever knows where the seed falls, or what grain may chance from it. No one can ever tell when the ripples from the stones thrown into the pool will end on some farther shore.

So we have lectures at a high level (probably from the most distinguished scholars in two Continents), seminars at all levels, and discussions — wherever you will. Nothing is more admirable than the way in which students, in this sort of setting, begin to *teach one another;* and themselves learn as they do so. And if the time is short, a mere thirteen days, it provides at least some of the tools (such as those in our Bibliographies and other papers) for those who want to use them in the future. No university course, in whatever subject, can be more than a springboard for the future; unless indeed we were to return to the happy days of the Druid Bards, and prescribe a fourteen years' course for the final examination.

$viii

This is, perhaps a time at which we might reflect, not only on the Place of Shells, and on music, and poetry, and history; but upon the fact of this International School. If it had been pre-planned instead of growing up spontaneously because of the character of the Town and of the Society, it might have been more logical to have held it in one of the great Irish universities; where accommodation, administration, transport and the like would have lain to hand. It is not, I think, a secret that several American universities would have gladly caught it up into the resources of their wealth and scholarship. But this bad world seems to me (at times) to be over-planned. One of you said to me last year: 'This is the only place left where a poet can read his poetry without feeling self-conscious and over-organized.' I suspect that that was — is — only partly true: yet I know that many of the Poetry Competitions, Festivals and such-like have not been altogether happy places. I like to think that here we are still casual, carefree, with no papers to write for credits, no prizes to compete for; and that we use to the full this unique and magical and very ancient place. Yeats's father boasts to his son of his family "We have given a tongue to the sea-cliffs". But the son gave more than that to sea, mountain, lake.

§ix

Yet I would not have it thought that one of our functions is less than that of providing a meeting-place for the most advanced and famous scholars. We are indebted to very many who have taught here over the past decade, and to those who are not with us whose inheritance we use. Among these last are my own friends. Among them, Joseph Hone, the first of the Yeats biographers; Una Ellis Fermor, whose account of the Irish Dramatic Movement remains a classic; my friend and pupil Peter Allt.

§x

Yet there is so much more to be done: in scholarship, and in teaching. One day there must be a definitive edition, properly edited and cross-referenced to the plays and poems, of the Collected Prose. Remember two things; that Yeats's work, like Shakespeare's, or Milton's, or Arnold's, must be seen as a unity: and also that the volumes of essays, papers and prefaces that you know and use differ in some respects from their originals. When all the manuscript materials of *A Vision* are made available it will be possible to make a calm assessment of two important books, round whose walls so many scholars of note have marched blowing on a variety of rams' horns. When Warner's long-promised edition of Cornelius Agrippa is completed some new light will be thrown on Yeats's so-called 'magical' preoccupations being the end of the long road that led back from Blake through Swedenborg and Boehme; though I myself would question Yeats's contention that there was a time when Agrippa was familiar to every Irish farmer.

§xi

Such scholarship is vital; yet there is always the danger that Sligo might be tempted to keep its eyes fixed too closely on the sea-shore, on the smaller shells (however delicate) at its feet. We dare not view a great poet in a lesser setting than that of his time, his friends, and his age, his predecessors and contemporaries; and, ultimately, against the tradition of Western Europe. It would be only too easy, here, to fall into some kind of bardolatry, to let the appetite sicken, surfeit, die. Some form of dilettanteism is an ever-present danger. So far we have tried (and it is my hope that we shall continue) to set beside him some of his great contemporaries: 'A.E.', Synge, George Moore, James Stephens, Lady Gregory. Nor would it be wrong to predict that, as well as hearing them read their own work, some of the living here may join that tradition. Among the host of excellent books there is as yet no 'great' one to lead us through the whole labyrinth of the Irish Literary Revival. I use the word labyrinth with deliberation; for surely there is no literary movement or history of which the setting is so complex, the shifts of emphasis so pronounced with the veering of its intrinsic history and politics, the friendships and hatreds so intense. Out of that comes, of course, the energy of the time; for − again −

Out of Ireland have we come.
Great hatred, little room.

§xii

The mystery of Sligo remains, and I would have it remain a mystery: as of something which has grown organically, and (as some would say) by chance; out of a map of the 'Yeats Country' in a chemist's shop, a request for a single lecture at the height of the tourist season. It has grown as the ancient universities have done. Some years ago the Yeats Society consulted me about the possibility of a University here. As I remember, my estimate of the cost of such a foundation today closed the discussion. But indeed with all the money and plant, the power of buying professors, you cannot make a University. This some have lately found; to their cost. Here at Sligo I would like to think that men and women will continue to come, as they have come from the time of Plato's academy onwards, to sit at the feet of famous scholars and poets. That, and not a degree or a diploma, is the essence of education. Granted that the time is all too short (though this may be one aspect of its strength); granted that many things are lacking in materials and accommodation (though there may be one day a worthy building[1] for us and the Museum); there is yet this fact that, year after year, men and women of the greatest eminence have come here to make this School. And I

1. This came to pass, by the generosity of the Allied Irish Banks, in 1973.

can find no reason other than the charity of great minds, the certainty of unjealous friendship and a passion for poetry, and the genius of the Place of Shells, of its people, and of the Society who have made a reality of what was once no more than a 'surmised shape', a living memorial.

NOTE

Tom Henn died barely a week after he had finished correcting the galley proofs of this book. I was to have visited him to discuss the changes in the next essay which he wanted and we felt were necessary in the light of the Birmingham bombings and the general political situation at the time, but I left it too late. I therefore decided to leave the essay as it was, in its 1972 version, knowing that the reader would bear this point in mind. It does, however, include some notes added later.

                                                                Colin Smythe

II

THE WEASEL'S TOOTH

$i

We, who seven years ago
Talked of honour and of truth,
Shriek with pleasure if we show
The weasel's twist, the weasel's tooth.

Yeats, 'Nineteen Hundred and Nineteen', IV.

Twice in this poem Yeats uses the image of the weasel; and once,
notably, in *The Countess Cathleen:*

— though the whole land
Squeal like a rabbit under the weasel's tooth.

The animal is of some interest in the imagery of poetry, and we may
pause to consider some of the connotations suggested here. Yeats
had little natural history; the list given in the Princeton Concordance
of his 'fish, flesh and fowl' is more remarkable for its birds than for its
animals. The weasel occurs seven times. He would not have known
that there are no weasels in Ireland, since we use the term as synony-
mous with stoats, which are abundant. Nor does the monosyllabic
stoat (which is probably a *mot bas)* lend itself so readily to a metrical
line, or even to rhythmic prose. We remember Synge's *Deirdre of the
Sorrows* with its cadenced music:

I see the flames of Emain starting upward in the dark
night, and because of me there will be weasels and wild cats
crying on a lonely wall where there were queens and armies
and red gold, the way there will be a story told of a ruined
city and a raving king and a woman will be young for ever.

Clearly the beast is associated with ruins and desolation, the encroach-
ment of the wild upon what was once civilized: there is, perhaps,
Isaiah:

But the cormorant and the bittern shall possess it, the
owl also and the raven shall dwell in it; and he shall stretch
out upon it the line of confusion, and the stones of emptiness.[1]

The Biblical rhythms are those adopted and modified, as so often,
by Synge.

The polecat (also disyllabic, and with a violent explosive sound, as
opposed to the verbal sinuousness of the weasel) is used by Yeats, in a
Donne-like image, to convey a similar kind of desolation:

---

1. 34:11. N.E.B. has *horned owl* and *bustard* for the first two birds: thus re-
moving the imagination of a marsh as well as of desolate stony places, perhaps
of a ruined and deserted village or place of tombs. The weasel is mentioned
only once in the Bible, and then (together with mice) as unclean; *Leviticus*
11.29.

Conduct and work grow coarse, and coarse the soul,
What matter? Those that Rocky Face holds dear,
Lovers of horses and of women, shall,
From marble of a broken sepulchre,
Or dark betwixt the polecat and the owl,
Or any rich, dark nothing disinter
The workman, noble and saint, and all things run
On that unfashionable gyre again.[1]

Better, perhaps, to turn to Shakespeare's folklore. The weasel sucks
eggs:[2] it is 'tossed with spleen': an encounter with it is still said to
be unlucky. It may be a witch's familiar. Packs of weasels are known
as 'fairy packs', a terrestrial equivalent of the Seven Whistlers, and
the *Cwm Annwm,* the ghost-hounds of the sky. It is furtive and
treacherous:

For once the eagle England being in prey,
To her unguarded nest the weasel Scot
Comes sneaking, and so sucks her princely eggs . . .[3]

§ii

So far we have accepted as traditional connotations the beast's
furtive character, bloodthirstiness, even treachery of 'kind'. To those
familiar with its habits we may note (always remembering the inter-
changeability in Ireland of stoat and weasel) the sinuous swift graceful
movement; the preferred dens in old stone walls, or in banks; its habit
of hunting in families or packs; the characteristic scream, on a still
night, of a rabbit that has been tracked down, and fastened with that
deadly hold, used by all the ferret tribe, just above the eye.[4] It was this,
no doubt, that Yeats had in mind in the image in *The Countess
Cathleen.* James Stephens remembered that curdling night-sound
(though this was of a snared rabbit).

Little one, oh little one,
I am searching everywhere.

Go deeper, and we are aware of a compressed ferocity in the tiny body:
of a reported mesmeric quality when it confronts its prey: the blood-
lust which, like its cousin the otter, can drive it to kill far more extensively than it needs for food. And on any estate where game is preserved
one may still see, close to the keeper's cottage and his testimony to his

---

1. 'The Gyres': I do not think he realized that the polecat may also be an image
   of chastity.
2. As You Like It, II.5.13.
3. *Henry V,* 1,3,107. I am indebted, here as elsewhere, to E.A. Armstrong's
   Shakespeare's Imagination and *The Folklore of Birds.* In the former her cites
   an article (which I have not read) T.S. Duncan, *The Weasel in Myth, Super-
   stition and Religion,* Washington University Studies, XII. Hum.Ser. No.1.
   St. Louis, 1928.
4. So I have found. Others speak of an attack on the throat.

zeal, the 'gallows': bodies of stoats, rats, hawks, owls, jays: even wild
cats that, once tame, had become predators on the game. They are
dishevelled, blackened (like Villon's gibbeted thieves) by wind and sun.
And they provide yet another Marlovian image in *The Countess
Cathleen.*

> Destroyers of souls, God will destroy you quickly.
> You shall at last dry like leaves and hang
> Nailed like dead vermin to the doors of God.[1]

But we may return to 'Nineteen Hundred and Nineteen'. 'Seven years'
bring us to 1912. It is clear from the poem that, though Yeats was
emerging from a kind of dark night of the soul into the bitter clarity
of *Responsibilities,* and though there were political controversies, detractions, and slanders too familiar to quote, he saw the time, in retrospect, as one of comparative tranquility, justice, a progress towards
civilized behaviour:

> O what fine thoughts we had because we thought
> That the worst rogues and rascals had died out.[2]

By the forth stanza we are in the midst of The Troubles, the incident
described in 'Reprisals':[3] then —

> The night can sweat with terror as before
> We pieced our thoughts into philosophy,
> And planned to bring the world under a rule,
> Who are but weasels fighting in a hole.[4]

§iii

My theme is the ambivalent position of Anglo-Irish writers and
of their audiences since the turn of the century. The status, values and
credibility of those writers are still the subject of bitter and unending
controversy. Is there, in the first place, such a thing as Anglo-Irish
literature? Is it to be confined to men and women, of Irish birth and
breeding, writing in English? Is there implicit in it a further conflict of
religion, Protestant *versus* Catholic? and even a further set of social
divisions according to supposed race and lineage? Is this whole corpus
of literature in a sense illegitimate, or at least deserving of some other
title: because it should have been written in Irish?[5] or is it basically
defective because the members of the 'Ascendancy' must be *ex
hypothesi,* ignorant of the innermost soul of Ireland? (One thinks of
Lionel Johnson, Wilfrid Scawen Blunt). How far can the acceptance of

1. *Collected Plays,* p. 15.
2. 'Nineteen Hundred and Nineteen'.
3. *Variorum Edition of the Poems,* p.71. Peter Allt and Russel K. Alspach. (New
   York 1957) p.791.
4. 'Nineteen Hundred and Nineteen'.
5. It is common indictment of Yeats that he did not so write; but then he had
   not the knowledge of the language.

nationalistic ideals and politics be seen as capable of redeeming the misfortune of religion or of birth? Does Yeats's membership of the Irish Republican Brotherhood in 1897 weigh in the scales against the current indictment of him as a Fascist? Is Lady Gregory's slow but whole-hearted conversion to the Nationalist cause to be allowed to mitigate her position in the same category?[1] Was it Synge's failure to write in Irish that caused him to be accused of misrepresenting the Irish people; and how might *The Playboy* or *Well of the Saints* be re-written now in order to be described as 'patriotic'? And if the 'curse of historical memories', unsoftened by time, are indeed living, how far back does this influence persist? Do hatred and suspicion of the 'Ascendancy' go back to Dermot and Dervorgilla, or to Cromwell, or to the Flight of the Earls, or to the Rising of '98, or to the great Famine half a century later? How far does (for example) the rhetoric of John Mitchel affect the 'historical memory'?

Three million and a half men women and children were carefully prudently and peacefully slain by the English government. They died of hunger in the midst of abundance which their own hands had created; and it is quite immaterial to distinguish those who perished in the agonies of famine itself from those who died of typhus fever, which in Ireland is always caused by famine.

Further, this was strictly an artificial famine — that is to say, it was a famine which desolated a rich and fertile island which produced every year abundance and superabundance to sustain all her people and many more. The English, indeed, called that famine a dispensation of Providence, and ascribe it entirely to the blight of the potatoes. But potatoes in like manner failed all over Europe, yet there was no famine save in Ireland. The British account of the matter, then, is first a fraud; then second a blasphemy. The Almighty indeed sent the potato blight, but the English created the famine[2].

Or should we set against it an ironic passage from A.E.:

"Why, who created the spirit of this revolt? Who led the people to quit the beer which gives peace, to drink the heady wine of imagination? Who ransacked the past and revived the traditions of the nation? Who but you have found in the fairy-tales of its infancy the basis of a future civilization? The

---

1. All three — Yeats, Lady Gregory and Synge — were classified as 'Fascist traitors' by a Maoist group at The Yeats Summer School, 1970.

2. John Mitchel, *History of Ireland*, p.243. See the essay on *John Mitchel and the Jail Journal* by Thomas Flanagan *(Irish University Review*, Autumn 1970) and compare Cecil Woodham-Smith. *The Great Hunger*. (London, 1962); Edwards and Williams, *The Great Famine* (Dublin, 1956).

For a balanced account of the historical circumstances, see Edward Norman, *A History of Modern Ireland*, Chapter V, (London, 1971).

wine has gone to people's heads. What are they doing? Thinking they are building a heaven on earth while they are fighting like devils."[1]

English misrule, corruption, iniquitous taxation — these are favourite
themes so often disinterred, and the bones elevated, or re-buried, under
conditions of high emotion.

What is the estimate, in nationalist terms, of the writers who were
not of the Ascendancy, yet among the greatest — Shaw, O'Casey, Joyce,
Beckett? It is legitimate to attack Yeats for having lived half his life
away from Ireland? How are these delicate and tenuous threads to be
disentangled?. And how much of the debate is necessary, or fruitful, and
why should modern Ireland, and the Irish in America, return to it so
constantly and with such venom?

Memories are kept alive, inflamed, by historical myth. Much of the
Irish history taught in the South is slanted (as in all such circumstances)
to emphasize the ethics of liberation. The murder of the British Officers
on 'Bloody Sunday' has been translated into an epic action, the judicial
execution at great personal risk of British spies, and its title transferred
to an event in Londonderry on 30th January 1972, which was followed
by the burning of the British Embassy in Dublin. We should not fail
to notice the conjunction of the adjective with 'Sunday', and its
religious overtones. Every destructive act is romantically and unilater-
ally exploited. The compulsive psychological power of the *Todentrieb*,
so efficiently cultivated in the German songs of both World Wars, is
conspicuous in two centuries of Irish Ballads. It is not without significance that George Moore and Shaw both turned to Wagner, and Yeats
to Nietzsche. On one level there is Yeats himself:

> 'But where can we draw water',
> Said Pearse to Connolly,
> 'When all the wells are parched away?
> O plain as plain can be
> There's nothing but our own red blood
> Can make a right Rose Tree'.[2]

On another:

> St. Mary in Heaven has written the vow
>   That the land shall not rest till the heretic blood,
> From the babe at the breast to the hand at the plough

---

1. *The Interpreters,* p.13, (1922). As regards the beer, it will be remembered that
   Meredith, Housman, Chesterton made the same democratic point.

2. 'The Rose Tree'. This was apparent in the Resistance Movements, and their
   aftermaths, in France and Italy, 1943-5. The myth of the blood-sacrifice was
   a feature of Nazism: as well as of many African tribes. A well-known writer
   in Ireland recently went so far as to invite a comparison with the Christian
   doctrine of the Atonement.

Has rolled to the ocean like Shannon in flood.[1]

Mr. Conor Cruise O'Brien, in a recent broadcast, paid tribute to the popular ballad in its power to keep alive patriotic and violent emotions. So Yeats:

> It is the attempt to repeat an emotion because it has been found effective which has made all provincially political literature — the ballad movement of Germany, for instance - so superficial.[2]

It will be rememberred that Bishop Ulfilas refused to translate for his Gothic parishioners the books of Kings: lest they should stimulate unduly the warlike propensities of his people. And Bernard Shaw remarked of *Cathleen ni Houlihan:* "When I see that play I feel it might lead a man to do something foolish".

§iv

Let us face reality. There is among all nations a habit as well as a tradition of military or para-military action. A tiny country with a negligible army and a ludicrously small navy has no warlike activity for half a century. It has not been prominent in what might be termed its altruistic military expeditions.[3] A nation that has been accustomed to some form of warfare, whether tribal or national, for a thousand years does not take kindly to conditions in which the possibility of war is remote, and in which little attempt is made to proffer to the more adventurous spirits a legitimate military career. It was for this reason that Yeats wrote:

> If human violence is not embodied in our institutions the young will not give them their affection, nor the young and old their loyalty. A government is legitimate because some instinct has compelled us to give it the right to take life in defence of its lands and its shores.

> Desire some just war, that big house and hovel, cottage and public house, civil servant - his Gaelic certificate in his pocket - and international bridge-playing woman, may know that they belong to one nation.[4]

It is a wholly irresponsible statement, yet it emphasizes a technique that has been constantly used by politicians and dictators, as a method of consolidating, or diverting, popular sentiment.

1. Kipling: 'The Mutiny of the Mavericks'. The story (from *Life's Handicap)* concerns the attempted subversion by an American 'secret society' of an Irish regiment in India.
2. *Memoirs*, p.247, 1972 (ed. Donoghue). London, 1972.
3. There were, in fact, two: O'Duffy's Brigade of Blue Shirts which attempted to fight for Monarchist Spain in 1934: and a smaller body of 200 which fought effectively (for half of them were killed) for the Republican Forces. Both were subjected to ecclesiastical censure.
4. *On the Boiler*, (1938), p.30. The passage is also of some interest in relation to the philosophy of neutrality.

That there was, and is, a fierce and noble idealism in this continuous conflict is beyond question. That it thrives on myths, that it is nourished on every spring of emotion that man's intellect can imagine or release, is clear. This vision of a United Ireland, freed at last from three or five hundred years of the influence of the invader; unified in its ancient language, religion and social aspirations; drawing strength and inspiration from a common mythology, is an attractive one. It lends itself readily to an emotional exploitation of the past: by the demagogue, the rhetorician, the politician. It has been, and is, an attractive target for highly-trained mercenaries of many countries, as well as for idealists of many political shades. It is an admirable subject for scientifically-designed propaganda, and indeed the I.R.A. engaged as consultants a well-known commercial firm with experience of civil war propaganda, for this purpose; and the mass media have played a remarkable part in dubious support. Text-books (and much experience of subversion) have taught the guerilla how to destroy, the politician how to curse. To achieve it no sacrifice would be too great; even the lack of money, arms and men, and a voice in the councils of the world after 1918. We may quote from a responsible American writer in 1920:

> Gunmen from the United States are being imported to do killings in Ireland. That is an established fact from Associated Press dispatches.
>
> According to underground gossip in New York and Chicago, every ship that leaves for England carries its one or two of these weasels of death bound for where the hunting is good.
>
> In the Red Island they do their job of killing, collect their price and slip back to England. It is said that the price for a simple killing, such as a marked policeman, is 400 dollars and for a well-guarded magistrate or official 1,000 dollars.

This sadly topical-sounding report in fact appeared in the *Toronto Star Weekly* in 1920. It was filed from Chicago by a young reporter called Ernest Hemingway.[1]

§v

We should not underestimate the capacity for self-destruction, and its cost; the Civil War which succeeded the Treaty will serve as an exemplar in a repeating pattern. Shaw's comment on de Valera's opposition to the Free State is relevant:

> Of course he can enjoy the luxury of dying for Ireland after doing all the damage he can.[1] 'What matter if for Ireland dear we fall' is still the idiot's battle song. The idocy is sanctified by the memories of a time when there was really nothing to be done for Irish freedom but to die

---

1. Quoted from *The Daily Telegraph*, 11 October 1971.

for it; but the time has now come for Irishmen to learn to live
for their country.[1]
In the Civil War Military Courts were set up, and empowered to deal
summarily with those who had prejudiced the safety of the state. By
the beginning of 1923 there were over twelve thousand Republicans
in gaol or internment camps. We may contrast this figure with those
interned in the 1969-71 conflict, whose release, as a prior condition for
any negotiation, was made into a world political issue. Among them
were several of the younger writers who afterwards became famous.
The short story became a favourite vehicle for making public the
complexities of a divided patriotism, the ironies that are always implicit
in a civil war, and something of its pity and terror; though only Sean
O'Casey had given it voice in a major key. Seventy-seven Republicans
were executed; the most notorious case was that of Erskine Childers,[2]
shot in November 1922, while his case was still pending before the
Court of Appeal. The total of casualties on both sides at the conclusion
of the Civil War was said to be equal to those in Ulster by the end of
1972. The burning of the houses of the newly-elected Senators began;
they had to be protected, though not very effectively, by armed guards.
Gogarty was kidnapped, and his escape was celebrated in a picturesque
though inaccurate ballad. Another kidnapped Senator was 'allowed to
escape' when the Free State announced that twenty Republican prisoners were to be shot if he were not immediately released. The bridge leading to Yeats's Tower was blown up by the Republicans. He had asked
permission to remove his children to a place of safety; this was refused
but time was given to remove them to an upper room before the laying
of the mine.

$vi

The Civil War was in fact the result of the rejection by one party of
a democratic process: admittedly carried at the Treaty negotiations by
a very narrow majority: and exposed, in retrospect, to allegations of
chicanery by Lloyd George and his cabinet. The decision was subsequently endorsed by a people sickened by continuing violence and
destruction. To Yeats this was an additional cause of ambivalence. In
his view democracy had failed: not only in Ireland but throughout
Europe, where Mussolini and his 'Incomparable Fascists'[3] were in process

1. *The Matter with Ireland*, ed. Greene and Lawrence. (London 1962). p.256.

2. Contemporary malice ascribed this to the fact that he was 'an Englishman'.
   By 1973, when his son was elected President, the wheel had (with rare justice)
   returned full circle.

3. The phrase is from a letter of Ricketts to Yeats. O'Higgins, the 'sole statesman', was known to some as 'the Mussolini of Ireland'.

of attempting to redress the balance; and in that process he seems to
have believed that 'violence upon the roads' was inevitable. But as
early as 1922 the Roman Catholic hierarchy had issued a pastoral
condemning the Irregulars "for having done more damage in three
months than could be laid to the charge of British rule in three decades".[1]
Allegations of tortures and atrocities, which are endemic in all civil
or guerilla wars, were common on both sides. Not infrequently these
accusations had substance. The mutilation of enemy bodies after an
ambush at Sixmilebridge in 1919 has parallels in the campaigns of
1969-72. So, of course, in Homer. The Free State had to deploy
sixty thousand men to deal with the Republicans, rather fewer than a
contemporary estimate by a British general of the forces which would
be needed. Shaw's comment on the Civil War is worth quoting:

> In spite of these despotic measures, reinforced by savage,
> unauthorized floggings by the soldiery, armed young men and
> boys raid shops, seize bicycles and motor cars on the high
> roads, burn mansions, wreck railway tracks and bridges and
> trains, throw bombs about and keep up fusillades in the
> streets of the cities, kidnap senators and officials, and blow up
> their offices and houses, and behave generally as if they were
> in an enemy country with no Government, no police, and a
> population of imbecile cowards.[2]

$vii

It is, I think, arguable that the Anglo-Irish writer has, since the
early 1920s, been conscious of a climate that has been inimical to
creative work in his particular tradition. A number of the 'big houses'
were burned, or their occupants forced to leave the country, between
1918 and 1921. These were mainly Prostestant. 1922 saw the burning
of many of the homes of the newly-appointed Irish Senators. The
threat by the I.R.A. to shoot any deputy who had voted for the Treaty
was ineffective only because the Free State had threatened to shoot
I.R.A. prisoners in reprisal. The next decade was one of sporadic
lawlessness, particularly in the South-West; the most dramatic incident
celebrated in poetry being the murder of Kevin O'Higgins on his way
to Mass, in 1927. This, the supreme act of cowardice and sacrilege,
produced no counter-myth; only some good poems.[3] Michael Collins,
for three days head of the Irish Free State after the murder, had boasted
that no fellow-countryman would ever shoot him: he was killed in an

---

1. E. Norman, *A History of Modern Ireland.* London 1971, (See Chapter 11).
2. *The Matter with Ireland op,* cit. p. 259. This was written in March 1923.
3. Yeats's 'Death', and 'Parnell's Funeral'.

I.R.A. ambush. The cumulative reaction against this (for the Troubles smouldered on) resulted in the Blue-Shirt Movement under O'Duffy. Violence, the intimidation of voters, and the disruption of government were common: particularly in certain counties of the South-West in which such conduct was traditional.

For an example of a recurrent pattern, only too familiar in its variations, we may quote from a ballad of 1885 called 'Moonlight Attack on Curtin's House'.[1]

Now listen awhile the truth I will state,
How those moonlighting heroes of late made a raid,
Down in Castlefarm in John Curtin's place,
They entered the kitchen with masks on their face,
And boldly demanding firearms with rifles presented they
      followed his son
Right into the parlour in search of a gun,
From the top of the stairs two bullets did come,
      Which murdered the poor widow's darling.

Murder and politics have traditionally gone hand in hand:

They never told the ramping crowd to card a woman's hide,
They never marked a man for death — what fault of theirs he
      died? —
They only said 'intimidate', and talked and went away —
By God, the boys that did the work were braver men than they!

. . . . . .

The secret half a county keeps, the whisper in the lane,
The shriek that tells the shot went home behind the broken pane,
The dry blood crisping in the sun that scares the honest bees,
And shows the boys have heard your talk - what do they know
      of these?[2]

But there still seemed hope, though 1934 seems in retrospect to have marked the end of an era, not only for Ireland but for Europe. Perhaps, too, we may see in it the end of the Irish Literary Renaissance. Lady Gregory was dead and the long service of Coole was over.

§viii

The background for the Anglo-Irish writer from the period from the turn of the century, perhaps even from the 1880s onwards, was one of an emotional ambivalence and of his confrontation with intermittent physical violence that is probably unique in literary history. It included one minor and two major wars in which his loyalty was for the most part pledged, by tradition and emotion, to the country under whose laws he lived. A very large number of Irishmen fought for England in the

1. From *Irish Political Street Ballads and Rebel Songs*, Geneva 1966 (No. 88).
2. Kipling, 'Cleared'. This is dated 1890: 'In Memory of the Parnell Commission'. It will be remembered that his poem 'Ulster' (dated 1922) produced a violent reaction from A.E. himself an Ulsterman. The first line is of special interest today (I am revising this in 1972) in view of the torture of young girls.

First War. Many of them suffered for this half a century later. Until the pendulum swung back as a result of the Easter Rising the Irish Regiments were filled with anger and contempt for those who, they felt, had attempted to stab them in the back. The history of Anglo-Irish labours for Ireland has never been written, still less weighed: much of it is on record in the Protestant churches and their graveyards. The numbers of his race were steadily diminished by material and psychological pressures. One alternative was that of emigration to the more tolerant climate of England or of Scotland. Few of the great Irish writers died at home. Only one had the distinction of having his bones returned.

In 'the witches' cauldron' (the phrase is Yeats's) that had been simmering since the 1880s there were countless incidents in which the Anglo-Irish writer came under attack. It did not matter that he had raised his country's literature to a level that, for the first time since Swift and Berkeley and Burke, commanded world attention. In the new Free State it was in the nature of things that he should become isolated by his opposition to the Censorship and to other doctrines to which, by its composition and constitution and *mores,* the government was committed. The developing ideology was watched anxiously by the North; less for theological reasons than for the treatment of the vital problems of education, health, censorship, and economic welfare.

And this vision has always been simplistic; it over-rides at every turn the immense complexities of mire and blood, the very destiny of Ireland, and particularly her geographical position in Europe. The historic landmarks are well charted: the Elizabethan and Cromwellian Wars, the Plantations, the infamous Act of Union, the Home Rule Bill, and finally the necessary folly of partition: which was to ensure, as did the Yalta Conference which split Europe, that there should be no peace in our time.

The 'national consciousness' has undergone a wave-like motion, but one increasing steadily since the Eighteenth Century. It is related to the European revolutionary movements; Kossuth, Mazzini, Garibaldi, the troubles in Israel and in Cyprus, all served as graphic *exempla* for Ireland. The leaders of the Rising had pondered much on the Hungarian revolt[1] as a possible model for the future. Nor is it the prerogative of the Catholics or of the political organizations that have given it historical support. The Protestant Unionists have always been as critical as anyone of the stupidities and misgovernment of England. Shaw's Preface to *John Bull's Other Island* still contains, with all its perversity

---

1. Arthur Griffith wrote, in 1904, a book called *The Resurrection of Hungary.* Yeats described him as "a slanderer of Lane and Synge, founder of the Sinn Fein movement, first President of the Irish Free State and at that time an enthusiastic anti-cleric". (*Autobiographies, p.416).*

and its begging of the vital question, much sense, much that throws light on the situation and on the psychology of idealism. To us England was proverbial for a certain obtuseness, insensitivity, slow-wittedness, insularity. Equally it was clear that English justice and integrity offered the one valid defence against misgovernment, corruption, a breakdown of the rule of law, and what Joyce called 'The Day of the Rabblement'. It was also clear that only in England, after the mid-Nineteenth Century, could the Irish schoolboy find the kind of education that would lead on to the traditional professions - trade being still unthinkable, as Yeats naively pointed out[1] — though he might well plan to return to Ireland for his university courses, or to practise his profession.

One reason was pointed out by Yeats as long ago as 1908:

> The education given by the Catholic schools seems to me to be in all matters of general culture a substituting of pedantry for taste . . . I have never met a young man from an Irish Catholic school who did not seem to me to be injured by the literature and the literary history he had learned at it.[2]

Again and again Yeats returns to this theme; of 'the schoolboy thought of Young Ireland', and of his hopes for a more enlightened age.

> The Irish people till they are better educated must dream impermanent dreams, and if they do not find them they will be ruined by the half-sirs with their squalid hates and envies.[3]

Of actions of his own that were apparently altruistic but which were susceptible to every kind of misrepresentation, we might select some examples to reinforce the poems of *Responsibilities* that concern Lutyens, Lady Gregory and Synge.

The Countess Cathleen is not a good play, but has much auto-biographical interest. In most European countries it would have been considered inoffensive. It might even have been thought of as posing an interesting moral problem of a Faustian kind. But here is a specimen of the response:

> Nowhere is there a single gleam of manliness, intelligence, or bare civilization. The Catholic Church only appears in Shrines of the Virgin that are 'kicked to pieces' by Celtic peasants, and in priests who are killed by devils in the shape of pigs. We are told that the land is full of famine, and that it is the Ireland of old days. Where was the aid of friendly and generous chiefs and clansmen to the suffering district? Where was the charitable hospitality of a hundred monastic foundations,[4] which were afterwards to be 'kicked to pieces' not by Celtic peasants, but

1. See his assumed and (unjustified) pride in blood that 'had not passed through any huckster's loin', and Moore's comment on this in *Hail and Farewell*.
2. *Memoirs,* op. cit. p.187.
3. Ibid. p.185.
4. This is probably a refraction of the Chesterton-Belloc myth.

by the reformed chivalry of England? Mr. W.B. Yeats seems to see nothing in the Ireland of old days but an unmanly, and impious and renegade people, crouched in degraded awe before demons, and goblins, and sprites, and sowlths, and thivishes, — just like a sordid tribe of black devil-worshippers and fetish-worshippers on the Congo or the Niger.[1]

Cathleen ni Houlihan is also a play of no great dramatic merit, but yet of considerable political importance:

> — Did that play of mine send out
> Certain men the English shot?[2]

but to the Cork Realists she was —

> . . . a grasping middle-aged hag. She was avaricious, she was mean; for family reasons she would force a son into the Church against his will, she would commit arson, she would lie, she would cheat, she would murder, and yet we would write all our terrible words about her out of our love.[3]

The attack on the *Playboy* is too well-known to document. I have referred to some of its psychological aspects in a later essay. But this, and the pamphlet called *Souls for Gold,* are significant as representing the peaks of the attack: we might perhaps add the affair of The Municipal Gallery and the Lane Pictures, the poems 'To a Wealthy Man . . .' and 'An Appointment'. The abuse in the press, from many angles, is everywhere: but there seems to be one constant theme. We may attempt to summarise by quotation:

> The work, mostly amateur, done for the Abbey Theatre between 1902 and 1922 was for Ireland's self; it was, *in intention,* genuine Anglo-Irish Literature, but more than that one cannot say. We must not be waylaid into thinking that because it shed for the once its Colonial character it became genuine Anglo-Irish literature, or that because the world accepts it as Irish Literature, it may really turn out to be Anglo-Irish literature, or that because it is neither quite English nor quite Irish it must be Anglo-Irish.[4]

In this passage we have an attempted distinction between 'English', 'Irish' and 'Anglo-Irish'. Attempts to isolate and focus the characteristics of the last group have not been happy.[5]

A minor but important aspect of the Literary Renaissance has been

1. *Souls for Gold, Pseudo-Celtic Drama in Dublin.* (London, 1899).
2. 'Under Ben Bulben'. *The Old Lady Says No* (1939) was Denis Johnston's expressionistic comment on Yeats's play.
3. Lennox Robinson *Ireland's Abbey Theatre,* (London, 1951) p. 84.
4. Daniel Corkery, *Synge and Anglo-Irish Literature.* (London, 1931) p. 11. We may notice the frequency with which the emotive word 'colonial' is applied to such different writers as Somerville and Ross, Joyce Cary and Denis Johnston.
5. Terence de Vere White's *The Anglo-Irish* (Dublin, 1972) is relevant.

the question of compulsory Irish. Few of the great writers mastered the language. None produced works of major importance in it. As an aspect of re-emergent Nationalism and of 'de-Anglicization' it was clearly an admirable project. To foster pride in the language and literature was a fine literary ideal. In practice it proved an expensive and unsatisfactory experiment. The two major political parties have long been divided over it. For many years the minority party, the Language Reform Association, fought a losing battle with a subject which, though minor in its incidence on the national life, provoked the most fierce emotions from the patriot spirits. Compulsory Irish became a prescribed subject for the Intermediate Certificate in 1932, and the Leaving Certificate in 1934. The requirement was not lifted till 1973.

There were many objections to Irish as a compulsory subject. The enthusiasm shown by converts such as George Moore and Lady Gregory is a matter of history, and there was everything to be said for it as a scholar's language, with a rich literature and tradition. There was little to be said for its attempted revival − as Shaw noted long ago − as a popular or current language, with a vocabulary which was wholly unfitted to the modern world. The duplication of official language and formulae, at some inconvenience, are not of great moment. The most serious effect was the expansion of the language to meet the conditions of a modern civilization. Those who produced so much misery in pursuit of this idealism went to the lengths of ordering that infant teaching was to be through Irish alone.[1] The difficulties in teaching modern science and technology through a medium which does not possess an adequate vocabulary are considerable. Any mention became highly emotive. The expensive and romantic dream of the Gaeltacht, the settlement in which Irish speaking is encouraged by subsidy, seems to have slowly faded under economic pressures: not least those of the Common Market. To insist on its essential qualifying role might result in mere lip-service:[2] but the school-time spent on it has the effect of diminishing the time available either for the Classics (or at least Latin) or for a modern language.[3] And there are clear warnings in the events in other countries, particularly in India with its experience in Hindi as a national tongue.

1. This was the work of General Richard Mulcahy, Minister for Education in the Coalition Government of 1948.
2. As polar extremes, we may quote from two statements of Kevin O'Higgins. "It (the Gaelic League) learned that we had a language, a literature, 'a muse of our own, better, purer, sweeter by far than the dreary tongue of the conqueror − or would-be conqueror." This in 1922: later, "I deprecate the tendency to use the Irish language as a spearhead for jobbery." (Terence de Vere White, *Kevin O'Higgins* (London 1948)
3. French, and the ties with France, have long been traditional, but only Joyce, Synge and Beckett took full advantage of them.

Of all problems that of the land has proved to be the most intractable.

> . . . a rich man's flowering lawns,
> Amid the rustle of his planted hills.[1]

could be, at worst, a perpetual source of jealousy, irritation. At its best, the Big House might offer to the people a focus of loyalty, of employment, of what would now be called, in derision, paternalistic care. At worst, the evils of absenteeism, the traditionally rapacious agent, the human tragedies of the evictions, offered a continual temptation to erosion, violence, and ultimately destruction by fire. There was no tradition of settled tenancy as in England; and the question of rightful ownership could readily be carried back far into a romanticized past. The hunger for the land is persistent, passionate. When the Big House passed, by penal rates, death duties or other economic pressures, it might readily be bought for a religious house or a mental home or a hotel: or by a purchaser from America, France, Germany. If it were destroyed by fire there would be its spoils; furniture and 'famous ivories'[2], the destruction of the 'planted trees'[3]. "Mean roof-trees" would be "the sturdier for its fall"; the squared stones would make farm buildings; the land itself fenced out into small-holdings which could never be economically viable, but which as grazing offered a sufficient and indolent living. More than religion, more than the nationalist consciousness, the land was, and remains, an insoluble problem.

Much had been done by a succession of Land Acts, notably that of 1903; but Yeats's poem 'Upon a House Shaken by the Land Agitation', with its allusion to Sir William Gregory's diplomatic and political work, recalls the fact that Coole had been threatened with destruction, and its owner with death, thirty years before. And the I.R.A. advocated, much to the disgust of Kevin O'Higgins (as of all trained lawyers) the resurrection of Brehon Law as a substitute for English in order to assert communal rights over all land. The chain of Norman Castles, the 'Square Houses', testify that the land — however granted and whatever the titles — had to be held by force of arms. Spenser at Kilcolman lamented its burning: and he was not the first of those defeated in such a manner:

> "But what could he 'gainst all them do alone?
> It could not boot; needs mote she die at last!
> I only 'scaped though great confusion

1. 'Meditations in Time of Civil War', I.
2. 'Nineteen Hundred and Nineteen'.
3. The destruction of woods has been endemic. So 'Kilcash' —
   > What shall we do for timber?
   > The last of the woods is down.

   Planting, public or private, demands a higher 'time-horizon' than is common; yet one should not refrain from paying tribute to the work of the Irish Forestry Commission.

Of cries and clamours, which amongst them past,
In dreadful darkness, a dreadfully aghast . . ."[1]

In the meantime there was, is, a further cause of division. To a loyalist and Unionist the nationalistic parties, of whatever colour, had aided and comforted England's enemies: from George Moore's ludicrous telegram to the Boer leaders and Major MacBride's brigade that fought for them, through Casement's attempted formation of a brigade from the prisoners among the Irish Regiments, the repetition of the same plan in 1940 (even to landing from a German submarine at the same strand in Kerry) down to the series of explosion outrages in 1939, the use of Dublin as a centre for espionage, and the official telegram of condolence on the death of Hitler.

There was another cause of division and bitterness that has received little attention from the social historians: the matter of the Irish Regiments disbanded after the Free State came into being. Though the territorial claims were never so strong as in Scotland or Wales or England, nor the traditions so ancient, the pride in them was very real. Such were the Dublins, Munsters, Leinsters, Connaught Rangers. The officers of these regiments were often, though not invariably, drawn from both the Protestant and Catholic gentry. Their destruction, and that of their battle honours, the flags which had hung in many Protestant Churches and in the cathedrals of Dublin, were other factors that conduced towards alienation; but these again were ambivalent. As in the Southern States of America, the virtues and sometimes the vices of the soldier had been long cherished. Kipling celebrated the proud record of the Irish Guards, in whose service his only son had died; and in verse –

For where there are Irish there's bound to be fighting,
And when there's no fighting, it's Ireland no more.

But the soldier returning from the first war was often subjected to harassment, various kinds of social injustice, denial of elementary voting rights. For the ex-officer the fact that he had served with the Irish Regiments might well be a pretext for future burning or expulsion. A very few of them it is true, did join the Free State Army and the Civic Guards: and stiffened those bodies with their experience of discipline and war; but in general both the I.R.A. and Free State forces were officered by a different class, with wholly different traditions; not least in the system of pensions and rewards, politically as well as militarily: so that the past readily became (and will no doubt become again) fertile soil for a continuing heroic myth. And these were again divided, for comedy or tragedy according to one's angle of vision, by the forces of religion, nationalism, idealism, pressure from political, military and commercial interests. Here history was repearing itself: to the North

1. *Faerie Queen* VI, xi, 32.

symbolically in the Williamite Campaign; to the South, the Risings of 1798, the landing of Casement. And all was complicated by the intricate events such as the Curragh Rebellion, Carson's arming of the North, the Howth gun-running, the Volunteer movement.

The Anglo-Irish writer, of Protestant stock, has thus been in a peculiar position. He has seen and suffered intermittent violence from the Norman Conquest onwards. He has seen the majority of the 'race' to which he belonged (there are various terms, loaded in various directions, to denote it) gradually eliminated from much of Southern Ireland.[1] He has seen the parishes of his own faith shrunken, even to the point of vanishing, as the familiar processes of burning and attrition proceed. Nor should we underestimate the element of *Schadenfreude*, particularly for the immature, in the acts of destruction by explosives or by fire. Such exploits are often safe and easy of execution, more so, perhaps, in the countryside than in a city. One aspect is given Wagnerian expression in *The King's Threshold:*

> And I would have all know that when all falls
> In ruin, poetry calls out in joy,
> Being the scattering hand, the bursting pod.
> The victims' joy among the holy flame,
> God's laughter at the shattering of the world.

On June 12 (1968) the Republican Publicity Board issued a statement accepting responsibility for the burnings carried out by the units of the I.R.A. "in accordance with our policy of resistance to foreign take-over of our land, fisheries, industries and other assets that belong by right to the Irish people".[2] The same commination has extended (at least in theory) to English capital and enterprise. At the same time the few Big Houses that are left struggle for existence under rates deliberately set at punitive levels: and, when an estate is administered by official channels, there can be more than a suspicion of gross mismanagement.[3] And if a house is burned, an estate dismembered, he knows that the romantic idealism that underlies the action will have its economic consequences: he will also be aware of the irony of a situation in which the government of the Republic has encouraged foreign investment in industry, mining, land, by means of tax concessions to some who had been historic enemies of the United Kingdom.

1. Because of the intermittent nature of the Census, firm statistics are not easy to obtain. It has been said that between 1936 and 1961 the Protestant population in Eire decreased by 1% per annum. This is in line with my own impressions, particularly as regards the population of farmers in my own county, where Protestants have been virtually eliminated.

2. J. Bowyer Bell, *The Secret Army*, p.361. (London, 1971). The Germans seem to have been the main object of attention: but farms bought by Frenchmen were also attacked.

3. The case of the Gore-Booth Estate of Lissadell offers a complex but illuminating example.

§ix

It is arguable that the myth, fostered by Matthew Arnold's famous essay (following Renan) of the uniqueness of the Irish race, is much to blame. The view has been propounded with cogency[1] that the 'average' inhabitant, from whatever rank or trade or profession, is much the same in both countries; that the great majority of the people in Southern Ireland wish to live peaceably with their neighbours, enjoying the steadily-increasing standard of living, and the wage-structures that inevitably (for migration is unhindered, and the force of Irish workers in England and in Scotland is formidable) tend to relate ever more closely to those of England. In any war, whether guerilla or declared, it is not uncommon to find large areas of a country in which there is no overt disturbance and where races or creeds may live together in apparent amity for long periods of time. So in Ireland: 'Terrorist' activities have fluctuated greatly over the sixty years or so that I have taken as a base from Yeats's quotation. English, French, German 'Settlers' have come and often gone: come for a whole number of reasons, gone because this Eden in which one foot had been tentatively planted had shown the serpent as well as the weasel in the undergrowth. After each war the 'visitors' had acquired houses or property: whether in the hope of farming, the pursuit of lower taxation and cheaper living (a hope to be quickly shown to be illusory), domestic help, or various sporting amenities. And even though there was often an initial honeymoon period in which all went well, the gradual withdrawal of large numbers to Scotland, Devonshire, or to the pensioner-havens of Cheltenham or Bath has testified to the reaction to this second, or maybe twentieth invasion from across the water. Nor is the 'excuse' of the 'quiet man', who takes no part in local politics, a certain safeguard against jealousy and acquisitiveness. 'Service with the British', in whatever capacity, could and can be readily inflated into a pretext for robbery, or murder, or both.[2]

§x

Yet whatever the immensity of complexities in creed, wealth, social standing, it is clear (as I have written elsewhere[3]) that the Anglo-Irish race failed: perhaps through

> . . . natural declension of the soul,
> Through too much business with the passing hour,
> Through too much play, or marriage with a fool . . .[4]

1. Notably in the B.B.C. Broadcast in October 1971.
2. There is little point in recapitulating the incidents. Those of 'The Troubles' of 1917-22 are well documented: more recent examples are familiar.
3. *The Lonely Tower*, Ch. 1.
4. 'Meditations in Time of Civil War', IV.

In the event they failed either to lead rebellion, or to crush it. Perhaps that aristocracy had too many dead. The young Free State, in its attempt to compose a Senate from the landed aristocracy and from the intellectual élite, failed to establish an Upper House of any considerable moral or cultural authority. And this was understandable when the price of membership might well be the burning of the Senator's house.[1] The failure to achieve outstanding leadership among the new politicians was celebrated by Yeats in 'Parnell's Funeral', in words of unparalleled bitterness:

> Come, fix upon me that accusing eye.
> I thirst for accusation. All that was sung,
> All that was said in Ireland is a lie
> Bred out of the contagion of the throng,
> Saving the rhyme rats hear before they die . . .

$xi

Perhaps the last words are again those of Yeats. He perceived that Irish politics were indeed a 'witches' cauldron':

> Out of Ireland have we come:
> Great hatred, little room.[2]

But overall there was, is, the fantasy of unity, whether based on a romantic examination of the miscellaneous wars of Celtic Mythology, the perception of a mystic unity in the poetic imagery of 'rock and hill', the evocation of ghosts of heroes in the immediate present, so that the ghost of Cuchulain would 'stalk through the Post Office'.

> We had fed the heart on fantasies,
> The heart's grown brutal from the fare; . . .[3]

The fantasies were on both sides. Was the end of it all a sanctified and peaceful island, the last bastion in Europe in which 'the workman, noble and saint' might coexist in amity; a community that might resist indefinitely the incursion of modern industrialism; one to which writers and poets might be attracted by taxation relief? Was it to be a drastic and impossible reversal of history, Hyde's de-Anglicization, the elimination of all evidence of the English 'conquest', English achievement and English law, while maintaining all the advantages of trade and reciprocal employment? Was it to become the last defence of European Christianity and Culture, Byzantium maintaining the ancient parapets against Imperialist Rome? One proof was the piety of the peasant that (as Corkery noted) made a religious idiom, often ejaculatory, integgral with his speech; sometimes in conjunctions which, as recorded by

1. See, generally, Oliver St. John Gogarty: in particular his memoir *It Isn't that Time of Year at All.*
2. See, again, *The Lonely Tower,* Ch. VI. 'The Study of Hatred'.
3. 'The Stare's Nest by My Window'.

Synge, might easily be taken to demonstrate blasphemous comedy. Such piety, too, provided a social-religious barrier of a kind inconceivable in Britain. Mixed marriages were discouraged, often with some violence, by both sides; conversion acquired, not without justification, a certain odium.[1] The Treaty of 1921 showing the worse features of surreptitious pseudo-diplomacy, was destined to leave a dissident minority for half a century, to present the successive Free State governments with a Swiftian tight-rope act, and to present the I.R.A. — itself split since the Easter Rising — into factions that divide, coalesce, unite again so that new ideologies and neo-Marxist opinions take hold — with the perfect guerilla situation for exploiting its policies against the North.

§xii

I am writing this in 1972, in the midst of an undeclared war which duplicates in many respects that which I knew as a boy, half a century ago, save that the new sciences in weaponry and explosives have increased beyond all reckoning its arbitrary terror, and modern highly-professional methods of propaganda have made all truth more clouded than ever. New factors have been added to the complexity. First, there is the certainty that several powers unfriendly to Great Britain have exploited the 'war' (at every stage of its development) in accordance with their political philosophies. An idealistic form of anarchism found a voice in Westminster Hall and was heard with sentimental applause; there are parallels to be drawn, not inappropriately, between Maud Gonne and Bernadette Devlin. Contacts and mutual assistance have been maintained, perhaps with no great efficiency, between the I.R.A. and subversive 'nationalist' groups in Scotland and Wales; but those with the Middle East, Czechoslovakia[2] and Mexico[3] have been of importance. The United States provides a subvention which is credibly estimated at a quarter of a million pounds annually. Fund raising activities by politicians of varying beliefs are common, but the greater part of the money and arms are channelled through organizations which are able to take advantage of the powerful emotions among a population estimated at thirteen million American-Irish. Among the most active are those known as The Irish Northern Aid Committee, The National Association for Irish Freedom (which works largely through the Civil Rights movement), The American Committee for Ulster Justice, The Irish Republican Club; with many smaller clubs and soc-

1. Here the novelists provide much evidence. Perhaps *The Real Charlotte* (Somerville and Ross) is as good a documentation as any. George Moore's *The Untilled Field* is of interest here. (See Chapter X.)

2. The main source here is the state arms company, OMNIPOL.

3. A charge of gun-running from that country is now under investigation at Forth Worth. There have also been exchanges with the 'guerilla schools' behind the Iron Curtain.

ieties. Pride in Irish ancestry, the heart-warming recital of ancient wrongs, the search for ancient homesteads or tombs, offer a major preoccupation for many Americans. Slogans enhance the images of Latin-American, Chinese and African leaders. Propaganda can stage or distort 'incidents' at will: often using the naive idealism of the universities. The most common and perhaps the most fertile has been the outcry against internment, which is a military and political necessity when the process of law breaks down because witnesses will not give evidence nor jurors convict. It is a minor irony (among many) that the Government of Eire have, of necessity, abandoned trial by jury for cases of this nature.

A second factor is the changed atmosphere of religious toleration. In 1968 it seemed as if some form of ecumenicism was at last in view. Within a year all had changed. The Constitution of Eire, drafted by de Valera in 1937, propounded as a central tenet that of a wholly Catholic State, though overtly guaranteeing freedom of conscience to all.[1] At the same time it legislated for a single united Ireland, holding that any enclave there might be in the North was essentially of a temorary nature. Its hieratical strictures, the most rigorous and stringently defined in Europe, had been strengthened by the educational policy of the State, both ecclesiastical and secular.

The Irish schoolboy has been taught aspects of history and of literature that would be largely unrecognizable by his British contemporaries. The doctrine of a holy war, sometimes enunciated by priests in English parishes, has given a voice to the long-term unease. And the liberal theology encouraged by the Second Vatican Council has had no intellectual room to develop in Eire as it has elsewhere in Europe, and to discuss those problems of theology that have the most intimate relationships to the social sciences.[2] Against these forces the Southern Protestant has been, as his Northern co-religionists have noted, relatively helpless; in the period 1936-1961 his numbers have been approximately halved.

There are, therefore, the most powerful religious, economic and social impulses towards the subjugation, or elimination, of the North. To these we might add the judicial situation. We recall again Yeats's lines

> We too had many pretty toys when young:
> A law indifferent of blame or praise,
> To bribe or threat; habits that made old wrong
> Melt down, as it were wax in the sun's rays . . . [3]

1. Particularly as set out in Article 44.2[c]
2. In particular, birth control, the censorship and certain aspects of the health services. These are of course political problems; the North sees itself as ultimately overwhelmed by the rising Catholic population within its gates.
3. 'Nineteen Hundred and Nineteen'.

Some experience of Irish legal history suggests that, by 1912, the judiciary was, on the whole, as free from corruption as that of its English prototype. By 1923 Yeats, as a Senator, could express public doubt as to whether the judges might not be in danger of being overruled by the executive. Such fear was not unjustified. Pressure upon the Eire Prime Minister to control 'the wild men' who in pursuance of that 'war' against Ulster had contravened the laws of her own country, has resulted in few prosecutions, and fewer convictions; whether for robbery, arson, the bearing of arms illegally, or murder.[1] We need not be surprised at this. The Attorney-General of Eire has the right to decide which prosecutions shall be followed up. In the lower courts, a profound and widespread sympathy for the 'freedom fighters' makes it unlikely that conviction, if it occurs, will result in more than nominal penalties. We may quote from one who is a Roman Catholic as well as a most distinguished scholar, with a European and American reputation:

The government's holding action has given the I.R.A. a marvellous latitude in the Republic. A year ago, the Dublin I.R.A. Commanders were still careful to dissociate themselves, at least in public, from any specific action taken in the Six Counties, Now they are openly claiming credit for the Northern bombings, each faction insisting that its own particular brand of violence represents the right strategy and the proper patriotic goals. Northern terrorists who used to make their trips in secret are cavalierly commuting across the border, murdering in Derry, drinking in Donegal, and boasting that no policeman in the South would dare to stop them. Southern terrorists stand at the frontier, ten feet into the sanctuary of the Republic, and bombard the British soldiers on the other side with bombs and rifle fire, a kind of insane border war that leaves them free from any retribution. Arms smugglers hold press conferences in Dublin — so close to Leinster House, where the Dail meets, that people who want to can drop in to hear them, during a break in parliament — to recount in detail their adventures in evading the police. The Sinn Fein Provos have even staged a mock Ulster parliament in the Republic, complete with delegates, which they used as a recruiting platform, but which was nevertheless enthusiastically and openly attended by rural priests and politicians and several hundred Irish countrymen. And the Officials have distributed a broadsheet threatening any Southern judge or juror who convicts a republican 'for actions in the cause of a Free and United Ireland'[2].

1. One of the major anomalies in a Gilbertian situation is (a) that the I.R.A is illegal in the Republic, but not in England, and (b) that the Government is kept in power by the Right, or 'old' I.R.A. Only in 1973 has the situation been modified.
2. *Letter from Ireland* by Professor Denis Donoghue: *The New Yorker,* February 19th 1972.

It is not surprising that

> A law indifferent to blame or praise,
> To bribe or threat . . .

is not the least of its possessions that Ulster is reluctant to relinquish.

Nor should we underestimate the *Todentrieb* in all nations cursed with a messianic vision, and drawing its psychological strength from that impulse. Close to this *Todentrieb* lies the pleasure in sheer tragedy of an explosion, a burning house,[1] that (from childhood memory) became a dominant symbol in Yeats's mind. It is not to be doubted that there is in this zest for destruction a most powerful sexual component. The documentation by the psychologists of this subject is too familiar to require quotation.

§xiii

I do not know when the Irish Literary Revival, or Renaissance, ended; perhaps with the death of Lady Gregory in 1932, perhaps with the death of Yeats in 1939. Its background has been divided between peace and sporadic wars, violence upon the roads, that seem to show a series of peaks; which we may think correspond with the ripening of successive generations into unrest (at intervals of ten to fifteen years) and with the time it takes for 'loose emotion'[2] to cohere around a·real or imaginary grievance, and for money and arms to accumulate. A critical event in the outside world, some pretext (such as a centenary) can be made a basis for that now popular term, escalation. That all opportunities were laid open by political ineptitudes at Stormont and at Westminster there is no doubt. It has been said that if a proportion only of the tyrannies against the Catholic minority alleged by politicians in Eire and America were true, armed rebellion would be not only excusable but a duty. It has also been said with justice that the major casualty of the 1969-72 conflict has been Truth. That all events were intensified by the pusillanimity which believed that a war can be conducted with perpetually-varying policies, with alternating attempts to suppress violence and to placate it, there is no doubt. The desire to spare a civilian population which has adopted an active or passive paramilitary role against one's own troops is made ever more tentative by a fear of world opinion among enemies or allies, misled both by suborned mass-media and by the whole historical complexity of Irish 'mire and blood'; with which the cumbrous and uncertain mechanisms of the United Nations are wholly unfitted to deal. But it is clear that no one was concerned to suggest reasoned comparisons, or to hold a moral balance, between the events of 1917-22 and those of 1968-72.

---

1. I do not wish to use the term *Schadenfreude* which (to me) has a slightly different meaning. See, passim., my *Harvest of Tragedy*.
2. I use the word in the sense developed by Clutton Brock *(Essays on Life,* London 1925).

In all this no significant voice was raised by the writers, and the churches spoke in no more than generalities.[1] Since Yeats's death those who remained in Ireland (with occasional American expeditions) have not produced any men of the first rank, or with the stature to offer leadership. There are short-story writers who have achieved a high standard of technique. There are two excellent poets. But the bulk of the literature has been, and remains, wholly 'provincial'.[2] The short stories tend to centre on Cork or Dublin; the writers, now elderly, draw on their experiences of the Easter Rising, the Civil War or 'peasant quality' without the grace of Moore or the deep compassion of James Stephens. The one major figure, Samuel Beckett, followed Joyce into exile. I do not think there is apparent in Dublin the sense of European culture and tradition that the great writers showed. Again, Yeats's advice seems relevant, with its Shakespearean precedent:

> I can only wish a young Irishman of talent and culture
> that he may spend his life, from eighteen to twenty-five, out-
> side Ireland — can one prescribe duties to a developed soul? —
> and I suppose him to become conscious of himself in those
> years. If one can, I would wish him to return.[3]

The literary society of Dublin may be thought to have abandoned the salons, the famous 'at homes', for the euphoric and raucous fellowship of the pub.

Nor has any leader emerged to speak at large for the moral issues. The leaders of the Churches of all denominations have, as in duty bound, spoken many words in condemnation of the outrages. It does not seem as if these words have been effective. There are probably a number of reasons. The Roman Catholic Church, which possesses the traditionally supreme weapon of excommunication, is not prepared to use that weapon against a cause which has the support of its own adherents. The Protestant and Non-Conformist Churches seem to be uncertainly divided between militancy, traditional suspicion of the Catholics, and the slackening (after many promising developments) of the ecumenical movement. Behind all is the climate of religious confusion, the loosening of the provisions of the Decalogue. The much-discussed 'Protestant backlash' would be a countering of violence of the opposing 'holy war'; understandable but futile. Violence inevitably breeds counter-violence.

§xiv

It may be that the whole of the Irish Literary Renaissance is in some part to blame for encouraging long memories, for invoking ancient

1. Perhaps we should except the Pope's message of Easter 1973*, urging negotiation over the White Paper.
2. In Matthew Arnold's sense.
3. Memoirs, p.159.

myths, for thinking too long on the violence of Cuchulain, for failure to reassess the validity, in a modern civilization, of the traditional exaltation of the blood sacrifice. It may be that in spite of – even because of – the intensive study now devoted to it, the seminal energy has been dissipated in world confusion and violence. It may be that by rejecting (as George Moore thought) that stabilizing core of Protestant ethic once manifested in the Ascendancy there has been a loss of the traditional alignment with the Western European tradition; and here the ebb and flow of political and religious censorship seems to have been a determinant.

But in a larger context the writers since the death of Yeats have failed to confront what he himself called, when he criticized Shelley, 'the vision of Evil', as evidenced in the microcosm that is Ireland:

> The Christian world is now truly confronted by the princi-
> ple of evil, by naked injustice, tyranny, lies, slavery, and
> coercion of conscience . . . That outpouring of evil revealed to
> what extent Christianity has been undermined in the twentieth
> century. In the face of that, evil can no longer be minimized
> by the, euphemism of the *privatio boni*. Evil has become a
> determinant reality. It can no longer be dismissed from the
> world by a circumlocution. We must learn how to handle it,
> since it is here to stay[1].

That vision is only possible in a literature which is prepared to return to a basis in religion and philosophy; above all, one which is prepared to confront again the Christian and tragic principles of pity and fear. Events in Ireland over the past half-century seem to have given rise to a progressive induration, through repeated violence and bloodshed, of the primary charities. Of the Civil War Yeats wrote: "There is no longer a virtuous nation, and the best of us live by candle-light." Small candles have been lit since his death, often of great beauty, but no more than points of light. The time seems ripe for the re-emergence of a great and gracious literature.

---

1. C.G. Jung, *Memories, Dreams, and Reflections* (London 1963), p.303. This book is of profound interest for the study of Yeats's thought.

III
CHOICE AND CHANCE[1]

§i

If we look backward upon our lives it is usually possible to perceive events as falling into patterns or clusters in time. Such clusters form, perhaps, the Aristotelian 'beginning' of a play. A king dies, and his successor comes to the throne; the funeral baked meats furnish the tables for his widow's marriage. The state and its government go on; uneasily it may be, but in the normal processes of daily life. Then suddenly a ghost and a past sin, or it may be some ancient error or curse, irrupts upon the scene; and we are in the midst of the thick and sudden growth of dramatic events.

So, on a slighter scale, in our own lives and in those of others. Sometimes the logical or causal origins of events appear to break down; at others we may be aware of some greater if inscrutable power that seems to determine the patterns. We may even imagine, at times, that events themselves possess, in themselves, some mysterious quality of the nature of gravitational forces, that causes them to draw together, to coagulate. Pauli has called this the Principle of Synchronicity.[2] Yeats called the dominant components Choice and Chance; he saw them, at least from middle age onwards, as having been in operation throughout his life. They were apparent also to him in 'the great mutations of the world', the movements of the historical gyres set against the almost inconceivable perspectives of 'the Babylonian starlight', of the Platonic Great Year. In the strange quasi-deterministic matrix of *A Vision* we may see how he set statesmen, generals, artists, poets, philosophers in a kind of kaleidoscope, lit by the waxing and waning moon. And he foresaw how, in the last of the Phases of the Moon, Chance and Choice converging on it, were to give, at the end, a Unity of Being,

Chance being at one with Choice at last[3]

My purpose this morning is to suggest to you, first, some considerations as to the nature of the experiences presented by Choice and Chance: and, secondly, what Yeats made of them when Isaiah's coal had come to purge his lips. I am thinking now of the Lesson read at the Drumcliffe Service a month ago: for which I recalled the two lines from 'Vacillation':

---

1. Sligo: the opening lecture, 1965.
2. Jung and Pauli: *The Interpretation and Nature of the Psyche* (London, 1955).
3. 'Solomon and the Witch'.

The Soul: Isaiah's coal, what more can man desire?
The Heart: Struck dumb in the simplicity of fire![1]

§ii

It is very clear, from the Lives of the Poets (and the living poets among you may test it from your own experience) that our childhood and youth are not only the most important subjects for our subsequent reveries, but are also the treasuries of the uncut gems that may be split and polished later, whether in prose or verse. So Wordsworth:

Fair seed-time had my soul, and I grew up
Fostered alike by beauty and by fear.[2]

When we know enough to form a coherent picture, whether through the biographical studies of the great Romantics or Victorians, or through the autobiographical indiscretions of our modern poets, we can see these early influences at work. (One temptation, indeed, is to go back too far in time what Sidney called *ab ovo:* as Amy Lovell began her biography of Keats with a description of the house in which Keats's parents spent their marriage night.) And for the young poet today, we have the same phenomena. Childhood experiences are enough to provide, perhaps, one 'slim volume' of early verse; though (if we are wise) we will have suppressed much, having in mind the embarrassing juvenilia of most of the great poets. Perhaps they will supply one quasi-autobiographical novel, on the standard formula. This is now fairly well defined. "The Novel, if it is to be best-seller, must surprise by a gross excess." In that pattern an unhappy childhood, uncomprehending parents, sexual perversion, sadism or masochism, may serve as swelling prologues to one's first love affairs. It is easy and agreeable to assume a degree of youthful martyrdom; and martyrdom, if we may trust Bernard Shaw, is the only road to fame that is open to a person of mediocre talents. But once we have extracted the maximum pathos or drama from our childhood miseries, we are faced at the age of, say, twenty-five, with a dilemma which is peculiar to this age. For between then and, perhaps, thirty-five, is the testing time: when we can gain some idea whether the poetry has possibilities of greatness, or is merely 'good'.

Now this is the dilemma, as it seems today. It is seldom that the young poet has either private means, or some employment that is both wholly congenial to himself and at the same time ancillary to his poetry. Perhaps Shakespeare was fortunate as an actor-manager: more fortunate in his infinite capacity to register, absorb, transmute all the life about him. It is probable that Spenser gained something from his public service in Ireland, but more from that solitude at Kilcolman that made the dusty

1. 'Vacillation', VII. *Kundalini* is the Condition of Fire in Indian Mysticism.
2. *Prelude,* 1 301.

dreams of the Arthurian Legend come to a peculiar kind of life in the *Faerie Queene*. John Donne's great work is inextricably linked to his calling as a priest and to his experiences as a lover; but there is no 'complaint to his purse'. T. S. Eliot turned from banking to literature, and appeared to find in the transition some liberation of his own personal conflicts. But the young poet as a schoolmaster (we may think of Robert Bolt, Christopher Fry) or as publisher, or as a Civil Servant or don, is under a double disadvantage. He has his primary work that (if he does it properly) is in itself exciting and rewarding. If he reduces it to a part-time activity he and it, as well as his family, are likely to suffer. In any profession today opportunities for travel, even for adventure, are strongly limited, though Shakespeare's saw is as true as ever:

> Home-keeping youth have ever homely wits.

Those fortunate ones who are released to follow the calling of a dedicated poet are indeed few. Such a release you may read of in the recent autobiography of my friend and sometime pupil, Patric Dickinson; and in the poem he wrote to his mother whose death had set him free to write. And, in spite of the patronage of the B.B.C., too many writers suffer initially a genteel and protesting poverty, and, even worse, the frustrations of wholly uncongenial employment.

§iii

I wish to put before you today some aspects of the operation of Chance and Choice in Yeats's life, and to stress a little this aspect of his uniqueness. He shared something of the hardships and uncertainties of certain of those whom he called 'The Tragic Generation', but he shared in, and boasted of, the integrity of that company of The Rhymers' Club, who

> never made a poorer song
> That you might have a heavier purse ... [1]

As a struggling poet-journalist in the London of the early Nineties, Choice sent him to the two English poets most likely to fertilize his genius. There was Spenser from whom he learnt (as I think) 'music and motion', the chiming of the vowels that you get, say, in 'Lullaby', the delight in the heroic that was to blend for a time with the Cuchulain legends, till Maud Gonne became aligned with Helen of Troy, and both with Deirdre of the Sorrows. There was Blake whose vision and visions drove him back, ever deeper into the traditional mines of neo-Platonism, Plotinus, Swedenborg, Cornelius Agrippa, More; Blake whose illustrations to Job and Dante and Young showed him how closely poetry and

---

1. 'The Grey Rock'.

painting could intertwine. Shelley he knew already and, however much he might rid himself of 'Shelley's Italian Light', the great Shelleyan images of Tower, Cave, Ship and Desert remained as foundations for his thought. (I think of W. H. Auden's memorable book, *The Enchaféd Flood.*) It was, perhaps, the choice of literature (at the long price of relative poverty until the Nobel Prize came) that drove him to publish, piece-meal, so much of his early work, and to furious and painful revision as his taste stabilized and matured. It was Chance, or perhaps the sheer accident of two centenaries, that caused the anniversary of the 1798 Rising to coincide so nearly with the Jubilee of 1897: when, at the Spithead Review, the armed might of England seemed to have reached its zenith: to merge so soon into the Boer War and its defeats, and the rising sympathy with the smaller nations that was to find its voice so strongly in the next decade: when in Chesterton's words,

> . . . sword in hand upon Afric's passes,
> Her last Republic cried to God.[1]

It was Chance that postponed the Rising planned for 1898, but which substituted the slow-maturing myth of Parnell, his greatness and his tragic fall. It was Chance, I think, that gave rise to that strange meeting in the low white house called Duras, near Kinvarra: where the Count de Basterot — that most romantic figure — met with Lady Gregory and Yeats and Synge, and talked for the first time of the possibility of an Irish Literary Theatre. None of us can tell, as we watch the great movements of literary history, how an idea, a series of ideas, is born; by what intention of predestination Wordsworth and Coleridge met at Nether Stowey, or how Tennyson at Cambridge drifted into the company of the Apostles with their 'passion for reforming the world'. We only know that it happened: that Miss Horniman came to the help of the young Abbey, that Synge abandoned Paris for Aran, Wicklow, West Kerry; that the hospitality of Coole, and Lady Gregory's motherly care, should have resulted in an imaginative alignment with Urbino, its great rooms where the travelled men and women met, and made *The Courtier.*

Behind all this first phase of the Irish Literary Renaissance moves the figure of the femme fatale, Maud Gonne: was it Chance, or Choice, or *The Wanderings of Oisin* that brought her, in 1889, to Yeats's lodgings in Bloomsbury? Without that magnificent flaming, exasperating presence the boy from a Dublin suburb, the child who once walked to Lissadell to be given cast-off shoes and stockings,[2] would never have had the chance to remember with nobility and ever-growing breadth of perception.

1. 'A Song of Defeat'.
2. I would have thought this improbable, had it not been told me by the late Maeve de Markciewicz, who was at Lissadell at the time.

— All I had rhymed of that monstrous thing
Returned and yet unrequited love.[1]

And no poet in the world's history has had a love affair that endured for forty years, that sustained his imagery with Helen of Troy, with Deirdre, with the procession of queens whom Villon and Synge had sung.

Again, Chance is powerfully at work. No one could have foreseen the death of Synge, killed, perhaps like Keats, by the malice of the Dublin mob (so Yeats thought) at that critical stage of the Abbey's fortunes: yet, as we look back we can see how vital were those five or six years of rejection, in the wilderness, when so many things seemed to have been set awry: the Municipal Gallery, the Lane pictures, his own professorship at Trinity College[2] ('that wicked temptation'), the attack on Lady Gregory. Then the chance friendship with Grierson, the meeting with Ezra Pound, the opening of the World of the Noh plays that seemed to offer (so strongly) so much in thought and imagery, the life of the ghost and the expiation of sin that he had already pondered and that seemed to provide him with a solution to his problem of a form which could combine lyric, song, dance, a stylization of setting: all these cheaply, and for a small, perhaps élite audience.

Above all, there was the supreme 'fortunate tragedy' of the 'Easter Rising', and maybe of the Troubles that followed: anarchy, murder, the horrors of civil war. Never before in human history had a poet had the chance of seeing, even by glimpses, such a war: whose aims like its origins were clear-cut, and both capable of imaginative alignment with the great heroic and epic traditions of European literature. It was small enough to be perspicuous; its tragedy, as he explained in a famous letter to Grierson, was not only local but metaphysical:

"I think things are coming right slowly though very slowly; we have had years now of murder and arson in which both nations have shared impartially. In my own neighbourhood the Black and Tans dragged two young man tied alive to a lorry by their heels, till their bodies were rent in pieces. 'There was nothing for the mother but the head', said a countryman, and the head he spoke of was found on the road side. The one enlightening truth which starts out of it all is that we may learn charity after mutual contempt. There is no longer a virtuous nation and the best of us live by candle light."[3]

I have sometimes wondered why Yeats, who delighted in perceiving patterns in history, did not in this context refer to his own archetypal image of Troy; and Hector, Tamer of Horses, dragged by the heels at the tail of his enemy's horse, though his version of the Troubles

---

1. 'Presences'.
2. See Philip Edwards. *'Yeats and the Trinity Chair'*: Hermathena, CI, 1965
3. Wade, *Letters,* p.690.

has an imaginative rightness. So, too, in 'The Road by My Door', 'The Stare's Nest by My Window'. Yeats, of course, took no part in the fighting though his personal courage is not in question. In 'The Stare's Nest by My Window' he is aware both of the envy for the 'liberation' of the fighting man that he stresses again in 'Under Ben Bulben', yet has given us what I take to be (and I return again and again to this quotation) a fair assessment of the Irish mind and of the Irish dilemma:

> We had fed the heart on fantasies,
> The heart's grown brutal from the fare;
> More substance in our enmities
> Than in our love; O honey bees,
> Come build in the empty house of the stare.

§iv

While he was still relatively young Yeats wrote an important essay, on William Morris, called 'The Happiest of the Poets'. A recent essay on the subject of his debt has not, I think, exhausted the matter of the relationship between the two. Morris, whom he had known as a boy, remained to the end a great figure in Yeats's mind; though he was not haunted by Morris as he was by Swift. It is not difficult to see why. Morris's poetry and prose embodied much that was congenial to Yeats's mind. There was the ceremonious worship of women, women with long pale faces and clouds of dark hair that might have come from a score of portraits, or from Mrs. Morris, or even from the Women of the Sidhe:

> Her great eyes, standing far apart,
> Draw up some memory from her heart,
> And gaze out very mournfully;
> _Beata mea Domina!_
> So beautiful and kind they are,
> But most times looking out afar,
> Waiting for something, not for me.
> _Beata mea Domina!_[1]

Yeats found in Morris 'the make-believe of a child who is re-making the world, not always in the same way, but always after its own heart'. He tells one story, again and again, 'how some man or woman lost and found again the happiness that is always half the body', who saw the abundance of the earth and of men and women 'as when they came from the divine hand'. The Morris idylls, the 'pleasant popular land', could be seen against the purity of the pastoral idylls of Palmer, of Calvert, of 'the sheep of God'. The women of the pre-Raphaelites could themselves be aligned with the Renaissance:

---

1. 'Praise of My Lady'.

> Paul Veronese
> And all his sacred company
> Imagined bodies all their days
> By the lagoon you love so much,
> For proud, soft, ceremonious proof
> That all must come to sight and touch . . . [1]

But however much we may remake and discipline ourselves, however
loudly we may cry, with Keats, 'Get wisdom, get philosophy', whatever
silences of ten years we may impose upon ourselves to heal a reviewer's wounds; the fact remains that we make our best poetry out of the
love or affliction or tragedy that Chance deals us. We prepare ourselves
by Choice and discipline; we write out of 'the events that come upon us
like waves'. And we may not expose ourselves consciously to these
waves; they must come from some further shore.

Five such events cut sharply across Yeats's life. The first was the
marriage, in 1903, of that brilliant, erratic, intolerable Maud Gonne;
whom he had wooed ineffectively for fourteen years, who had glittered
through the early poems and *The Countess Cathleen* (which he rewrote
to show himself as a suppliant before her). She had married one who was
destined to achieve momentary fame as one of the martyrs of the Easter
Rising:

> This other man I had dreamed
> A drunken, vainglorious lout.
> He had done most bitter wrong
> To some who are near my heart,
> Yet I number him in the song . . . [2]

Maud Gonne divorced her husband in 1905; for a time Yeats's hopes
revived. Then came two more blows. *The Playboy* Riots of 1907, though
directed in a half-comprehended reaction against Synge's complex and
profound irony, involved the whole Abbey Theatre; and with it Yeats's
dream of a theatre, deep-rooted in myth and legend and peasant life, that
might one day unify Ireland, awake her to a consciousness of her
heroic destiny. Out of his failure appears that ambivalence of bitterness
which we find throughout the bulk of Anglo-Irish literature; from Swift,
perhaps from Spenser even, down to Joyce and the long list of the expatriate writers. Ireland is, perhaps always has been, the supreme
exemplar of the *odi et amo* theme. Yeats had grown to hate Dublin in
its mob moods, 'this blind bitter town'; to hate the provincialism and
the religious intolerance that had rejected Lutyens, Lane, Lady Gregory.
"The Irish are like a pack of hounds, always ready to pull down some
noble stag"; so he quotes Goethe.

The third impulse is not, of course, the first World War; which

---

1. 'Michael Robartes and the Dancer'.
2. 'Easter, 1916'.

touched him mainly through Lady Gregory, and which gave rise to the four elegies on her son. Robert Gregory is seen as Renaissance man, with a side-glance at the Wilton Elegy. It is not, I think, profitless to attempt to adjust the portrait to the reality. But Yeats's imagined desire for the courageous horseman, for the solitary fighter-pilot, for his 'battle-joy' (though the death was accidental, and not from the enemy)—these are magnified out of *pietas*. Over the portrait there is, I think, some glaze or gloss of William Morris whom he had met and admired in the beginning, and to whom (he tells us) he returned in old age. This may have been the second haunting; the first was Swift. To one who had

> — thought Cuchulain till it seemed
> He stood where they had stood

the figure of Morris, with his multitudinous activities in printing, tapestry, the making of carpets and furniture, the loving elaboration of the embellishments to *The Kelmscott Chaucer* may have seemed to provide a comparison with the glowing picture he had conceived of the unity of the arts in Byzantium.

But there was also the primitive violent side of Morris that appealed to him also; as in 'The Judgement of God':

> 'Swerve to the left, son Roger', he said,
>   When you glimpse his eyes through the helmet-slit,
> 'Swerve to the left, then out at his head,
>   And the lord God give you joy of it!'

or again, from *Sigurd the Volsung,*

> Then he rented the knitted war-hedge till by Hogni's side he stood,
> And kissed him amidst of the spear-hail, and their cheeks were wet
>   with blood.

Perhaps in Yeats's eyes Morris had achieved, in some measure, a kind of fullness of Renaissance man, the maker of so many things: verse, books, paintings, houses, furniture; a kind of craftsman's 'unity of being', a fore-runner of Major Robert Gregory. And there follows at the end of the essay a notable passage by Yeats, which others have repeated recently, though in different words:

> He knew clearly what he was doing towards tne end, for
> he lived at a time when poets and artists have begun again to
> carry the burdens that priests and theologians took from them
> angrily some few hundred years ago.

The historic Apologies are gathered into Bronowski's summary, *The Poet's Defence*, (Cambridge, 1939), but the debate is perennial.

And this in turn raises the whole question of the moral function of the poet and the artist. I am clear that Yeats held passionately to his views that these functions were of central importance. I have tried elsewhere to emphasize the significance of Yeats's views on Dante's triad, the central themes (in whatever combinations, under whatever cloaks of symbols or myths) of Love, War, Death. I believe that if we do not take these with all seriousness and test them against the statements of other poets and (above all) of such experience as we can muster at the different stages of our lives, we do them a gross injustice. It is a lie at the root of the soul if we do no more than pay lip-service to poetry of this kind: reading with a smug superiority because we are not prepared to consider the validity of the beliefs, or because we shrink from the implications of death and war.

It is in this context that I would call Yeats, not the happiest but the most fortunate of the poets. And his fortune, or Chance, seems to me to consist in these things. A boyhood in the countryside: and then exile from it; exile to keep the memories clear-cut, and the related emotions warm. A poetic training in the company of poets who were then technically more accomplished than he; Dowson, Johnson, Le Gallienne and the rest. Perhaps, too, there were negative examples: as of Oscar Wilde. An apprenticeship to the literary life which brought him to those two seminal influences, Shakespeare and Blake. An emergence from that stage into the far more rigorous and frustrating discipline of the Theatre, which no one who has not practised it can judge. A simultaneous pressure, in part financial, in part ideological, to turn out, during this critical period between the ages of twenty-five to fifty, work which had to be published quickly and often in strange places, and which then had to be filtered, filed through revision, for the collections of poetry, plays, essays. A 'dark night of the soul', something which all must pass through, when it seemed that he and his friends were confronting the forces of malice, stupidity, misunderstanding and defeat. That period was, perhaps, from 1909 — the death of Synge — to 1914.

In 1912 he was forty-seven. Many writers have indicated his period of study, of regeneration by the rediscovery of Seventeenth Century English literature and of Japanese plays, at about this time. This too was a piece of fortune that is not given to many; for poets are often by then atrophied in their imagination, or bound by the burdens of family or affairs: by hostages given to fortune, or by the memory of some real or imagined sin. Yeats (for all his unhappiness) was free to read and think. How far he was helped by Ezra Pound is not yet, I think, wholly clear;[1] I do not think the influence was as powerful as that of Pound on Eliot.

But perhaps the supreme act of Chance was the Easter Rising. Yeats could not have foreseen, in the middle nineties, that a heroic war, small enough to be perspicuous, would one day overtake the whole Irish Literary Renaissance; would lay in ruins much of the culture that

1. But see K.L. Goodwin, *The Influence of Ezra Pound* (Oxford 1966): Ch. V.

had fostered it; and would provide him with endless material for the great period to come. Of that event I have written elsewhere. Slowly the Rising and all that it meant swung into changing alignments: the 'terrible beauty', 'the crazy fight', the burning of the houses, his choice of The Tower for his bride. Was that Choice or Chance — that within range of his beloved Coole a so-called Norman Tower was to be purchased cheaply, that had a long history in connection with Gort and its legends, and could become a powerful and multiplex emblem? It is clear that his Choice, his characteristic violence of metaphysical imagination, made it so: its significance ranging back through Irish history, the story of Deirdre, to Troy, to Alexandria; to coalesce with the arrogant imagery of his own great love affair:

> Why what could she have done, being what she is?
> Was there another Troy for her to burn?[1]

Choice or Chance gave him the Tower, Choice drove him from that domestically impossible dwelling, to Oxford and a new period of study. Choice and the genius of Lady Gregory gave him those immensely fruitful journeys to Italy:

> I have prepared my peace
> With learned Italian things
> And the proud stones of Greece,
> Poet's imaginings
> And memories of love,
> Memories of the words of women. . . [2]

And among that gallery, or the processional figures of that winding stair, I wish to pay tribute to the memory of Mrs. Yeats, and to join the many scholars who know her full measure of patience, hospitality and wisdom. In her Chance and Choice met, and perhaps rejoiced. It was fortunate that Maud Gonne and her daughter had rejected him, and at critical moments. In 'my wife George' he found one who was familiar with the majority, perhaps, of his esoteric interests: who understood his weaknesses: who repeatedly made a background for him in the 'lovely intricacies of a house'; who understood his need for 'memories of the words of women'. Behind all the comprehension of his mind there was her own indomitable courage, her essential practicality, even a certain dominance in domestic affairs that is still remembered in Gort. But above all she understood him, and was capable of deflating, on occasion, his pretensions. To the poet in the company of young people at Oxford (this was perhaps his most truly happy period) she acted as a kind of catalyst to his brilliant talk; and like him she seemed to possess the gift of instant and profound insight into the character of those who came to visit.

1. 'No Second Troy'
2. 'The Tower', III

For this perhaps was Yeats's supreme fortune (though not his happiness) in the long gallery of women who loved him, served him, gave him the inspiration of their friendship and physical presence. Was it these women, or some chance reawakening of the body, that aroused and kept aflame in the

     . . . sixty-year-old smiling public man.[1]

this incredible access of poetic energy and vitality that throbs through *The Tower* and *The Winding Stair,* and continues (changing a little in quality but not in kind) in *Supernatural Songs and Last Poems?* On such things critics will continue to speculate. My desire is only to put before you the elements of this infinitely strange patterning of Choice and Chance, these series of conflicts and tensions, of changing relationships, that seem to provide, at every turn, new and wholly unexpected creative energy. For all things served his turn; even the malice of his enemies:

> The finished man among his enemies?—
> How in the name of Heaven can he escape
> That defiling and disfigured shape
> The mirror of malicious eyes
> Casts upon his eyes until at last
> He thinks that shape must be his shape?
> And what's the good of an escape
> If honour find him in the wintry blast?[2]

Perhaps one of our functions here is to see that the mirror does not distort unduly.

§v

Nor did Chance desert him in the manner, and the time, of his death. The old age of poets makes, in the course of literature, depressing reading. But not only was he spared the worst symptoms of

> . . . the wreck of body
> Slow decay of blood,
> Testy delirium
> Or dull decrepitude,
> Or what worse evil come —[3]

but he had kept, as he wished, his 'intensity'. Within five months of his death he had written four important poems. He had been able to jest, in a kind of parody of his joy in the gustation of words, on a Spanish doctor's description of him as 'an elderly arterio-sclerotic': "I had rather be called arterio sclerotic than Queen of Lower Egypt."[4] Only the greatest can jest in this way in sickness, I know only of Donne and Voltaire and Dr. Johnson who have done so with passion and irony.

1. 'The Tower'.
2. 'A Dialogue of Self and Soul'.
3. 'The Tower' III.
4. A letter, unpublished, to me.

The dominant images, Cuchulain, the Tower, Ben Bulben and its horse-men, his masters in painting and poetry, his concern with the Anima Mundi, remained with him: to produce a vitality characteristic of the whole of the final period.

And it is also arguable that he died at an auspicious time, as war gathered over Europe. If anything could have disturbed him on his death-bed it might have been the crumbling of all ancient parapets[1] in the succeeding spring, but neither his imagination of politics or of war-fare could have led him to foresee that destruction. If, as I believe, 1934 seemed to him a kind of turning point in the history of the world, it was in 1939 that we saw the consequences of the Night of the Long Knives and the rise of Nazism. Whatever the date it was a fitting time for *Last Poems,* with a flicker of the old rhetoric, in 'The Black Tower', in the decay (as he saw it) of the new Ireland under de Valera, the rising of 'this filthy modern tide'.[2]

§vi

It is clear to me (and one day the history of this School will be written) that Choice and Chance have operated powerfully in its beginning, its development, its fantastic growth. Chance: a request for a single public lecture for summer visitors: the sight of a map of the Yeats Country in a chemists' shop in Wine Street: the advice of a lecturer (now a Professor) from University College, Dublin. Choice: because those who founded The Yeats Society had some idea (however vague it may have been at its inception) of founding some organization at which visitors to the town and countryside could combine a pilgrimage with a holiday, and both with instruction. It was Choice that determined the calendar, the availability of the two grammar schools, to whom we owe so much. It was something between Choice and Chance that learnt through experience how to improvise in many different ways, with the most tenuous financial support; rather than seek the help of some body that was already organized for such an academic task. Choice preferred to let this gathering grow as an organic unity, divorced alike from those religious or political influences that might have modified its direction had the policy of the Society been less liberal and less wise.

It was something between Choice and Chance (I confess I do not yet understand this operation of things) that has brought to us during the past years many, perhaps most, of the important Yeats scholars of two continents. Certainly it has not been for academic gain, nor, I think, to increase academic reputation; for though a good deal of

1. 'Je regrette l'Europe aux anciens parapets'.
2. 'The Statues'.

the work that was shaped here has been published (and the excellent Dolmen Press papers are one aspect of this), we believe that there is a difference in shape, texture, purpose between a good lecture and an academic essay. This year, indeed, has seen a flood of Yeatsian criticism, explanatory and evaluatory, in all forms. Some of the most impressive volumes we owe to scholars who are here with us now: Jeffares, Mulryne, Skelton, Donoghue. Yet I sometimes wonder whether, when the flood has washed over us and we can take stock of this fertilizing silt that all these books have left, there is anything better than the living intercourse of a society of scholars and students, who seek to draw from the work, and to give to it, that abundant life which grows when we talk, not with books, but with each other and with the poetry.

For these conditions the environment, though it is not everything, is of immense importance. Sligo has altered very little in half a century; and nothing that our successors do to it can change the changing beauty of lake, mountains, sea. You will have the opportunity of seeing the superb photography of the new film.[1] You will visit the many scenes of the poems and plays, and decide what *numen* resides there. The Yeats Society has arranged much for your pleasure and entertainment, but for my part I recognize always the need, at times, to be alone, to meditate much. It is a valid criticism of many conferences, summer schools, and such like things that they allow too little time for this, alone or with a friend or two. We have tried to make room for this.

$vii

And now for a sort of valediction I want to quote some short passages, not from Yeats, but from James Stephens; and its relevance to us this morning you will, I think, perceive:

This is the Thin Woman speaking; for one of the Three Absolutes, in *The Crock of Gold;* which I take to be among the wisest of books:

"It is not lawful to turn again when the journey is commenced, but to go forward to whatever is appointed; nor may we return to your meadows and trees and sunny places who have once departed from them. The torments of the mind may not be renounced for any easement of the body until the smoke that blinds us is blown away, and the tormenting flame has fitted us for that immortal ecstasy which is the bosom of God."[2]

Then, as you remember, Angus Og takes his bride Caitilin, and they move towards Kilmasheogue for the hosting of the Sidhe; so that the roll-call of the names of the Host thunder like a passage from Homer.

---

1. *The Yeats Country:* Patrick Carey.
2. p.297

The Happy Monarch gathers its warriors and its strength, and this song merges into a dance. They are going to release the Philosopher, the hero, who has been imprisoned 'in the big City, in order that he might be put on his trial and hanged. It was the custom'.

"They swept through the goat tracks and the little boreens and the curving roads. Down to the city they went dancing and singing; among the streets and the shops telling their sunny tale; not heeding the malignant eyes and the cold brows as the sons of Balor looked sidewards.
And they took the Philosopher from his prison,
even the Intellect of Man they took from the hands of the doctors and lawyers, from the sly priests,
from the professors whose mouths are gorged with sawdust, and the merchants who sell blades of grass — the awful people of the Fomor . . . and then they returned again, dancing and singing, to the Country of the Gods . . . "

IV

THE CENTENARY YEATS[1]

*It is fifteen years since I gave the Yeats Memorial Lecture.
T.S. Eliot was my predecessor. Joseph Hone was in the Chair,
and he and H.O. White walked with me from the College to the
Abbey. A few months later the Theatre was burned. As I
stood on that stage I was aware of many ghostly presences;
and Hone and White, names of power in Dublin, have joined
them. I am grateful for the invitation that Trinity has extended
to me.*

§i

I am to speak on the poetry of Yeats; in some sort of anticipation of
the Centenary Year of 1965, though antedating Yeats's birthday by
some few months. It is possible that you may share my own feelings in
not wholly approving of literary centenaries. They are apt to release a
flow of essays, commentaries and miscellaneous criticism, much of which
we could well have spared. Publishers in particular become, as in
Coriolanus, 'waking, audible and full of vent'. The television screens
glaze with superfluous broadcasts. and in the 'confusion of the death-
bed' we are apt to neglect other centenaries of significant figures, such
as those of Marlowe and John Clare. A flood of sentiment, not always
judicious or desirable, is loosed, especially when the writer has a national
or nationalistic image; I am told that the gravel on Burns's grave has to
be renewed periodically to fill the pockets of his admirers who seek some
mana from it. So far we have not had to do that at Drumcliff Churchyard;
and, though a lucrative *tourisme* is growing up round the Lake Isle of
Innisfree, we have dissuaded its owners from planting either beehives
or bean-rows there. (They would not in any event know that, in Ovid,
Nine Beans are one of the offerings for the Dead, and I doubt whether
the poet was aware of this added complexity.)

There are other less harmless aspects. A centenary may be the
occasion of the real or symbolic opening of a grave, to denigrate in the
name of 'objective criticism'. My first book on Yeats, *The Lonely
Tower* was written (to some extent) out of some anger and disgust at
Yeats's image projected in 'the mirror of malicious eyes' of post-war
Dublin. A recent critic of Yeats, J.R.Loftus, has noted that there
are now current among Irish critics persevering attempts to depreciate
Yeats; whether for religious, or national, or social reasons. One is
tempted to quote the words from *Love's Labour's Lost:*

> 'The sweet war-man is dead and rotten: sweet chucks,
> beat not the bones of the buried; while he lived, he was a man.'

1. Trinity College, Dublin: 22 January 1965. I have incorporated certain material
   used in The Skemp Memorial Lecture at Bristol in the same year.

But there is, of course, a sense in which these Festivals of the Dead offer a valid and valuable opportunity for reconsideration. Poetry, and the images out of which it is built, shifts a little in time. It has to be read anew by the light, however 'broken by the leaves' of new contexts in thought, morals, politics, perhaps even of civilization itself. The co-ordinates which determine it as a moving point in literary history may have to be re-considered. We must attempt to make other measurements to define the operative changes, as well as those important curves and angles related to the credentials and personality of those who offer criticism. Yet – I continue my metaphor from physics – it is unlikely that both measurements, in space and time, will have more than an approximate accuracy. My task tonight is to attempt the impossible, or perhaps, in the phrase Yeats was fond of quoting 'of all tasks not impossible the most difficult': to set the poetry of Yeats, first, against his background, and to some extent my own: and then against our own climate of opinion forty years after he wrote his greatest poetry, *The Tower* and *The Winding Stair*. As I do this I shall, inevitably, reveal something of my own background and beliefs.

§ii

Let us first stand back, as it were, from the whole body of the work, and try to celebrate (provocatively, for that is part of my intention) the uniqueness of Yeats.

He is the only poet in our literature who forged a new and vital style after his fortieth, perhaps his forty-fifth winter. I am thinking of those memorable lines from 'Vacillation' – once part of 'Coole Park and Ballylee, 1931' – whose exhortation we neglect at our perils:

> No longer in Lethean foliage caught
> Begin the preparation for your death
> And from the fortieth winter by that thought
> Test every work of intellect or faith,
> And everything that your own hands have wrought,
> And count those works extravagance of breath
> That are not suited for such men as come
> Proud, open-eyed and laughing to the tomb.

He is the only poet in our literature who produced his best work between the ages, say, of fifty-five and sixty-six; in splendid contrast to the host of poets who have spent themselves much earlier: whether in drugs or drink, or in vain attempts to recall dead passions, past intensities, carrying, maybe, 'their mistress in their brain'. Are poets indeed like mathematicians, whose flame – we are told – has often guttered and burnt down by their early thirties?

He is the only poet I know of, who believed, or half believed, that he had started a war; and that war compact, perspicuous, heroic, as it might have been in the Middle Ages or Renaissance history. Was it not

the only successful war in five hundred years of miscellaneous Irish
rebellions? Had its flame been fanned by his own work for Irish
Nationalism, and, at the last, by his play *Cathleen-ni-Houlihan?* It was a
sobering thought:

> Did that play of mine send out
> Certain men the English shot?
> Did words of mine put too great a strain
> Upon that woman's reeling brain?
> Could my spoken work have checked
> That whereby a house lay wrecked? ... [1]

He is the only poet since Milton (should we except Marvell and
Prior?) who held a place of honour in the councils of his country, as
a member for six years of the Irish Senate; and that place, as the recently
published *Speeches* show, by no means negligible.[2] Nor do we commonly
realize that his life and property were, because of that service, in peril
at the hands of the Irish Republican Army, who would have none of
the Treaty.

He is the only poet since Coleridge — should we except Walter de la
Mare? — who has voiced a compelling though intermittent awareness of
the supra-natural; using it, as I believe, between utter conviction and a
kind of defensive ridicule, in the manner of our race: but aware
constantly of the seductions of the séance, of the possibility that truth
might issue from 'a medium's mouth', the strange manner in which the
Twilight of Gods, ghosts and fighting men appeared to certify some
undefined but powerful incursions of *The Middle Kingdom*[3] into human
life, particularly in the West of Ireland. Much later, after his work on
folklore with Lady Gregory, it seemed that these paranormal phenomena
might be as it were legitimized by a symbiosis of philosophy, science
and poetry. In the 'Twenties two physicists of some repute[4] had given
psychical research at least the semblance of respectability. I myself
heard Conan Doyle lecture at Cambridge, with spirit photographs like
those of d'Ochorowicz, whom Yeats mentions with some reverence a
generation later. He showed us the ectoplasm issuing from the medium,
and forming into shapes; one thought of Donne's 'Aire and Angels',
and of the medieval doctrine that angels might take their simulacra
from the 'condensation' of a kind of air. It even seemed possible, for a
moment, that some modification of Berkleian views might be shown,
ultimately, to converge. Perhaps there might even be a new Sacred Book,
in which the physicists and even the philosophers would have a part.

1. 'The Man and the Echo'.
2. (London, 1961) See chapter XII, infra.
3. This is the title of a notable book by D.A. MacManus (2nd edition, Colin
   Smythe Ltd., Gerrards Cross, 1974).
4. Sir Oliver Lodge and Sir Arthur Conan Doyle.

This is, I believe, of profound importance in helping us to understand Yeats's theories of perception. For a key sentence: "The thing seen is never the vision, the thing heard is never the message." The world as perceived by the poet or artist is extensible and extended beyond the normal range of the human sensory powers. The light of Ribh's illumination is 'somewhat broken by the leaves', though it may cast a circle upon the grass.[1] Or, to change the image a little, the light-rays that issue from the Idea may be bent or refracted in the transmission. What is seen, or heard, differs from the ultimate reality; but may and does assume forms which, though symbolic, lead to an apprehension of the truth. Into this process of bending or refraction there is apparent the personality of the artist, poet or prophet; and the quality of his own sensitiveness to the whole metaphysical world. Other variables are the tradition which is inherited, the 'Great Memory', the ability of the individual to draw upon it.

From this arise several consequences. For Yeats himself there is a constant 'dramatization' (his own word) of that which is perceived. It may be an image out of Spiritus Mundi,[2] or from the Tarot Pack, or from arcane rituals such as those of the Golden Dawn. The metaphysical 'apprehension of similitudes' may draw on Classical or Indian or Egyptian or Celtic mythology. They may be assisted by the 'student's lamp'; they may be highly personal, as (for example) his own personal emblem of the hawk. They may acquire a special validity and force by the apparent coincidence, in different cultures, of the same emergent image; and, then or afterwards, be certified by repetition in his own poetry and prose, and be perceived at their most powerful condition when they have some correlative in the natural world of his own experience.[3]

He is the only poet (and I do not forget Blake) who attempted to frame, as a scaffolding for his imagery, perspective of history, and his views on the progress of the soul, what I would call (following Jung and Kerenyi[4] and to break free of the many misleading associations of the word 'myth') a philosophic 'mythologem'; in that strange, erratic but by no means negligible work A Vision; which was first published in 1926, and, eleven years later, in a heavily-revised form.

He is the only poet who has made use of the pictorial and plastic arts, not merely to provide 'metaphors for poetry', but to incorporate these artists and their works into a layered and laminated view of history;

1. 'Ribh at the Tomb of Baile and Aillinn'.
2. 'The Second Coming'.
3. e.g. such birds as the heron, curlew.
4. Introduction to a Science of Mythology trans R.F.C. Hall (London, 1954). For some aspects of the Indian Influences, see H.R. Bachcham, W.B. Yeats & Occultism, (Delhi, 1965).

perceiving through them a kind of pageant of cyclic movements in 'the great mutations of the world', which were illustrated and as it were certified by painter and sculptor. From them came a wide range of archetypal imagery; as well as his view of one major function of the artists, that of guiding men and women to make their sexual choice aright:

> That girls at puberty may find
> The first Adam in their thought,
> Shut the door of the Pope's chapel,
> Keep those children out.
> There on that scaffolding reclines
> Michael Angelo . . . [1]

Yeats's literary output is vast in sheer mass and scope: lyrics, narrative poems, dialogues; folk-lore and fairy-tales; a wealth of letters most of which — but by no means all[2] — are available in Wade's great edition; reviews, criticism, propaganda for the theatre, support of lost causes as different as those of the design of the coinage and the ethics of Irish divorce; some of the greatest satiric poems since Dryden; a mass of plays of many types and magnitudes.

He is the only poet — and I am not omitting by accident Corneille or Coleridge — who has written profoundly on the subject of tragedy. How profoundly, you may read in Edward Engelberg's book *The Vast Design*.[3]

He is the only poet in literature who retained his poetic vitality, coarsened yet unimpaired, through his seventieth year, so that he could write two characteristic poems, both concerned with violence and death, within a few weeks of the end.

If we let our minds rove back, dispassionately, over English literary history, with whom can we compare him? Keats? (have they not something profound in common?) Dryden (Also a poet of political and social concern, but the kinds are wholly incomparable)? Milton? There is no one in the Nineteenth Century to challenge him, though he drew something from Tennyson and Browning, and more from William Morris. And then I remember what I.A. Richards said to me as we walked back, late one night, after reading the newly published *Winding Stair* together:

'This man is the greatest poet since Shakespeare'.

§iii

Against such a background, which I have outlined, deliberately, as a

---

1. 'Long Legged Fly'.
2. The remainder, several hundred at least, are being collected and edited by our own scholar, John Kelly (1972).
3. *The Vast Design: Patterns in W.B. Yeats's Aesthetic*, (Toronto, 1964).

challenge (remembering Bishop Berkeley's words to the mathematicians of Europe 'We Irish think (or do not think) thus') we may sketch some lines of a portrait; in full awareness of the uncertainties when we speak of a personality so complex, so defensive and, at times even contradictory.

He was, from first to last, fully confident of himself as a poet in the professional tradition: composing with notable slowness — was Moore being merely malicious[1] when he spoke of a set maximum of nine lines per day, and of Lady Gregory's rejoicing when the poet had produced five and a half by lunch-time? — and revising meticulously and with infinite labour of the spirit. It is probable that we know more about those revisions than of the work of any other poet, thanks to such scholars as Allt, Alspach, Parkinson, Stallworthy, Bushrui. For his interpretation of the poet's role a certain dramatic isolation was necessary if his work was to be as he himself wanted it to be 'distinguished and lonely'; an aim which seems at variance with an oft-repeated desire to write from 'the book of the people'. The black cloak (which led Moore to compare him to 'an elderly rook', an insult to which Yeats replied with suitable violence in *Dramatis Personae*), the flowing tie, an ignorance (in striking contrast to some of his successors) of the pubs of Dublin, were the outward symbols of one who assumed a somewhat hieratical mask, and who did not easily put his singing robes off and on. Yeats had seen Tennyson and Morris plain; he had admired 'Irving and his plume of pride'; and he had been intimate, as far as he was capable of intimacy, with those whom he called the Tragic Generation; Lionel Johnson, Dowson, Le Gallienne, Beardsley, Wilde. Perhaps it was something of the Irish Protestant in him, or a certain fastidiousness, or the assumption of an aristocratic pose that held him back from the doom of his friends; in whiskey, absinthe, emotionalized religious conversions, and the confused amours of the Strand or the brothels of Dieppe. The straw of that generation blazed up for perhaps a decade; but it serves to remind us that Yeats was no more than twenty-four when *The Wanderings of Oisin* brought Maud Gonne to his Bloomsbury lodging; that he read poetry aloud to fellow-poets who saw in Walter Pater the prophet of the time; that Huysmans' *A Rebours* must have seemed the last and logical step in the pursuit of essences of sensation and sensuality; that Axël, which he was so fond of quoting, seemed almost a sacred book. Those years among the Decadents might have set an irrevocable stamp upon him. Perhaps he was saved by being compelled to re-read Spenser to make his *Selections* from that poet, and by the editing of Blake, which drove him back from the wits of the Cafe Royal, the Strand by gaslight, the bachelor rooms in the Temple, to Thomas Taylor and Plotinus, to Swedenborg, Boehme, Cornelius

1. *Ave* p. 20.

Agrippa, More. If he had died at the turn of the century we might now be arguing his position among the minor pre-Raphaelite poets. It is well to remind ourselves, occasionally, that Blake has his roots in the Eighteenth Century; and that Yeats lived for thirty-six years of his life in the Victorian Age.

§iv

For the purposes of his poetry he named two factors in his life which he called Choice and Chance; which is the title of a previous chapter. As we grow older, we can see them, or their like, forming patterns in our lives. As to Choice, there were, I think, four periods in his life when he set himself out, quite consciously, to equip or re-equip himself for his task as a poet. The first was shortly after the turn of the century, when we can see the first deliberate rejection of a young man's sentimentality, of 'Shelley's Italian light', of what he called 'remorse'. I think we may connect this with the widening insight which his practice at the Abbey Theatre, 'the period of the drudge' that continued till 1910, had given him; though indeed he doubted afterwards whether it had not killed his lyric gifts. The second was, perhaps, from 1911-1914, the end of what we call the 'bitter period' that followed on the death of Synge in 1909. He was then reading under the tutelage of Ezra Pound, discovering Donne in Grierson's great edition, and corresponding with the editor.

The third period of Choice was at Oxford in the early 'twenties; when some leisure, some freedom from a long if genteel poverty, combined with the riches of the Bodleian to set him reading widely and erratically. There is much evidence to suggest that this Oxford period was the happiest in his life.[1] Here too the pictures of the Ashmolean, the Italian journeys with Lady Gregory, the correspondence on philosophy with Sturge Moore, combined with Egyptian thaumaturgy, memories of Plato and of Henry Moore, much miscellaneous information that had long been stored in his mind, found an outlet in Mrs. Yeats's automatic writings and the strange Instructors, to form the patterns of *A Vision*. Finally there is a fourth and less determinate period, linked to the severe illness at Algeciras, and the end, as he saw it, of a new phase in Irish politics and the larger European scene which they seemed to mirror. By 1932 it seemed his world was disintegrating, and a gyre was nearing its end. We who can now look back on the Europe of 1932-4, the rising tide of Fascism, may think he was not far wrong. 'The Second Coming' is too familiar to quote, but we may recall the first few lines:

1. The best and most gracious account of his life at this period is in L.A.G. Strong's *Green Memory* (Methuen, 1961).

> Turning and turning in the widening gyre
> The falcon cannot hear the falconer;

(as Hamlet in his hysteria calls on his father's ghost as he sweeps an imaginary lure round his head)

> Thing fall apart; the centre cannot hold;
> Mere anarchy is loosed upon the world,
> The blood-dimmed tide is loosed, and everywhere
> The ceremony of innocence is drowned . . .

The brutal murder of Kevin O'Higgins, the 'sole statesman', in Yeats's view, of the new Free State, combined with de Valera's return to power and the rule of the New Democracy, emphasized the need for the political thinking that runs through the later work. And here Swift and Berkeley, Mitchel and Parnell, stood as strong ghosts beside him: less strong, but serving the dramatic needs of the moment, shades as diverse as those of Goldsmith and Nietzsche.

The important events seemed to have converged, grouped them-selves into a pattern, in the period 1916-23. His mind had been cleared by the bitter wisdom of *Responsibilities*. In quick succession we have the Easter Rising, the proposal of marriage to Iseult Gonne, his marriage: the purchase for his bride of The Tower that he was to set up as a power-ful emblem, and which was to acquire additional symbols and ironies from the events of the Civil War. Lady Gregory's grief at the death of her son Robert, killed as a fighter-pilot over Italy, had provided him with a subject for two elegies, and with the traditional opportunities of the elegist to meditate on wider issues, and upon his own philosophical outlook. There were precedents from the pastoral tradition, and above all from 'Lycidas' and 'Adonais'. But all elegies seem to lie open to denigration of one kind or another; perhaps they call in question the perennial problem of what is meant by 'sincerity'. These events from 1916 to 1923 we still call, generically, 'The Troubles'. To the poet they give the valuable experience of watching, from The Tower, the end of three hundred years of our civilization; of being linked, ambivalently, to warfare, the operation of politics and nationalism, and the destruction, perhaps by his own hand, of what he had valued so highly. This too I knew as a boy, and as an undergraduate, my own home being then under sentence of burning, a sentence not completed till half a century later.[1] In the confusion the English and the Black and Tans were as much enemies as the Free State or Republicans: by whom my house was raided in turn.

Of that period Yeats wrote in verse that mirrored my own mood:

> We are closed in, and the key is turned
> On our uncertainty; somewhere
> A man is killed, or a house burned,

1. See Chapter XII

> Yet no clear fact to be discerned:
> Come build in the empty house of the stare.

And, for the answer, perhaps, to all the dreams of Ireland:

> We had fed the heart on fantasies,
> The heart's grown brutal from the fare;
> More substance in our enmities
> Than in our love; O honey bees,
> Come build in the empty house of the stare.

Two other incidents, perhaps of Chance, which seem significant. In 1917 he was staying with Maud Gonne in Normandy. He proposed marriage to her daughter, a girl of eighteen: seeing in the daughter — as old men are apt to see their Perditas and Mirandas — the image of her mother twenty-seven years before. She refused him, and became the dancing girl of 'A Long-Legged Fly'; more prophetically

> O you will take whatever's offered
> And dream that all the world's a friend,
> Suffer as your mother suffered,
> Be as broken in the end.[1]

His marriage to Miss Hyde-Lees followed immediately. It gave him what he had always lacked: stability, a home, children, and reassurance of many of his views as to the supra-natural world. To these she added much of the wisdom in affairs that the poet lacked; her wise and tolerant understanding of his friendships and his needs; and the foresight to recognize the importance of the scraps of paper from his workshop which have proved of such value to scholars.

The last significant event was the death of Lady Gregory, and the final end of Coole for which Lady Gregory had fought so long and so courageously, that she might hand it on to her grandchildren, (so the Anglo-Irish thought that their work would endure): after more than three decades of friendship, collaboration, care for his health and comfort; above all, the gift of leisure and attention in that ancestral house. Long before he had speculated on its possible ruin: now no stone of it stands.[2] Wiser councils, and a new generosity towards monuments have kept the Tower from decay. And this was perhaps the crowning irony where Choice and Chance converged; that his own actions had culminated in the destruction of Urbino, of the civilization that he had valued, of the whole Anglo-Irish literary tradition. He had been powerless to stop the clock that he had helped to wind.

$vii

Yet with all its qualities, his immense reputation, the bibliography —

1. 'Two Years Later'
2. This is no longer true: some care has of late been given to the house and woods. (1973).

some fifteen hundred books and major articles —that have clustered upon
his work like limpets on a sea-washed rock, it is possible to argue that
Yeats's poetry is now almost wholly against his age. Let us try to set out
what Yeats himself, writing of the death of Synge, called 'Detractions'.

In the first place it is poetry of the older kind, embodying a strong
and even violent rhythmic energy; which permeates even the speaking
voices of his poems in dialogue, and — in my view — tends to preclude
subtleties of character-in-tone in most of his verse plays. It is a rhetorical
poetry, relying (as Rosamund Tuye has shown) on many of the traditional devices of Elizabethan rhetoric. These were, I think, absorbed
unconsciously, and this must happen to anyone who has what Yeats
demanded from his readers, 'a rich poetical memory'. Always he remembered the lines from *Sailing to Byzantium,* and the Keatsian references
in that poem:

> Nor is there singing school but studying
> Monuments of its own magnificence . . .

We may remember, too, Rabindranath Tagore:

> 'That training is most intricate which leads to the utter
> simplicity of the tune'[1]

I see no critical significance whatever in Professor Yvor Winters's pejorative use of the term *bardic* in connection with Yeats, except perhaps
in *The Wandering of Oisin, The Shadowy Waters,* and in one or two
ballads. One might retort that this part of his poetry is meant to be
'bardic', for it is founded on Celtic saga. But it is a poetry written, in the
tradition, to be read aloud; not perhaps imitating Yeats's method of reading — the records seem to be far too heavy, rhetorical, the lines too
heavily end-stopped — but in the manner of, for example, the late Poet
Laureate:[2] allowing the strong and subtle resonances of the imagery,
the overtones and cadences of Anglo-Irish speech, to emerge.

Secondly (and here I find a certain obtuse simplicity in Professor
Yvor Winters's strictures), it is a poetry based on presuppositions which
are not acceptable; therefore the poetry is unacceptable too. It is a
strange view, which, if pressed home would seem likely to dismiss much
poetry that is founded on or related to many kinds of myth. But the
attack also comes from other sources. Yeats is a 'spook-monger', the
amateur in magic, the member of The Ghost Club, the believer in
horoscopes. So, too, over the faery-aura of the earlier poetry; we may
remember Max Beerbohm's cartoon, and the parody of the *Daily Express*
headline on his death in 1939: 'Scoffed at Fairies, But THEY MADE HIS
LIVING'. Now there is some truth in the first accusation. Yeats was interested in the occult; so were Blake and Milton. He used the fairy world
for decoration; so did Shakespeare and Collins. The strong Theosophist

1. *Gitanjali,* 12.
2. Cecil Day Lewis.

and allied movements of the '90s and later, and their renewed prominence in the 1920s, form a fascinating by-way of social and poetic history. So too the wave of Spiritualism after the First World War not unrelated to its three million dead. Behind and above what we may, on occasion, concede to have been mystery-mongering, a dramatic satisfaction in the occult, a 'stirring at the roots of the hair', I would set out what I take to be the basic facts.

I am clear that Yeats believed, with not disreputable theological authorities, in the communion of saints, and the resurrection or the return of the dead. The dead could influence, even guide the living; whether through a daimon (like those noted by Plutarch), or through the Great Memory, the Jungian Collective Unconscious. If one holds such belief, it is not unreasonable that one should explore, and use for images, the 'wavering and uncertain thoughts' of three thousand years of literature on those matters. Nor is it unreasonable to use the traditional formulae of invocation to recall the memory of dead friends; that, too, has precedents. (I think of 'All Souls' Night', 'A Prayer for My Son', 'Presences'). And if in a scientific sense our ancestors are (as we know) all about us, whether as a cloud of witnesses or as ribo-nucleic acid at the utmost centre of the cell, I am open to conviction through either persuasion. As a Christian I reject the idea (which Yeats seems to have held) of metempsychosis. I have no certainty in my mind (nor had More and Donne) as to the Progress of the Soul after death; but I prefer at least to listen to Yeats rather than to Donne. In short, speculation on this matter seems to me to be neither foolish nor misguided. I should hold by the lines from the third movement of 'The Tower':

> And further add to that
> That, being dead, we rise,
> Dream and so create
> Translunar Paradise.

— or from that noble poem to the theologian Von Hügel:

> Must we part, Von Hügel, though much alike, for we
> Accept the miracles of the saints and honour sanctity?
> The body of Saint Teresa lies undecayed in tomb,
> Bathed in miraculous oil, sweet odours from it come,
> Healing from its lettered slab. Those self-same hands perchance
> Eternalized the body of a modern saint that once
> Had scooped out Pharaoh's mummy. I — though heart might
> find relief.
> Did I become a Christian man and choose for my belief
> What seems most welcome in the tomb — play a predestined
> part.
> Homer is my example, and his unchristened heart . . . [1]

1. 'Vacillation', IV. But see Chapter XIII.

And in the explanation of the sixth line of the poem, in which Yeats imagines the ghosts of Egyptian embalmers coming across the sea to preserve the Saint's body, we might consider the third detraction, that of obscurity.

I do not think that there are more than six poems, and two plays, that deserve this indictment. Among them I would name 'A Bronze Head', 'The Statues' and the two 'death' poems, 'Cuchulain Comforted' and 'The Black Tower', together with three of the shorter poems in *Supernatural Songs*. A number of the others involve, of course, a certain amount of background knowledge; most of which can be drawn, as parts of an organic whole, from other poems, plays and prose. It is not a poetry that responds to analysis of single poems in complete isolation. We must be aware of some basic and perennial imagery, and we must learn to think, at times, in terms of Baudelaire's *correspondances*. Above all, we must have 'a rich poetical memory'. The common bogey, that of the need for an extensive reliance on Celtic mythology, is I think demonstrably false. It is true that there *is* a residue of arcane knowledge. Yeats was certainly not above a certain amount of mystification, and he ploughed with many heifers from the past. We do not yet know the significance (if it is significant) of the statement that the dice used by the soldiers at the foot of the Cross in Calvary 'were made from an old sheep's thigh in Ephesus'; or of the distinction between the Red and Grey Cocks in *A Full Moon in March* (though we remember that they are apparently so distinguished in certain of the Scottish Ballads); or why the flute was made from a heron's thigh in that still-mysterious play *The Herne's Egg*. But I am convinced that there is less commentary required on Yeats than on Eliot or Hopkins, still less than that which we use constantly for Donne or Milton or Blake.

A fourth detraction is that this poetry depends on values, both in the poet and his background, that are unacceptable today. It has to do with a world which is aristocratic, perhaps even authoritarian; it represents and celebrates the culture of a minority; and that minority, in the main, of no more than a section of the Irish aristocracy. There is a good deal of truth in this. The Celtic legend is of its very essence both aristocratic and warlike. The Eighteenth Century figures, the leaders of the two rebellions, who became his heroes, are of this kind. The hierarchy that he perceived in Byzantium, the Workman, Noble and Saint, is a social order to which he seems to look forward in 'The Gyres'. For a short time he flirted with O'Duffy and his blue-shirted comedians. Many at that time approved of Mussolini's operations in Italy on broadly similar grounds. And he assumed an ancestry which was not his by right: a fact which did not escape the notice of George Moore, the jests of some of his friends.

None of this I refute: but I observe only that he mirrors, sensitively and profoundly, the world which I knew as a boy, and which I saw pass, in bloodshed and in the flames of the great houses, in seven years. It was an age of violence, which seemed, perhaps intermittently, the price of Irish nationalism; to an ageing poet it seemed a memorable and cataclysmic experience. Again and again we return to Dante's triad, the great subjects of poetry: love, war and death. In war, with all its waste and horror, there is some purgation through fear, some valued exaltation, even in the prospect of tragic defeat. Yeats had learnt from Blake of 'War and hunting, the two fountains of the river of life . . .' He recalled Mitchel, the rebel of the '98 Rising, in the phrase from the *Jail Journal*.

> You that Mitchel's prayer have heard,
> 'Send war in our time, O Lord!'
> Know that when all words are said
> And a man is fighting mad,
> Something drops from eyes long blind,
> He completes his partial mind . . .
> Even the wisest man grows tense
> With some sort of violence
> Before he can accomplish fate,
> Know his work or choose his mate.

This, as all soldiers know, is true: however we, as armchair moralists, may deprecate it.

§viii

And linked, maybe, to this is a fifth detraction; that this is a *ceremonious* kind of poetry. Indeed 'ceremony' is a word that is often in his mouth. I think that he took it from Shakespeare and from Chapman, and we may recall the famous passage in Chapman's continuation of Marlowe's *Hero and Leander:*

> Thus Time and all-states-ordering Ceremony
> Had banished all offence: Time's golden thigh
> Upholds the flowery body of the earth
> In sacred harmony, and every birth
> Of men and actions makes legitimate;
> Being us'd aright, the use of time is fate.

It is true that Yeats's 'ceremony' extends in many directions: to the Dying Lady, Mabel Beardsley; to the ceremony of the Bride's homecoming in 'A Prayer for My Daughter'; to the new Urbino, 'that grammar school of courtesies' at Coole Park; to women of many kinds and characters. This, as he says, he had learnt from The Tragic Generation; but I believe the real source is Morris. That 'ceremony' seems to some old-fashioned now. Yet he can remain clear-sighted — after the period of the 'cloud-dimmed eyelids' of the girl with 'red mournful lips' — as few poets have been since the Seventeenth Century; and the clarity of vision seems to combine with an unexampled delicacy and tenderness

in *A Woman Old and Young*. I think especially of 'Three Things', of
the exquisitely-modulated 'Lullaby'; ringing the changes on the vowel
music, together with subtleties of alliteration, in a manner that he
may well have learned from Spenser:

> Sleep, beloved, such a sleep
> As did that wild Tristram know
> When, the potion's work being done,
> Roe could run or doe could leap
> Under oak and beechen bough,
> Roe could leap or doe could run . . .

We may perceive, and value, this insight into the minds of women
that is at its height in the lyrics rather than in the plays; it is an insight
that belongs to the wise tenderness of Shakespeare and to the clear
insight of Donne rather than to the Romantics. We may remember
Lucretius:

> medio de fonte leporum
> Surgit amari aliquid quod in ipsis floribus augat.

Here is another version, from 'Solomon and the Witch':

> For though love has a spider's eye
> To find out some appropriate pain —
> Aye, though all passion's in the glance —
> For every nerve, and tests a lover
> With cruelties of Choice and Chance.
> And when at last that murder's over
> Maybe the bride-bed brings despair,
> For each an imagined image brings
> And finds a real image there . . .

For this is a common experience, implicit in the human situation.
And it is a knowledge that I think has value.

Six

But maybe I am the worst possible person to pronounce or to
persuade on questions of value here. This is *my* kind of poetry. I share
with Yeats a love of his countryside, and people, and a knowledge of
its 'wilderness', its 'fish, flesh and fowl' greater perhaps than his. I am
prepared to value a poet who attempts to do what Yeats thought
Plato had done, 'to think all things into unity', to make me aware of
'our marriage to rock and hill'. I think of that strangely Wordsworthian
poem, 'Stream and Sun at Glendalough', where archetypal images of the
Archer and the Star come into phase or resonance with the imagery
derived, I believe, from a painting of the Annunciation. It is worth quoting:

> Through intricate motions ran
> Stream and gliding sun
> And all my heart seemed gay:

Some stupid thing that I had done
Made my attention stray.[1]

Repentance keeps my heart impure;
But what am I that dare
Fancy that I can
Better conduct myself or have more
Sense than a common man?

What motion of the sun or stream
Or eyelid shot the gleam
That pierced my body through?
What made me live like those that seem
Self-born, born anew?[2]

He is a poet that is rhetorical in the older sense. His description of himself as of The Last Romantics is surely too naive. It is dramatic, attacking, violent; concerned with strong and maybe arrogant statements on themes and variations of Dante's triad. With the exception of a few early poems, some of those that he hated, it is beyond parody. He has left no school, no successor. Dylan Thomas might lift a phrase or two, Auden and Vernon Watkins catch something of his accent in noble elegies. Recently a young Irish poet told that he was 'desperately trying to rid himself of Yeats's rhythms'. One merely asked' Why?' For Yeats's poetry rests on the very fortitude and integrity of his rhythms as much as on the 'masterful images', that have their peculiar quality of resonance: in their own, in other poems, in the past. It is a poetry to be read aloud. It is a poetry that wore well, when there were no books (only one's memory) in time of war. But also it is a poetry set in the stream of history, and I find a value in recognizing that, in imagination or in fact. 'The Seven Sages' will serve; where else if not here in Trinity?

The First My great-grandfather spoke to Edmund Burke
In Grattan's house.
The Second   My great-grandfather shared
A pot-house bench with Liver Goldsmith once.
The Third My great-grandfather's father talked of music,
Drank tar-water with the Bishop of Cloyne.
The Fourth But mine saw Stella once.
The Fifth Whence came our thought?
The Sixth From four great minds that hated Whiggery.
The Fifth Burke was a Whig.
The Sixth Whether they knew it or not.

1. See Donne on 'Imperfect Prayer' (Sermon LXXX) for such distractions to the religious mood.

2. See Plotinus, *Enneads*.

> Goldsmith and Burke, Swift and Bishop of Cloyne
> All hated Whiggery; but what is Whiggery?
> A levelling, rancorous, rational sort of mind
> That never looked out of the eye of a saint
> Or out of a drunkard's eye.

The Seventh All's Whiggery now,
> But we old men are massed against the world.

The First   American colonies, Ireland, France and India
> Harried, and Burke's great melody against it.

The Second Oliver Goldsmith sang what he had seen,
> Roads full of beggars, cattle in the fields,
> But never saw the trefoil stained with blood,
> The avenging leaf those fields raised up against it.

The Fourth The tomb of Swift wears it away.

The Third   A voice
> Soft as the rustle of a reed from Cloyne
> That gathers volume; now a thunder-clap.

The Sixth   What schooling had these four?

The Seventh   They walked the roads
> Mimicking what they heard, as children mimic;
> They understood that wisdom comes of beggary.

And then (this is, I hope, my only husk of egotism tonight) I remember that Swift wrote an epigram (which may well be spurious) on my great-great-grandfather's father; on 'The Pig that accompanied Lord Chief Baron Henn on the Munster Circuit in 1704': and that, a few yards from Swift's tomb in St. Patrick's, on the south wall, there is a monument of some eighty years ago that strikes me strangely whenever I visit it; for the name is mine.

V

YEATS AND THE POETRY OF WAR[1]

§i

In the Second Book of Blake's *Milton* there is a notable verse:
'Those Visions of Human Life & Shadows of Wisdom &
Knowledge
Are here frozen to unexpansive deadly destroying terrors;
And War & Hunting, the Two Fountains of the River of Life,
Are become Fountains of bitter Death & of corroding Hell.[2]
My subject today is the influence of war upon a poet's mind. Much
has been written on the poetry of the two great wars of our century;
and the pattern that it followed in 1914-18 is now, I think, sufficiently
distanced to have taken shape in our minds. Perhaps it would not be
too far from the truth to think of it as following the common trajectory
of all war-poetry; enthusiasm, disillusionment, cynicism, followed by
the despair and horror of each battlefield of the fifth day. But in our
recent European and Mediterranean wars the whole action seems to have
been too vast, too impersonal (except perhaps in Spain) for the individual poet to attain to any kind of perspective, still less to shape
from it even the fragments of an epic. It is true that from time to time
a single event, perhaps a sea-battle of small ships against great odds,
has produced poetry of this nature; though not, I think of the highest
quality. Too often we return, for the satisfaction of our mood, to
Shakespeare's *Troilus and Cressida*, and the two recurrent themes.[3]
And those of us who have seen Europe in ruin are aware that no poet
could do more than glimpse a fragment of that vision of human suffering. One was only aware of its frozen, unexpansive terror in the
mass, and the pitiful goodness and charity of individual men and
women.

There is, I believe, no instance in literary history that allows us to
study the effect of war upon a poet with the completeness and subtlety
that we are offered in Yeats's poetry. The Easter Rising, and the
Troubles that followed it, extend in their Protean forms from Easter
1916 till about the beginning of 1923: their aftermath of violence continues till 1928; that of political bitterness and dissension for much
longer. The abortive ten days' warfare in Dublin shades into the guerilla
fighting and burnings, the atrocities and counter-atrocities of the British
Irregulars, the so-called 'Black and Tans', the Treaty of 1921, the Civil
War between Free State and Republicans. It ended, more or less, in

1. The Warton Lecture: British Academy, 1965.
2. 34, 35.
3. "All the argument is a cuckold and a whore" - "Wars and lechery, all inconti-
    nent varlets"

the 'victory' of David over Goliath; it continued when David, not unexpectedly, raised his armed insurrection against Saul.

It is clear that Yeats was wholly unsympathetic to the poetry and drama of war as seen by his contemporaries. His exclusions from *The Oxford Book of Modern Verse* are as notorious as the inclusions of the work of his friends.[1] The quarrels with O'Casey, whose work was so essential to the continuing life of the Abbey, are too familiar to rehearse, but we may see in them, and in Lady Gregory's criticism, the misguided fastidiousness of taste that had tried to censor the language of *The Playboy*. The poets of the First War, as he saw them, were obsessed with recording its cruelty, futility, pathos, suffering. Wildren Owen was 'all blood, dirt and sucked sugar-stick'. 'On being asked for a War Poem' he refused:

> for in truth
> We have no gift to set a statesman right . . .

Robert Gregory's death as a fighter-pilot in Italy was carefully dissociated from the patriotism of war:

> Nor law, nor duty bade me fight,
> Nor public men, nor cheering crowds . . .

and had grown into a personal and elegiac myth. The anti-British sentiments of 1920 could be readily aligned with the personalities of the Easter Rising, and they in turn with gods and fighting men; but he had no sympathy with O'Casey's tenement-dwellers, or with the incantation in the second act of *The Silver Tassie*. War as a subject for poetry was valid only in so far as circumstances allowed him to celebrate the response to its challenge of the individual or of a small heroic group, and to return to his favourite concept of tragedy; the confrontation of the utmost obstacles to the hero's will, the resolution of conflict in the central paradox of 'tragic joy'. For his justification he refers to Arnold, and praises that critic's withdrawal of *Empedocles on Etna:* 'passive suffering is not a theme for poetry'. The tragic hero must find his mask, his complementary opposite, in defeat. Hamlet, Lear, Antony, Cleopatra, Coriolanus become archetypal figures. 'No tragedy is legitimate unless it leads a great character to his final joy".

If we stand apart and consider it dispassionately there were many factors that provided superb material and 'metaphors for poetry'; and, even more important, an utterly new range of experiences for an ageing poet of fifty-one. The Irish War was small enough, compact enough, to be 'perspicuous'; one man might hold in his mind many aspects of it together. The outbreak was the result of a long period of preparation — political, social; literary, ideological - from the middle of the Nineteenth

---

1. Notably, the space given to Gogarty, to Dorothy Wellesley, and to Frank O'Connor.

Century on: perhaps, indeed, from the battles of the Williamite Wars. It was born of an intensively-fostered patriotism which, in a somewhat artefacted renaissance, found support in myth, legend, allegory and the repeating patterns of history. It had even drawn on the mystical approach of 'A.E.' to Ireland's druidic past, her elder gods, and the sanctity of her soil and landscape. The very isolation of Ireland, the antiquity of her culture and religion, her ancient language that was to receive new life at a stage when English had exhausted its possibilities as a medium for poetry,[1] seemed to give form and energy to the vision of her as a bastion of the West; a strong tower against the commerical and philistine imperialism — this was Shaw's thought also — that had sought for four centuries to crush her, spiritually and physically. The fires of nationalism had been long-nursed, and fed with many twigs: the embers had been cherished, after each defeat, with the characteristic long-memoried bitterness of the Irish mind. Yet with the outward Aristotelian simplicity of the fable, there were factors of some complexity in the unravelling and reversals of the plot. These, in turn, provided the material for that intense irony without which, I believe, there cannot be poetic depth or universality.

§ii

A fifty-year old memory is notoriously treacherous; but since I have chosen to speak of the background against which I think this poetry must be seen, I must appear for a moment to be personal. I was a schoolboy of fourteen at the time of the Rising. My brother had been wounded with the Munster Fusiliers at Gallipoli: one of the many Irishmen who were serving in England's war. There was no virtue in that, as Kipling noted,[2] but we may remember that many of them had gone to war on the promise of the British Government that Home Rule, so nearly achieved in 1914, would be given in full after the war was over. But because some of us were serving, as also because of religion and ownership of land, one's family was suspect. Violence, even before the seemingly halcyon days of 1903-1914, was never far from one's life: I remember that the horse and trap went through a pool of blood as we drove to the train that was to take me to my preparatory school, and that my Father covered my eyes as we passed. (This was no more than a 'private' murder). There were times when one did not sit, of an evening, between the window and the lamp-light, particularly when the anonymous letters, signed with a red-ink coffin or 'Captain Moonlight', had been especially frequent. So in Yeats's 'Beautiful Lofty Things' of Lady Gregory's challenge to one who threatened her life by sitting at the open window. It was through such gestures that my Mother, widowed

1. Such was George Moore's view: and that of other contemporaries in England.
2. v. 'The Irish Guards.'

and alone, had kept the house intact through seventeen raids, from British, Republicans and Free Staters who looted with a fine impartiality objects that they thought useful. They included fishing tackle, cavalry swords from the days of the Crimea, even a sidereal telescope. Later, as an undergraduate, I returned for the Long Vacation of 1921 to what was virtually a state of siege, with bridges destroyed and roads barricaded. I remembered Spenser at Kilcolman, read all *The Faerie Queene,* and wrote of what I thought Spenser might have felt in those circumstances. Forty miles to the north, and thus infinitely isolated, were Lady Gregory at Coole, Yeats at Thoor Ballylee. By then three of my friends had been shot, one after torture. and about a score of houses in the county had been burned.

$iii

This burning of the 'great houses' requires some momentary consideration. Agrarian troubles, murder, destruction of woods and landmarks, the 'driving' and maiming of cattle and horses, had been the accompaniments of Irish land-tenure since the Norman occupation, and are perhaps endemic in any society in which that tenure has been arbitrary in its imposition, inequitable in its maintenance, and subject to a racist mythology. "No Irishman ever gets anything from you till he goes to you with the head of a landlord in one hand and the tail of a cow in the other," said Barry O'Brien to a Cabinet minister in 1877. Yeats's 'Upon a House Shaken by the Land Agitation' is a relatively early poem; it is only of interest as a statement of his admiration for that aristocratic life, and for the prophecy that was exactly fulfilled when the stones of Coole were carted to new housing estates in Galway to make

mean rooftrees . . . the sturdier for its fall.

Even before 1914 the ruins were everywhere, though the systematic burnings belong mainly to the period 1917-23. Yeats's imagery that is connected with them is of peculiar interest.

As a boy he had been greatly moved by a burning house: Castle Dargan, which is remembered in a song in *The King of the Great Clock Tower.*[1] The play *Purgatory* centres upon a house in which the ghosts re-enact their marriage (as in a Noh play) in a blaze of light, while the son and grandson of that union watch them. 'The Curse of Cromwell' also ends with that scene:

> I came on a great house in the middle of the night,
> Its open lighted doorway and its windows all alight,
> And all my friends were there and made me welcome too;
> But I woke in an old ruin that the winds howled through . . .

But the burning of Troy, its destruction for a woman's sake, became the dramatic symbol (turning many ways in the mind, between Leda, and

1   'Castle Dargan's ruin all lit
   Lovely ladies dancing in it.'

Helen, and Deirdre) for his love for Maud Gonne. That in turn formed part of the repeating pattern of history. Nor should we forget the archetypal symbolism of the ultimate resolution by fire.

Any military action that involves direct and necessary destruction brings in its train, both in war and in the uneasy peace that so often follows it, events which have no intrinsic connection with the main action. A house may be burnt because of a suspicion that it may be harbouring enemies, that munitions of war are concealed there, that the owner is a spy or informer. (I have instances of all three in mind, and by both protagonists in the Civil War.) But in all guerilla warfare there are actions which arise from very different motives, greed, revenge, racial hatred, religious bitterness. We were familiar with this in the invaded territories in the Second War. A certain city in North Italy counted thirty murders nightly, long after the battle was over. The atrocities committed against the collaborators were often far more horrifying than those of the German invaders against native suspects, and emphasized once more the truism that cruelty is always close to the surface.

So it was in the burnings and murders of the 'Troubles'. Behind many of them, whatever the ostensible pretext, there was the hunger for the land of the demesnes; often looking no further than squatters' rights or the building of squared stones into byres, once the owners had gone. There was in fact a rationalized and heaven-sent projection of the land-wars of the Nineteenth Century. The religious fanaticism, which divided the priests when the Civil War came, might partake on occasion of the character of a holy war[1]; forgetting that the great leaders of past rebellions had been mainly Anglo-Irish and Protestant.

Yet here again there were paradoxes. The memories of the peasantry were often long and warm, much concerned with ancestry, and with the virtues, real or imagined, of aristocracy. Here as elsewhere Yeats is completely faithful to experience. One's own people, within, say, a ten-mile radius, would not, as a rule, combine to burn or murder; but unlike a Highland clan they would not move to save you, being easily frightened (as Synge had noticed) of their own people in conspiracy. So in 'Nineteen Hundred and Nineteen':

> But is there any comfort to be found?
> Man is in love and loves what vanishes,
> What more is there to say? That country round
> None dared admit, if such a thought were his,
> Incendiary or bigot could be found
> To burn that stump on the Acropolis,
> Or break in bits the famous ivories
> Or traffic in the grasshoppers or bees.

1. These words were used by a Birmingham priest in December 1971. He was 'admonished' by his superiors; but there were repetitions.

Lorry-loads of Republicans would arrive, brought from a neighbouring
county. I saw such a burning, through a summer's night, two miles
away across the valley. Those who burnt it were too drunk to come
on to burn my home, as (I was afterwards told) they intended. So
one walked the demesne woods at night, with all the folly of a boy,
waiting for

> armed men
> Who'd ring the house before the lorries came
> Laughing, a little drunk, their rifles blessed from the altar,
> To pay three conquests, hunger of the hill fields . . .

Yet that war, like all wars, had its comic side. I still have the photo-
graph of a firing party who came to shoot me, early one summer's
morning. One of the 'weapons' they discovered was the sound-box of
an old-fashioned gramophone, in a circular case: its delicate mehanism
suggested a bomb. It was necessary to demonstrate by producing the
gramophone and playing a record. We gave them breakfast, and the
party posed for me, kneeling, with rifles at the ready.

§iv

From a military point of view the Easter Rising was a gallant farce;
'that crazy fight', as Yeats calls it in 'The O'Rahilly'. It was ill-prepared
and ill-armed; its organization was rudimentary. Too many Irish volunteer armies had been the subject of Gilbertian comedy for them to be
taken quite seriously. Yeats has noted this with precision, as well as
giving us his relationship to the leaders:

> I have met them at close of day
> Coming with vivid faces
> From counter or desk among grey
> Eighteenth-century houses.
> I have passed with a nod of the head
> Or polite meaningless words,
> Or have lingered awhile and said
> Polite meaningless words,
> And thought before I had done
> Of a mocking tale or a gibe
> To please a companion
> Around the fire at the club,
> Being certain that they and I
> But lived where motley is worn:
> All changed, changed utterly:
> A terrible beauty is born.

There were 'mocking tales' in plenty; of the travesties of military rank,
of the route-marches to the public houses; of that officer who shot
himself when he dragged a loaded rifle after him by the muzzle
through a quick-set hedge near my house; more bitter, of the British
troops in the pubs who sold their opponents .303 cartridges to kill

them, at the price of one pint of porter for each round. The 'crazy fight' was precipitated by British political ineptitude. As a concerted plan it depended, on the Irish side, on a number of wished-for but unlikely possibilities. A country-wide rising in sympathy, a massive reinforcement of weapons from Germany, the arrival from that country of an Irish Brigade composed of renegades from the prisoner-of-war camps – all these were hoped for, but were mere fantasies. So in 'The Stare's Nest by My Window' Yeats pondered, in words of great profundity, on the meaning of the idealism that lay behind the wars. Again and again he expressed the thought; as in 'Easter 1916':

> We know their dream; enough
> To know they dreamed and are dead . . .

When the Rising broke out one was aware first of a stunned silence, as communications were cut and rumours began to spread. There followed the politically inept executions, which seemed to confirm so clearly the patterns of 1798 and 1848. A year later came the reprisals of Bloody Sunday, the murder of British officers in their beds.[1] The chain-reaction had begun; 'the blood-dimmed tide' was loosed, though it was little enough in comparison with the slaughter in France.

Yeats mirrored faithfully the period of numb horror of 1917-21:

> Now days are dragon-ridden, the nightmare
> Rides upon sleep: a drunken soldiery
> Can leave the mother, murdered at her door,
> To crawl in her own blood, and go scot-free[2] . . .

In times of war certain incidents, terrible or comic, etch themselves on the mind. One of these occurred when a lorry full of Black and Tans fired a burst from a Lewis gun down the village street at Kiltartan, and killed a woman. The lorries, protected by wire roofing against grenades, roamed the countryside at high speed, with the avowed and militarily senseless object of terrorizing the people. The pattern was a familiar one in France, Italy, Greece. I have memories of being machine-gunned by a lorry-load of Auxiliaries as they passed below a wooded hill where the main road ran through our demesne. This was nothing but sheer nerves; the place was an attractive one for an ambush, and raw troops will spray fire aimlessly under such conditions.

But the episode of the murdered woman was complicated by Yeats's *pietas* towards Major Robert Gregory, the 'Irish Airman', who was killed in action over Italy on 23rd January 1918. The familiar poem was written that year. Of it I would only draw attention to the manner in which Yeats isolates Gregory's service with the Royal Flying Corps from political considerations; there is, I believe, a back-handed reference

---

1. This is now celebrated, in a popular paperback, as the liquidation, by heroic liberators, of nearly all the British 'secret agents' in Dublin.
2. 'Nineteen Hundred and Nineteen'.

both to Redmond's recruiting campaign of 1914-15, and to the threat
of conscription for the Irish which followed:

> Nor law, nor duty bade me fight,
> Nor public men, nor cheering crowds,
> A lonely impulse of delight
> Drove to this tumult in the clouds.

Because of the Kiltartan shooting Yeats's mind swung violently towards
nationalism.[1] Robert Gregory's death had been rendered futile by the
betrayal of the loyalist element among the gentry. (The same thought
was in my mind when, under sentence of burning by the Republicans,
we were refused military protection by the British.) And since the poem
is not easily available, and is of some importance in relation to Yeats's
attitude to war, you will forgive me if I quote it in full.
I use the American Variorum text.

   In the opening lines Yeats picks up the thought of 'The Irish
Airman . . .', the exaltation of the fighting man which we shall see later
in 'Under Ben Bulben'; and a kind of Celtic saga-ecstasy, that recalls
the description of Cuchulain in battle:

> Some nineteen German planes, they say,
> You had brought down before you died.
> We called it a good death. Today
> Can ghost or man be satisfied?
> Although your last exciting year
> Outweighed all other years, you said,
> Though battle joy may be so dear
> A memory, even to the dead,
> It chases other thought away,
> Yet rise from your Italian tomb,
> Flit to Kiltartan Cross and stay
> Till certain second thoughts have come
> Upon the cause you served, that we
> Imagined such a fine affair:
> Half-drunk or whole-mad soldiery
> Are murdering your tenants there.
> Men that revere your father yet
> And shot at on the open plain.
> Where many new-married women sit
> And suckle children now? Armed men
> May murder them in passing by
> Nor law nor parliament take heed.

---

1. Lady Gregory's 'conversion' from Unionism to Home Rule goes back to 1895.

> Then close your ear with dust and lie
> Among the other cheated dead.[1]

It is violent and rhetorical, and Yeats could be both; but it emphasizes
from yet another angle the dichotomy in Yeats's mind, loyalty to the
Gregorys and what they stood for in the aristocratic tradition, set
against the death to which the aftermath of war had lent this bitter irony.

§v

We make poetry, not out of the experiences which we go out to
seek, but of those 'events which come upon us like waves'. The dualism
which Yeats uses, Chance and Choice, will serve as well as any to express
the patterning of a poet's life. At isolated moments the two had
appeared to converge. Some of them are clear: the long love-affair
with Maud Gonne, the death of O'Leary; the engagement (I use the
word deliberately) with the Abbey and its affairs, the death of Synge, and
the 'dark period' that followed it; the Lane pictures, the friendship
with Ezra Pound, the reading of Grierson's *Donne;* the chance that gave
him a home at Coole, and the love and encouragement that all poets
seek from women; the revelation of Italian and Byzantine art on the
journeys with Lady Gregory. All these events faded before the Easter
Rising.

He had no part in its planning. It is said that he was disappointed
because he was not consulted as to the date. He had founded the Irish
Literary Society. He was a member, though not an active one, of the
Irish Republican Brotherhood. His association with Irish nationalism
went back to his early years in London; and in particular to the sense
of isolation, of mixed shame and pride, that is a not uncommon
experience of the Irish schoolboy in England.[2] In the guerilla and civil
wars he had played the part only of spectator. From 1918 the Tower
had given a multiplex symbol of the past and of the present; an
alignment at once with 'Milton's Platonist', with the poet's defence, with

---

1 I am not satisfied with the text of this, which is the one given in Allt and
Alspach, (Var.) p. 791. This in turn seems to have been taken from Rann,
1948. But I have a version taken down from Allt himself, in 1947, which
seems to me more Yeatsian. I give the variants:
1,2 Although you had shot down, they say / Some nineteen planes before you
died.
5,6 I had more happiness in a year / Than in all other years, you said.
7 And battle joy.
9 It chases common thoughts away.
13 Upon the cause that you and we / Imagined such a fine affair.
23 Nor parliament nor law.
24 Then stop your ears . . .

2. See Chapter XII, infra.

the imagined continuity of Irish history from the Norman invasion onwards, with its domination of the countryside as well as the protection of the storm-beaten cottages beside it. As the spectator in the Tower there lingered a sense of disappointment at his inactivity. One of his chosen masks was that of the Swordsman who had repudiated the Saint (and had taken fencing lessons to give substance to the rhetoric); in his private myth he had thrown in his lot with Oisin rather than St. Patrick. In 'The Road at my Door' he talks with both Irregular and Free State soldiers; then —

> I count those feathered balls of soot
> The moor-hen guides upon the stream,
> To silence the envy in my thought;
> And turn towards my chamber, caught
> In the cold snows of a dream.

Who could resist the thought that he had launched the only Irish insurrection that had been successful? or silence the age-old envy

"We fought at Arcques, brave Crillon, and you were not there."

After an event of magnitude the resultant poetry seems to be generated in several waves. One is immediate; the poem written within weeks or months after the event: the imagination may be stirred by some phrase — such as 'A terrible beauty is born' — or by a rhythm, or a phrase from Shakespeare. Round them the images cluster and thicken. Of this kind are the Elegy on Major Robert Gregory, 'The Irish Airman', 'Easter 1916'. These were the first fruits; 'Easter 1916' is in 'Michael Robartes and the Dancer' of 1921, together with 'Sixteen Dead Men' and 'The Rose Tree'. These last are, I think, over-rated.

Then the experiences seem to lie fallow for a time. *The Tower* in 1928 is, by common consent, the summit of Yeats's poetic achievement. Here the poems directly concerned with the War and the Troubles are 'Ancestral Houses' and 'Nineteen Hundred and Nineteen'. Afterwards we have a more mature and meditative movement. There are changing perspectives of politics, national aspirations, responsibilities, friendships. It is pertinent to suggest some aspects of their particular combinations of Choice and Chance.

By 1921 the burning of the great houses appeared complete; yet they carried over into the Civil War, when more than twenty houses of Senators, most of them from the landed gentry, were burnt by the Republicans. Expropriation in various fields had driven others out. The returned ex-soldiers of the British Army were often widely and violently persecuted. By the middle twenties it was clear that a particular aspect of the Anglo-Irish tradition had been destroyed.

This was not, I think, the dilemma, but rather the great instrument that strung and tensioned Yeats's mind. If indeed he had been, however remotely, responsible for the Rising and what followed, then he had destroyed the civilization which had made possible his poetry; into whose ancestry he had aligned himself in imagination,whose personalities, men and women, he had celebrated and valued. If he had not been responsible, then the whole heroic aspect of the Rising was empty; his own vanity appalled or ridiculed. It was now clear that the maintenance of an aristocratic tradition was impossible:

> Many ingenious lovely things are gone
> That seemed sheer miracle to the multitude,
> Protected from the circle of the moon
> That pitches common things about . . .[1]

and

> But he killed the house; to kill a house
> Where great men grew up, married, died,
> I here declare a capital offence.[2]

It did not matter that his vision of the country houses was idealized in the extreme; that for every family with pretensions to culture there were many whose Philistinism was as blatant as anything in Victorian England.

§vi

There was to be a third phase, from the early Nineteen-Thirties onwards. Again it is complex. By 1934 Coole and Lady Gregory were dead, and Yeats was beginning to seek the company and encouragement of Lady Dorothy Wellesley. A kind of malaise, something like the onset of Jacobean melancholy, seemed to have descended on Ireland! It seems possible that Yeats believed that a gyre, a great movement of history, had ended. There was the rise of the Nazis, the Spanish Civil War, the preparations for rearmament. In 1932 de Valera returned to power; Yeats and many of his friends regarded him as responsible for the Civil War:

> Had de Valéra eaten Parnell's heart
> No loose-lipped demagogue had won the day,
> No civil rancour torn the land apart.[3]

One of his first acts was to bring forward a Bill for the Abolition of the Irish Senate, and the seats of the University Representatives: both containing elements which might have moderated political opinion and given much stability and wisdom to the Government. Yeats's term of office as a Senator had expired. An abortive Fascist movement, led by General O'Duffy, was a counter-protest against authoritarianism; for it, Yeats wrote the somewhat disjointed *Marching Songs*. Into one of them is incorporated (strangely, but a sign of factitious composition)

---

1 'Nineteen Hundred and Nineteen' Notice the 'vulgar' *pitch*, the deliberate allusion both to Empedocles and to the street-corner game of 'pitch and toss'.
2 *Purgatory*.
3 'Parnell's Funeral'. II.

a phrase of Mrs. Yeats's, when a neighbour's dog was supposed to have killed her chickens:

> 'Drown all the dogs', said the fierce young woman.

But violence still continued. De Valera did not finally outlaw his former comrades of the I.R.A. till he came to power. Of the episodes in that 'warfare' the one which horrified Yeats above all others was the murder, in 1927, of Kevin O'Higgins; his life-long friend, shot in the back by five men as he was going to Mass. The death is mourned twice; once in that most noble poem, 'Death':

> Nor dread nor hope attend
> A dying animal;
> A man awaits his end
> Dreading and hoping all;
> Many times he died,
> Many times rose again.
> A great man in his pride
> Confronting murderous men
> Casts derision upon
> Supersession of breath;
> He knows death to the bone —
> Man has created death.

It is recalled in 'Parnell's Funeral':

> Had Cosgrave eaten Parnell's heart, the land's
> Imagination had been satisfied,
> Or lacking that, government in such hands,
> O'Higgins its sole statesman had not died.

In the same poem we have the full and bitter indictment of the wars, of which these senseless violences seemed the culmination:

> Come, fix upon me that accusing eye.
> I thirst for accusation. All that was sung,
> All that was said in Ireland is a lie
> Bred out of the contagion of the throng,
> Saving the rhyme rats hear before they die.
> Leave nothing to the nothings that belong
> To this bare soul, let all men judge that can
> Whether it be an animal or a man.

We cannot assent to the romantic view of the I.R.A. of 1921 as set out by Frank O'Connor. 'They were simply high spirited, generous, adventurous boys, escaped from farms and classrooms'.

A.E. whose integrity was absolute, left Dublin in disgust to die (so inappropriately) at Bournemouth. A new and more stringent censorship was driving the poets and writers abroad. There was left for Yeats little but a proud and formal withdrawal, as he thought of Berkeley's phrase:

> We Irish, born into that ancient sect
> But thrown upon this filthy modern tide

And by its formless spawning fury wrecked,
Climb to our proper dark, that we may trace
The lineaments of a plummet-measured face.[1]

$vii

So the 'casual comedy' that preceded 'Easter 1916' had passed
through a 'terrible beauty', to become embodied in a government that
was the anti-type of all that he had valued. Coole was desolate; most of
the great houses of the south and west were in ruins. Even Gogarty's
house at Renvyle had been wantonly burned; and Gogarty, the wit, poet,
and athlete had been something of a hero in Dublin. All that was left
was an Ireland which might one day be educated into alignment with
the European tradition; which might achieve the Greek virtues of proportion, symmetry, control. So in 'The Gyres':

. . . Things thought too long can be no longer thought,
For beauty dies of beauty, worth of worth,
And ancient lineaments are blotted out.
Irrational streams of blood are staining earth . . .

He thought of the women he had loved, whose voices had grown shrill
in the politics which he detested, their bodies bent in old age:

Dear shadows, now you know it all,
And the folly of a fight
With a common wrong or right.[2]

Yet the country might be unified, and a golden age return — he
had used Virgil's thought before[3] — with the returning gyre. The tones
are resonant and prophetic, as if they had been borrowed from that
favourite poem, the 'Nocturnall' of Donne:

—shall,
From marble of a broken sepulchre,
Or dark betwixt the polecat and the owl,
Or any rich, dark nothing disinter
The workman, noble and saint, and all things run
On that unfashionable gyre again.

'It must be a terrible thing, when one is old, and the tomb round
the corner, to think of all the ambitions one has put aside; to think
perhaps, a great deal about women.'[4]

I have quoted this out of context from *The Resurrection;* but I think it
is relevant to this phase of *Last Poems.* Women move, in painting or
statuary, as queens or harlots or dancing girls, through its pages. Their
rustling shadows throng the stairway to his room; their words are
'remembered sweetness'. They are, in a sense, part of the gaiety of

1. 'The Statues'.
2. 'In Memory of Eva Gore-Booth and Con Markiewicz'.
3. 'Two Songs from a Play'.
4. *The Resurrection.*

mood. The volume is in a sense a gathering up of what had gone before; and a return (this is the normal cycle) to the experiences of his boyhood.

§viii

By 1935, and in his seventieth year, the Rising and the Civil War had turned in a little on their axes. The first had lost, except for a spasmodic and I think forced celebration in strong and coarse balladic rhythms, all epic and bardic quality. There is little imagery of the heroic battle. The legendary heroes had long been discarded in favour of Parnell, The O'Rahilly, Roger Casement. Only Cuchulain remained as a symbol, embodied in the 'true faith' of statuary, for the last stand in the Post Office, and for himself in old age. Oedipus had failed to answer the riddle of the Sphinx,[1] on the Rock of Cashel or elsewhere. Perhaps he was now passing to an Irish Colonos.

So, "I count the links in the chain of responsibility, and wonder if any of them end in my workshop". More concisely, in 'The Man and the Echo':

> All that I have said and done,
> Now that I am old and ill,
> Turns into a question till
> I lie awake night after night
> And never get the answers right.

Yet there is pride as well as bewilderment in the tone:

> Did that play of mine send out
> Certain men the English shot? . . .
> Could my spoken words have checked
> That whereby a house lay wrecked?

It could not; and in this was the central conflict in Yeats's mind as he 'meditated on wounds and blood', the wars and their result. With 'fashion changed, that high horse riderless', there was little left but a strange tragic exaltation, such as that which Shakespeare makes his characters speak under the pressure of coming death or of achieved despair. There is now much of *Hamlet* and *Antony and Cleopatra* in Yeats's verse. He had written of a Nietzschean 'tragic joy' as early as *The King's Threshold*.[2] He was to celebrate the destructive exaltation of the soldier in 'Under Ben Bulben'. In this new tragedy he finds both an assertion of courage, an aristocratic pride and calm in the face of defeat. 'Lapis Lazuli' begins colloquially, almost cynically, with the hysterical women, the Siege of Drogheda and the Zeppelin raids of the first war: then —

---

1. 'The Double Vision of Michael Robartes'.
2. See p.42 *supra*.

> Yet they, should the last scene be there,
> The great stage curtain about to drop,
> If worthy their prominent part in the play,
> Do not break up their lines to weep.
> They know that Hamlet and Lear are gay;
> Gaiety transfiguring all that dread.

In a new gyre, with 'workmen, noble and saint', reunited in that impossible Byzantine hierarchy, war might yet unify the nation.

It was not clear where that war might be fought; South against North to abolish Partition? (this seemed possible in 1937) or against England if she attempted to reoccupy the Treaty Ports when de Valera had broken the agreement? (this again was a possibility in 1941). More likely — there are other indications in *Last Poems* and *On the Boiler* — he thought that the exaltation that only the fighting man knew might be recovered in war; however much 'the rattle of those arms' might affright the dead when Cuchulain comes to The Valley of the Dead.[1]

Six

The two final poems, written just before his death, are concerned with war. 'The Black Tower', perhaps on some Sligo or Galway headland, has ironic overtones from *King Lear* and Browning and Malory. It concerns the poet in his last defence; it is the successor to Thoor Ballylee. In it the King waits for the horn of Charlemagne or Arthur, who sleeps surrounded by his men and his hounds, under the castle of Sewingshields in Northumberland.[2] But it also contains, I believe, the sharp Yeatsian precision of allegory. When de Valera came to power he brought in a Bill for the Removal of the Oath of Allegiance, which he himself had signed, explaining his action with some naiveté: "I signed the Oath in the same way as I sign an article for a newspaper". To this Yeats's friend Oliver Gogarty retorted . . . "I uphold it because I signed it". A sequal three years later was de Valera's attempt to reconstitute the Senate; but on a very different basis from that in which Yeats had served with some distinction.

He and his friends were isolated in the Black Tower. 'The wine gone sour' was a phrase he had used earlier for disappointment in politics. The new order, the 'base-born products of base beds',[3] wished for his support:

> Those banners come to bribe or threaten,
> Or whisper that a man's a fool
> Who, when his own right king's forgotten,

---

1. This was the original title of 'Cuchulain Comforted'. See page 96 infra and especially Kathleen Raine's important essay. *(New Yeats Papers,* VIII. Dolmen Press, 1974).

2. I am indebted for this suggestion to W.J. Keith.

3. 'Under Ben Bulben'.

Cares what king sets up his rule.
If he died long ago
Why do you dread us so?

The strange incantatory refrain shifts and modulates as he remembers the ancient battlefields between Knocknarea and Ben Bulben, the warrior buried upright that guards Queen Maeve's tumulus:

There in the tomb stand the dead upright,
But winds come up from the shore:
They shake when the winds roar,
Old bones upon the mountain shake.

Against a rising storm the Black Tower stands ironically, stubborn in defiance of his last values.

The other war-poem is 'Cuchulain Comforted'. The legendary fighting man comes fresh from his last battle into a Dantesque valley of the shadows. We remember the multiplicity of the Cuchulain images: the fighter of 'the ungovernable sea'; the slayer of his own son, begotten on that fierce woman, Aoife; the lover of Emer and Fand of the fairy world (I do not press the parallels); the heroic ghost that 'stalked through the Post Office' to hearten Pearse and Connolly in their last stand.[1] Now the phantom is among the shrouds or shades. The warrior terrifies them. He must forsake the violence and blood by which he had lived. He must learn to cooperate with the dead, to unite with them in sewing a shroud; Yeats remembers Blake's image for the spiritual body. The soldier is accepted, after knowledge of those two fountains of the river of life, war and hunting. But the visions of human life and shadows of wisdom and knowledge, were to be tranfigured into the bird-spirits of the Celtic myth in the country Tir-na-n'Og when the preparations for death are completed, and they have learned to sing in unison.

They had changed their throats and had the throats of birds.

So the 'casual' comedy and the 'terrible beauty' end. As in all tragic plays the resolution must be through lyric speech. We might return to a play written for the beginnings of the Abbey,[2] to find a fitting epitaph for the poet of this war:

The first is spoken by the *Youngest Pupil:*

O silver trumpets, be you lifted up
And cry to the great race that is to come.
Long throated swans upon the waves of time,
Sing loudly, for beyond the wall of the world
That race may hear our music and awake.

The second is spoken by the *Oldest Pupil,* and will better serve for Ireland and for Yeats:

1. 'The Statues'
2. *The King's Threshold.*

Not what it leaves behind it in the light
But what it carries with it to the dark
Exalts the soul; nor song nor trumpet - blast
Can call up races from the worsening world
To mend the wrong and mar the solitude
Of the great shade we follow to the tomb.

VI

THE RHETORIC OF YEATS[1]

. . . "I am particularly indebted to you for your essay on Byron. My own verse has more and more adopted — seemingly without any will of mine — the syntax and vocabulary of common passionate speech. The passage you quote that begins 'our life is a false nature'[2] down to almost the end of the quotation when it becomes too elaborate to 'couch the mind'[3] and a great part of the long passage about Haidée — I got a queer sort of half - dream prevision of the passage the day before your book came with a repetition of the words 'broad moon' — are perfect passionate speech. The over childish or over pretty or feminine element in some good Wordsworth and in much poetry up to our date comes from the lack of natural momentum in the syntax. This momentum underlies almost every Elizabethan and Jacobean lyric and is far more important than simplicity of vocabulary."[4]

§i

I think that Rosamund Tuve was the first to point out how closely Yeats's technique seems to follow the traditional 'devices' to be found in the Renaissance text-books of rhetoric.[5] To these Yeats had been led by his early work on Spenser, and he knew the two books of Cicero called *De Inventione*, the four books of *De Rhetorica*, the *Ad Herennium*, and the Epistle of Horace to Piso. Are these the works that appear in that 'mechanical little song', 'Mad as the Mist and Snow', where 'Tully's open page' may be Cicero's *De Senectute:*

> Horace there by Homer stands,
> Plato stands below,
> And here is Tully's open page.
> How many years ago
> Were you and I unlettered lads
> *Mad as the mist and snow?*

Now we need not impute to any modern writer the conscious exploitation of the traditional formalities of rhetoric, though it is worth while to recall J.M. Manly's words:

"Let no one scoff at this method of producing interesting and attractive writing. It has been practised very commonly in

1. From the Centenary Tribute (though much enlarged) *In Excited Reverie.*
2. *Childe Harolde.*
3. *Ibid.* "The beam pours in — for Time and Skill will couch the blind". Yeats's use of 'mind' is due to a misprint in Grierson.
4. Yeats to H.J.C. Grierson, 21 Feb 1926; Wade, *Letters*, p.710. The book is *The Background of English Literature*, (1925); the reference is to the essay 'Byron and English Society'.
5. *Elizabeth and Metaphysical Imagery:* Chicago, 1947.

all lands and epochs. It is recommended and taught in a widely-used series of text books. It is the method recently revealed by that most charming of stylists, Anatole France, and is perhaps the only method by which he or Lawrence Sterne could have achieved such effects as they achieved."[1]

But in Yeats's work it is possible to trace many elements of the traditional technique, as for instance the *descriptio, meditatio, invocatio*, in the two Byzantium poems, and in 'All Souls' Night'. It is, after all, only natural that his wide, excited, and somewhat random reading (and the long retention of that reading whenever it fired his imagination) in the Elizabethans, Jacobeans, Romantics and pre-Raphaelites should lead him to the traditional *exampla:*

> Nor is there singing school but studying
> Monuments of its own magnificence...

He was 'intoxicated' by the 'Nocturnall on S. Lucie's Day'; "I have used the arrangement of the rhymes in the stanza for a poem of my own, just finished"; the Byron passage that Grierson had quoted was 'perfect passionate speech'. He lamented the passing of a rhetorical tradition:

> "Every generation has more and more loosened the rhythm, more and more broken up and disorganized, for the sake of subtlety or detail, those great rhythms which move, as it were, in masses of sound."[2]

As for himself, the re-making took many forms: in love, in nationalism, in the whole art of living. Here —

> " . . . I deliberately reshaped my style, deliberately sought out an impression as of cold light and tumbling clouds."

(We think, among others of 'The Three Beggars', 'The Fisherman', 'The Cold Heaven'). "I cast off traditional metaphors and loosened my rhythm, and recognizing that all the criticism of life known to me was alien and English," (this is not meaningful) "became as emotional as possible but with an emotion which I described to myself as cold."[3]

And when he compared modern writers (with the exception of Balzac) to Dante, Villon, Shakespeare and Cervantes, Yeats found, instead of 'strength and weight' something 'slight and shadowy'. This was partly because the great writers had attained to 'a vision of evil'; Shelley, in Yeats's view, had not. And of his own verse —

> "If I wrote of personal love or sorrow in free verse, or in any rhythm that left it unchanged, amid all its accidence, I would be full of self-contempt because of my egotism and indiscretion, and foresee the boredom of my readers. I must

1. 'Chaucer and the Rhetoricians': *Proc. Br. Acad.* 1926, p.95.
2. Preface to *Poems of Spenser* (1903), p. xliii.
3. *Autobiographies,* p.74.

choose a traditional stanza, even what I alter must seem traditional."[1]

My concern in this essay is to suggest some aspects of Yeats's
'rhetoric', not in order to engage in the unprofitable business of
classifying it under the headings of the manuals (though the poems
would furnish abundant instances of technical innovation and 'inventio'),
but to examine his 'rhetoric' in the older sense. It is perhaps unnecessary
to point out that I wish to reject in this context the pejorative overtones of 'rhetorical', as well as Yeats's own statement that 'we make
out of the quarrel with others rhetoric, out of the quarrel with ourselves,
poetry'; and the parallel view implied in the lines

> The rhetorician would deceive his neighbours,
> The sentimentalist himself . . .[2]

I wish to return to the older meaning of rhetoric, and the Aristotelian
definition, as a form of persuasion, and to consider a suggestive remark
by Miss Tuve:

> "The line the earlier period (The Renaissance) ignores is
> the line nervously drawn by modern poetic practice between
> *a poet himself moved and a poet persuading or convincing.*"[3]

The point is not without importance in the light of recent question-
ings of Yeats's 'sincerity'.[4]

§ii

Yeats is a professional and accomplished poet working in media where
a rhetorical bent, partly native and partly traditional, is given full
scope. An almost impeccable ear, a laborious method of composition
in search of phonetic 'decorum' and exactitude by repeated redrafting
and by *sotto voce* declamation until 'words obeyed his call', a method
of reading aloud that was close to ritual declamation; all these show
a love of 'those great rhythms that move in masses of sound'.
We may quote from 'The Cutting of an Agate':

> "Walter Pater says music is the type of all the arts, but some-
> body else, I forget now who, that oratory is their type.
> You will side with one or the other according to the nature of
> your energy, and I in my present mood am all for the man who,
> with an average audience before him, uses all means of per-
> suasion — stories, laughter, tears, *and but so much music as he
> can discover on the wings of words.*"[5]

1. "A General Introduction for My Work:" *Essays and Introductions,* p.522.
2. 'Ego Dominus Tuus'.
3. *op. cit.p.* 183. But see 'Longinus' *On the Sublime,* especially Ch. IX, XV and,
    passim, the writer's *Longinus and English Criticism* (Cambridge 1934).
4. *e.g.* by Yvor Winters, *The Poetry of W.B. Yeats* (Denver 1960) "a home-made
    mythology and a loose assortment of untenable social attitudes . . . " "Yeats'
    poems are inflated; they are bardic in the worst sense."
5. *Essays and Introductions* (1961) pp. 267-8.

This sounds very much like William Morris's poetic belief and practice and we do well to consider Morris carefully in such a context.

"My work in Ireland has continually set this thought before me: 'How can I make my work mean something to vigorous and simple men whose attention is not given to art but to a shop, or teaching in a National School, or dispensing medicine?' I had not wanted to 'elevate them' or 'educate them' as these words are understood, but to make them understand my vision . . ."[1]

Certain formative influences are clear. In the background are Spenser and the 'brightnesse of brave and glorious words': Donne, Ben Jonson, Byron and Shelley, Tennyson and Morris. Dramatic resonances are picked up from Browning and Rossetti. In the background there is the comparatively unknown popular Nineteenth Century Anglo-Irish tradition, from Moore, Keating, Allingham, Todhunter, Dowden, Davis, Ferguson, Mangan, O'Leary, O'Shaughnessy, Lionel Johnson, Katharine Tynan-Hinkson: together with Hyde's translations and 'that somewhat neglected poet, Basil Bunting.'[2]

The blank verse — and Yeats is not on the whole successful in this medium — owes something to Tennyson, particularly in 'The Old Age of Queen Maeve' (1903). He moves somewhat more easily in 'The Two Kings' (1914) but has not yet found the 'music and motion' that appear in 'The Gift of Harun Al-Rashid' (1923). The first two appear as technical exercises; the last carries a different excitement, pressure; probably because its statement is, of necessity, parabolic, its genesis highly personal. In the forefront, of course, are the 'Nineties and the Tragic Generation. For prose there was Swift who 'haunted' him, Berkeley in his more assertive and less mathematical modes, Burke, Grattan, Mitchel, O'Connell' Parnell; and for a time the rhythms of Pater to give a certain stilted quality, almost as of parody,[3] to *Per Amica Silentia Lunae;* though several contemporary poets have noted their strong response to this portion of the 'Sacred Book'.

Consider first the dramatic nature of traditional Anglo-Irish rhetoric. There is clearly an intense love of the powerful, the resonant; of strong cadences, of the 'great masses of sound'.

A few examples will serve; from Ferguson's 'The Burial of King Cormac':

> They loosed their curse against the king;
> They cursed him in his flesh and bones;
> And daily in their mystic ring
> They turned the maledictive stones . . .

1. *Essays and Introductions* (1961) p.265
2. *1930 Diary, p. 7 (Jn).*
3. 'He wrote of me in that extravagant style
   He had learned from Pater.' ('The Phases of the Moon')

— from F. R. Higgins's *The Ballad of O'Bruadir* which Yeats included in
The Oxford Book of Modern Verse.

> When first I took to cutlass, blunderbuss and gun,
> *Rolling glory on the water;*
> With boarding and with broadside we·made the Dutchmen run,
> *Rolling glory on the water;*
> Then down among the captains in their green skin shoes,
> I sought for Hugh O'Bruadir and got but little news
> Till I shook him by the hand in the bay of Santa Cruz,
> *Rolling glory on the water.*

— from George Fox's translation of Lavelle:

> 'Tis my grief that Patrick Loughlin is not Earl of Irrul still,
> And that Brian Duff no longer rules as Lord upon the hill;
> And that Colonel Hugh McGrady should be lying dead and low,
> And I sailing, sailing swiftly from the county of Mayo.

or from the poem that Lionel Johnson dedicated to O'Leary, and that
he himself quoted:[1]

> A dream! a dream! an ancient dream!
> Yet, ere peace come to Inisfail,
> Some weapons on some field must gleam,
> Some burning glory fire the Gael.
>
> That field may lie beneath the sun,
> Fair for the treading of an host:
> That field in realms of thought be won
> And armed minds do their uttermost . . .

The essays, reviews, and *Autobiographies* show us the rhythmic and
gnomic scraps which he treasured; the passage from Nashe's 'Bright-
ness falls from the air', the 'old hunter talking with gods' from Browning's *Pauline,* Blake's

> The gay fishes on the wave when the moon sucks up the dew.

He preferred Burns's 'Elegy on Capt. Matthew Henderson' to Shelley's
'Adonais', finding in it speed, energy, naturalness, 'a great voice'. It is
worth while to quote two stanzas from the Elegy that may have appealed
to Yeats:

> Mourn, sooty coots, and speckled teals;
> *Ye fisher herons, watching eels;*
> Ye duck and drake, *wi'airy wheels*
> *Circling the lake;*
> Ye bitterns, till the quagmire reels,
> Rair for his sake.
> Go to your sculptur'd tombs, ye great,
> *In a' the tinsel trash o' state!*
> But by thy honest turf I'll wait,
> Thou man of worth!

---

1. *Essays and Introductions*, p.258. Note the strong cadences of the second and
   fourth lines of each stanza; the whole must be read aloud.

And weep the ae best fellow's fate
E'er lay in earth.[1]

In prose too such memorable things are hoarded, tasted: "There are things a man must not do to save a nation", "I saw my thoughts going past me like blazing ships", "When the goddess came to Achilles in the battle . . . she took him by his yellow hair". "Where did I pick up that story of the Byzantium bishop and the singer of Antioch, where learn that to anoint your body with the fat of a lion ensured the favour of a king?". The dramatic, the esoteric, is woven into the cadences, themselves traditional. "I seek more than idioms, for thoughts become more vivid when I find that they were first thought out in historical circumstances which affect those in which I live, or, which is perhaps the same thing, were thought first by men my ancestors may have known . . . it is as though I most approximate towards that expression when I carry with me the greatest possible amount of hereditary thought and feeling, even national and family hatred and pride"[2] Such 'charged' words were clearly those in *The Seven Sages,* the 'heroic' names of 'Easter 1916'; The O'Rahilly, Macdonagh, Connolly, Pearse. The classical names as recommended by 'Longinus'[3] are, one suspects, used as much for their sound-savour as for their evocative effect; Plato, Plotinus, Parmenides, Homer, Smaragdine, Cretan, Salamis, Ledaean, Agamemnon, Callimachus are woven, usually with great skill, into the sound-fabric. But indeed there are many precedents: Homer, Aeschylus, Marlowe, Chapman,[4] Milton, and those poems of Macaulay from which (though with some shame-facedness), many poets have admitted that they learned the 'music and motion' of their earlier memories in verse.[5] In the Irish a famous collection of the names is the James Stephens's *The Crock of Gold;* in passages remarkable not only for the 'names' but for the consummate ordonnance of the cadenced rhythms:

> "There came Bove Derg, the Fiery, seldom seen, and his harper the son of Trogáin, whose music heals the sick and makes the sad heart merry; Eochy Mac Eláthán, the Dâgda Mór, the Father of Stars, and his daughter from the Cave of Cruachán; Credh Mac Aedh of Raghery and Cas Corach son of the great Ollav; Mananaan Mac Lir came from his wide waters shouting louder than the wind, with his daughters Cliona and Aoife and Etain Fair-Hair; and Coll and Cecht and Mac Greina, the Plough, the Hazel, and the Sun came with his wives, whose

---

1. The italics are mine. Various echoes which will be recognized in the poems, and in *The Herne's Egg,* are perhaps suggestive.
2. *1930 Diary,* p.6.
3. See, for example, Sections XVI, XXIII of *'A Treatise . . . '*
4. Especially in his continuation of Marlowe's *Hero and Leander.*
5. I take the phrase from Jeremy Taylor's famous sermon, 'Angry Prayer'.

names are not forgotten, even Banba and Fodla and Eire, names
of glory."

A classical example of the desire for rhetorical weight is the conversion of the earlier draft of the second stanza of 'The Sorrow of Love',[1]
from

> And then you come with those red mournful lips
> And with you came the whole of the world's tears,
> And all the sorrows of her labouring ships,
> And all the burden of her myriad years.

into the more grandiose

> A girl arose that had red mournful lips
> And seemed the greatness of the world in tears,
> Doomed like Odysseus and the labouring ships
> And proud as Priam murdered with his peers.

The complicated arguments for and against the two versions are well
known;[2] but the simplest and perhaps adequate explanation (for the
alteration does little but extend and universalize the alignment between
Maud Gonne and Troy) is the sheer resonance that the 'names' give. There
are many instances of the typical Yeatsian cadence:

> Troy passed away in one high funeral gleam,
> And Usna's children died.

> A shudder in the loins engenders there
> The broken wall, the burning roof and tower
> And Agamemnon dead.[3]

> Where seven Ephesian topers[4] slept and never knew
> When Alexander's empire passed, they slept so sound.
> Stretch out your limbs and sleep a long Saturnian sleep . . .[5]

> Hector is dead and there's a light in Troy
> We that look on but laugh in tragic joy.[6]

There are even times when one suspects that the sound has perhaps submerged the meaning:

> I mock Plotinus' thought
> And cry in Plato's teeth . . .[7]

1. 'The Rose of the World'.
2. They are best set out in Parkinson's *W.B. Yeats, Self-Critic* (London 1951).
   especially p. 165.
3. 'Leda and the Swan'
4. Again the traditional "Vulgar word which is not vulgar because it is so expressive" ('Longinus'); and "In later years, through much knowledge of the stage,
   through the exfoliation of my own style, I learnt that occasional prosaic words
   gave the impression of an active man speaking." *(Autobiography,* p.263).
   Compare (perhaps) Housman's 'Tis true there's better booze than brine, but
   he that drowns must drink it'.
5. 'On a Picture of a Black Centaur . . . '
6. 'The Gyres'.
7. 'The Tower', III.

Virgil's resonances (from which Tennyson learned so much) are placed
under tribute in the 'Two Songs from a Play':

> Another Troy must rise and set,
> Another lineage feed the crow,
> Another Argo's painted prow
> Drive to a flashier bauble yet . . .

and we can see the Yeatsian energy more clearly if we set beside it
Dryden's translation:

> Another Tiphys shall new seas explore
> Another Argo land the chiefs upon the Iberian shore;
> Another Helen other wars create,
> And great Achilles urge the Trojan fate.[1]

The sureness of touch is apparent even in the minute particulars. 'To a
Wealthy Man . . .' is a proud and aristocratic poem, whose quick nervous
rhythms are integral with its tone. We remember the consummate
ordonnance of

> . . . And when they drove out Cosimo,
> Indifferent how the rancour ran,
> He gave the hours they had set free
> To Michelozzo's latest plan
> For the San Marco Library . . .

— so that the poem comes alive and prepares for us the alignments
with Lutyens and the Municipal Gallery, which (we are persuaded)
have become part of a great processional movement in history. In the
lines

> What cared Duke Ercole, that bid
> His mummers to the market place . . .

the cutting edge of the rhythm would be blunted if we substituted
'Hercules' for the Italian form that picks up the hard consonants of
Duke. But indeed the whole 'attack' of the poem, the proud
triumphant rhetoric of hatred, is superbly done. We may think that
the similitudes between Coole and Urbino, between Michelozzo and
Lutyens, are slender enough; but the 'stride' and energy of the poem
combine with similar assertions elsewhere to make them convincing.
"It is in the arrangements of events as in the words, and in the touch
of extravagance, of irony, of surprise . . . that leaves one . . . caught
up into the freedom of self-delight."[2] All three terms — extravagance, irony, surprise, would be familiar to a Renaissance rhetorician.
But the integration of rhythm with sound is peculiarly a Yeatsian gift:

> "What are the tones that verse[3] sets ringing in the mind?
> What is the power, in which you are pre-eminent, of summoning
> to our understanding, with one swift, wrought phrase, a land-
> scape, a sky, a weather and a history? We do not think about it,

1. "The Fourth Pastoral" II. 41-49, *The Poems of John Dryden* ed. James Kinsley.
   Vol II (Oxford 1958).
2. *Essays and Introductions*, p.254.
3. He has just quoted a stanza from 'The Mountain Tomb'.

till we realize that in the words before us there is no logical
warrant for that rush of feeling and knowledge . . . It is a
precise and definite art; the cutting of an agate."[1]

We are reminded of

> . . . that stern colour and that delicate line

of the *Elegy,* and of Calvert's appraisal of Blake's woodcuts:

> "that intense, soul-evidencing attitude and action, and that
> elastic, nervous spring which belongs to uncaged immortal
> spirits."[2]

§ iii

It has been argued that the Celtic 'namings' are less successful,
and indeed an obstacle to Yeats's communication; partly because they
are difficult to pronounce, partly because their full significance can only
be ascertained by study. Synge used them effectively, but then he had
Villon's precedent and Villon's music behind him; and the admixture of
the classical relieves, as it were, the Celtic:

> Etain, Helen, Maeve, and Fand,
> Golden Deirdre's tender hand . . .
>
> We named Lucrezia Crivelli,
> And Titian's lady with amber belly . . .[3]

There seems to have been a significant change in Yeats's technique.
We may quote from the Morrisian 'Wanderings of Oisin' with its long
stumbling rhythms:

> Came Blanid, Mac Nessa, tall Fergus, who feastward of old time
>   slunk,
> Cook Barach, the traitor; and warward, the spittle on his
>   beard never dry,
> Dark Balor, as old as a forest, car-borne, his mighty head sunk
> Helpless, men lifting the lids of his weary and death-making
>   eye.[4]

At the end, the decorative effect has been abandoned, the names
tightened into the layers of history:

> Are those things that men adore and loathe
> Their sole reality?
> What stood in the Post Office
> With Pearse and Connolly?
> What comes out of the mountain
> Where men first shed their blood?

1. L.A.G. Strong A *Letter to W.B. Yeats;* London, 1932.
2. A.H. Palmer *Life and Letters* (1892) p.16.
3. 'Queens'. Again the 'vulgar diction'.
4. 111.89. It is interesting that Yeats does not seem to have attempted the
Sigurd metre.

Who thought Cuchulain till it seemed
He stood where they stood?[1]

In the early work there is some shade of Marlowe, and Yeats seems to fall to Longinus's frigidity or perhaps turgidity; the imagery fails to support the thought. There is the theologically-notorious

Sign with this quill.
It was a feather growing on the cock
That crowed when Peter dared deny his Master,
And all who use it have great honour in Hell.[2]

or the 'frigid' —

Men yet shall hear
The archangels rolling Satan's empty skull
Over the mountain-tops.[3]

Sometimes the rhetoric falls into pseudo-Jacobean not far from that of Beddoes:

O, look upon the moon that's standing there
In the blue daylight — take note of the complexion,
Because it is the white of leprosy
And the contagion that afflicts mankind
Falls from the moon. When I and these are dead
We should be carried to some windy hill
To lie there with uncovered face awhile
That mankind and that leper there may know
Dead faces laugh.[4]

We may assess something of Yeats's development in this mode from 'The Gift of Harun Al-Raschid' (1923). It is the last of the long traditional poems, and shows the 'interior variety' which he had looked for as far back as 1902,[5] as well as the movement between 'passion and reverie', 'turbulence and stillness'. Here is the progression of a paragraph towards the rhetorical cadence, with full mastery of all the resources of blank verse:

'That love
Must needs be in this life and in what follows
Unchanging and at peace, and it is right
Every philosopher should praise that love.
But I being none can praise its opposite.
It makes my passion stronger but to think
Like passion stirs the peacock and his mate,
The wild stag and the doe;[6] that mouth to mouth
Is a man's mockery of the changless soul'.

1. *The Death of Cuchulain,* see also that the last stanza of *The Statues* for a successful use of this myth.

2. *The Countess Cathleen,* Sc1.

3. Ibid. Sc.V.

4. *The King's Threshold.*

5. *Essays and Introductions.* 'Speaking to the Psaltery'.

6. See 'A Last Confession'.

— so that the final line seems mortised and tenoned by its weight
and alliteration. The whole poem rises and falls with its own peculiar
rhythms, to embody sound-masses locked home in the rhythmic
structure by alliterative subtlety:

> . . . Self-born, high-born, and solitary truths,
> Those terrible implacable straight lines
> Drawn through the wandering vegetative dream,
> Even those truths that when my bones are dust
> Must drive the Arabian host.

§ iv

It is worth considering what I would call the 'rhetoric of the ghost'.
A ghost must be called by a traditional invocation; only then will it
appear. So the openings of 'All Souls' Night'. 'A Prayer for my Son', the
second stanza of 'Byzantium'. These poems are for the most part
hieratical, measured. They project a pattern of sound and imagery to
work (often by repetition) as all invocations do; their own numinous
energy gives life, intensity, and some kind of suspension of belief
grows steadily. It returns as it were, to carry the poet himself into a
particular *kind* of belief generated by the poem itself. "The wheels
take fire from the mere rapidity of their motion".[1] The sense of the
supernatural in the West of Ireland (of both races and of both religions)
is highly ambivalent. The dead walk, or play on the roads at night;
Synge's Bride Dara sees the dead man with the child in his arms. In
certain moods and in certain psychological states[2] their acceptance is
complete. But it is a delicate thing, dependent for its life on the perfection of the incantation, of which the full force is felt only when the
poem is read aloud. I am myself now clear that Yeats wished to believe
in the supra-natural, and that the belief was an integral part of his dramatic
perception of life and death and the fate of the soul at the Gates
of Pluto. He had seen Coleridge achieving this, and he had borrowed
from *The Ancient Mariner* to strengthen 'Byzantium'. Into the structure of
the rhetoric of the supernatural he incorporates freely those aspects of the
Christian tradition which are dramatically appealing; to produce ironies ,
tensions, ambivalences which are carefully subordinated to the major
rhythms that 'move in great masses of sound'. So 'The Cold Heaven':

> Ah! when the ghost begins to quicken,
> Confusion of the death-bed over . . .[3]

We remember the account in *A Vision* of the events that follow closely

---

1. Coleridge, *Biographia, XVIII.*
2. As, for example, those which accompany the stimulation, by means of the
   manipulation of symbols or by meditation or ritual, of ultra-rational perceptions.
3. See Chapter XIII 'The Property of the Dead'.

on death, and what anthropologists tell us of the custom of leaving
the spirit in peace to find its bearings like a homing bird. And on the
roads the spirit becomes a wanderer, seeking to relive fragments of its
past, as Crazy Jane knew.

In the fourth stanza of 'Byzantium' — and in its source drafts —
the spirits or flames arrive on the Emperor's pavement. In the second
stanza Yeats has invoked the traditional Guide to the Underworld to
watch their coming. Behind them is a mass of converging imagery,
carried excitedly on an accelerated rhythm that culminates on the
rhetoric of

> The golden smithies of the Emperor.

Plotinus, Moore, Cudworth, Milton, Blake and Noh plays — the fire-
imagery is common form; with it, perhaps, Pentecost, Isaiah, and the
text "Who maketh His angels spirits, and His ministers a flame of
fire".

This 'rhetoric of the ghost' seems to demand, historically, for
its communication those massive strong rhythms, which 'trade with the
living and with the dead' to enrich it, to generate the excitement by
which its assertions are supported. So the processional *Presences,*
so the closely-laminated 'And must we part, von Hügel?' that moves
towards the orotundities of sound which he loves:

> Homer is my example, and his unchristened heart . . .

> Though mounted in that saddle Homer rode . . .

> A woman Homer sung . . .

> What theme had Homer but original sin?

Something of the peculiar Yeatsian quality may be seen if we
consider a poem by Oliver St. John Gogarty, which is included in
The Oxford Book of Modern Verse. It is called 'Non Dolet'.

> Our friends go with us as we go
>> Down the long path where Beauty wends,
> Where all we love foregathers, so
>> Why should we fear to join our friends?

> Who would survive them to outlast
>> His children: to outwear his fame —
> Left when the Triumph has gone past —
>> To win from Age, not Time, a name?

> Then do not shudder at the knife
>> That Death's indifferent hand drives home,
> But with the Strivers leave the Strife,
>> Nor, after Caesar, skulk in Rome.

Beside it we may set (though with the usual reservations about all such
comparisons) an example of Yeats's technique in 'The New Faces':

> If you, that have grown old, were the first dead,
> Neither catalpa tree nor scented lime

> Should hear my living feet, nor would I tread
> Where we wrought that shall break the teeth of Time.
> Let the new faces play what tricks they will
> In the old rooms; night can outbalance day,
> Our shadows rove the garden gravel still,
> The living seem more shadowy than they.

Yeats's variations of speed and tone, the economy and symmetry of his statement, make comparisons invidious. The poem turns as it were on a hinge with the proud

> Where we wrought that shall break the teeth of Time

where the hard *t's* are picked up on the wave-momentum of the previous line. 'Time' is the only abstraction, and that is no longer 'abstract' when we remember Ronsard. The rhetorical questions of the first poem are replaced by the strong assertions grafted on the opening conditional clause. We need not know that the background to Yeats's poem is Lady Gregory's sickness, nor that the catalpa tree was one of the glories of Coole. But we are aware of the triumphant rhythm of that second line, the circumstantiality of the setting: and we remember — after Blake —

> For what but eye and ear silence the mind
> With the minute particulars of mankind?[1]

It carries over, a little misted (as the syntax demands) to the fourth line. The second half of the poem uses the colloquialism approved by 'Longinus'

> Let the new faces *play what tricks* they will

which threw into relief the arrangement and deliberately evocative (for this is of iron, the heat, the forge of style) —

> Where we wrought that . . .

Behind it, of course, is Shakespeare's Sonnet LV

> Not marble, nor the gilded monuments
> Of Princes, shall outlive this powerful rime;

§v

There is, I think, something that we might call a 'rhetoric of war' and here it seems to me that, in general, Yeats is far less convincing. I have no doubt that in the famous passage from *On the Boiler* 'Desire some just war . . .' he was sincere, seeing in this at least one possibility of re-integrating the State after its fragmentation at the end of the gyre. But the earlier references to war seem to me strained, and too close to the Nordic ferocity of Morris; always excepting the magnificently ambivalent 'Who will go drive with Fergus now?' where this excitement comes from far other sources than the 'brazen spears'. Yeats, writing to order, as in

1. *The Double Vision of Michael Robartes.*

Three 'Marching Songs', and to some extent in the 'patriotic' balladry, seems to me to fail to attain either momentum or life. In this class I would include (against popular estimation), 'Sixteen Dead Men' and 'The Rose Tree'. I think that the integrity of the rhythm is apparent when the experience has been, as it were, within his own reach, to be meditated on, absorbed in relation to his own political position. And that, I believe, falls into two more or less distinct parts: a bardic but abstracted celebration of the Easter Rising, its actors, their epic part, his own imagined responsibility, through play or speech, in the events which led to it. On the other side there is the poetry arising out of the events which he was aware of at first hand. And example is 'The Stare's Nest by My Window', with its polarities that are stated in a letter to Grierson: "The one enlivening truth that starts out of it all is that we may learn charity after mutual contempt. There is no longer a virtuous nation and the best of us live by candle-light."[1] He could never compass the sense of the brutality and exaltation of remote Celtic war (which is best left in prose) and he recognized his father in 'The Circus Animals' Desertion':

> . . . vain gaiety, vain battle, vain repose.

though in that poem we occasionally get the strong Shakespearian accent —

> Cuchulain fought the ungovernable sea.

But indeed the Cuchulain thought seems to stimulate in the verse this weight; aided perhaps by the unique metrical potentialities and strange vowel-changes of that name. Only the episodes near Coole bit into his memory:

> a drunken soldiery
> Can leave the mother murdered at her door
> To roll in her own blood, and go scot-free.

and, from 'Reprisals' (where the rhetoric of war links with that of the ghost of Robert Gregory)

> Half-drunk or whole-mad soldiery
> Are murdering your tenants there.[2]

Beside it, the 'popular' poems about the Rising and its actors, and the Casement poems, seem forced; the image that they present appeals more strongly to an English than to an Anglo-Irish audience. On the other hand 'The Curse of Cromwell' lives by reason of its astounding energy, the rhythmical checks and substitutions embodied in the violence of popular Balladry which he has transcended. We touch the edges of rant in a favourite thought, that he had used before in *The Countess Cathleen* but which is now given a peculiar proud energy:

> And there is an old beggar wandering in his pride —

1. 21 Oct. 1922 Wade, *Letters*, p.691.

2. Variorum, p.791. Note the contemptuous *soldiery:* as in 'Byzantium'.

His fathers served their fathers before Christ was crucified.
> *O what of that, O what of that,*
> *What is there left to say?*

§vi

There is, too, a 'rhetoric of love'. That long-enduring 'imposthume' in the heart and brain could be in some eased by perpetual alignment and realignment with the heroic or aristocratic ideal. If (as I think) he was at times 'in love with love for its own sake', it was natural that Helen should be the chosen archetype, as he had seen her in any early essay on Morris,[1] contrasting her with Morris's vision of his own gentle and abundant women, as he knew them in the pastoral worlds of Calvert and Palmer. Troy is linked to Emain, and the story of Deirdre; perhaps to the burning house that had impressed him so deeply, and the burnings during the Troubles. So the image-clusters turn and fuse: perhaps in a heat of aggrandizing self-pity:

> Why, what could she have done, being what she is?
> Was there another Troy for her to burn?[2]

"The verses may make his mistress famous as Helen or give a victory for his cause, not because he has been either's servant, but because men delight to honour and to remember all that have served contemplation."[3] Both Yeats and Synge are much concerned with Queens; in 'Long Legged Fly' the rhetoric of Troy is picked up and refashioned from Marlowe and Shakespeare with a memory of *Antony and Cleopatra:*

> That the topless towers be burnt
> And men recall that face,
> Move most gently if move you must
> In this lonely place.
> She thinks, part woman, three parts a child,
> That nobody looks; her feet
> Practise a tinker's shuffle
> Picked up on a street . . .[4]

Women are exalted ceremoniously, in the tradition - itself moving between extremities - that he had learnt in the 'Nineties. Again and again there is this attempt at self-conviction, the alignment with aristocracy, the verse giving at times a forced tone. The word *common* - which may carry overtones in Anglo-Irish speech of a peculiar intensity - occurs often in this context. So, of Mabel Beardsley, and superbly done:

> She knows herself a woman
> No red and white of a face,
> Or rank, raised from a common

1. 'The Happiest of the Poets'.
2. 'No Second Troy'.
3. *'Essays and Introductions'*, p.255.
4. v *Antony and Cleopatra*, II.2.234.

Unreckonable race . . . [1]

Less successfully 'To Dorothy Wellesley', which seems to me an archi-
tected poem, a little tumid and pretentious:

What climbs the stair?
Nothing that common women ponder on
If you are worth my hope! Neither Content
Nor satisfied Conscience, but that great family
Some ancient famous authors misrepresent,
The Proud Furies each with her torch on high.

§vii

Many have noted the weight and resonance of the Yeatsian line.
It is not easy to say anything of value about it. The many scholars who
have attempted to analyse the metrical and phonetic aspects of, say,
'Innisfree', 'Lullaby' or 'Sailing to Byzantium' do not seem to me to
have contributed much that is helpful to understanding these poems
'in the marrow-bone'. It is, of course, useful, indeed essential, to have
a general knowledge of the English prosodic tradition, and to recognize
the many modulations which individual poets impose upon traditional
material and stanzaic forms. But it is useful in discussing Yeats's
'rhetoric' to remember Matthew Arnold's famous - and sometimes
misunderstood, to our confusion[2] - theory of the touchstones: "to
have always in one's mind lines and expressions of the great masters,
and to apply them as a touchstone to other poetry". The quality
revealed is essentially the finality, the 'rightness', the 'ring' of the lines.
It is the mark of the greatest poets; it is also clear that it is achieved by
working and re-working, by accepting, if need be, the criticism of other
poets,[3] by submitting always to the final and simple test: 'Does this
sound right?' And with our ears alert to the complexity of the sounds
(there is no acceptable notation for these) we may attempt to set out
some instances for comparison:

Nor the grey wandering osprey, Sorrow . . .

(And makes a pale light in your cypress glooms . . .
Keats, *Isabella*).

Though flame had burned the whole
World, as it were a coal . . .

(But, though the whole world turn to coal,
Then chiefly lives.
George Herbert 'Virtue'[4])

1. 'Upon a Dying Lady', V. See also 'The Mother of God'
2. Often through neglect of Arnold's proviso' "Of course we are not to require
   this other poetry to resemble them; it may be very dissimilar."
3. *Essays in Criticism*, (Second Series: 'The Study of Poetry'.) The Ezra
   Pound/TS Eliot collaboration is of special interest.
4. Not a plagiarism. Behind both images is the hymn *Dies Irae*.

> Who will go drive with Fergus now,
> And pierce the deep wood's woven shade . . .
> (While the deep-burnished foliage overhead
> Splintered the silver arrows of the moon.
>   Arnold).[1]
> Or dark betwixt the pole-cat and the owl . . .
>   (Light thickens, and the crow
> Makes wing to the rooky wood. *Macbeth)*
> For though love has a spider's eye
> To find out some appropriate pain
> For every nerve, and tests the lover . . .
>
>   (. . . The spider love, which transubstantiates all,
>   And can convert Manna to gall . . . Donne)

Not less striking is the rejection of 'resonant' rhetorical lines during
the drafting process. We may choose some instances at random:[2]

> Where the dark drowsy fins a moment rise
> Of fish, that carry souls to Paradise.[3]

> Whether by star or moon
> I tread the imperious town
> All my intricacies grown sweet and clear.[4]

> Tormented, cloud encumbered Connaught skies[5]
> Foreknowledge of the desolate day awoke[6]

— which stands comparison with Tennyson's *In Memoriam* (VII)

> He is not here; but far away
> The noise of life begins again,
> And ghastly thro' the drizzling rain
> On the bald street breaks the blank day.

As a final aspect of the traditional rhetorical devices we may turn
our attention to the attacking energy of common speech: remembering
Longinus's examples: "So vulgar idiom is sometimes much more
expressive than ornamental language. It is recognized at once as a
touch of common life; and what is familiar is on the way to be credible.
. . . These scrape the corner of vulgar idiom, but they are not vulgar
because they are so expressive."[7]
Among them we might instance:

> Because you have found me in the *pitch-dark* night . . .

---

1. The depth-images in these lines repay study.
2. I am indebted, as all students must be, to Jon Stallworthy's *Between the
   Lines,* from which these examples are taken.
3. 'Sailing to Byzantium'.
4. 'Byzantium' *(Intricate, intricacies,* are key-words; c.f. also *arrogant, wild).*
5. 'Coole Park' 1929.
6. 'Chosen'.
7. *On the sublime,* $XXXI.

> Last night they *trundled* down the road
> That dead young soldier in his blood . . .

(Hamlet's 'I'll lug the guts into the neighbour room'.)

> Where fashion or mere fantasy decrees
> We shift about — all that great glory spent —
> *Like some poor Arab tribesman and his tent.*

— where the cliché of the last line is used with a conscious and successful insolence.

Or, perhaps, the epigram 'On Those Who Hated *The Playboy of
the Western World',* 1907 — remembering always Ricketts's picture —

> Once, when midnight smote the air,
> Eunuchs ran through Hell and met
> On every crowded street to stare
> Upon great Juan riding by:
> Even like these to rail and sweat
> Staring upon his sinewy thigh.

§viii

Perhaps some mention should be made of Yeats's rhetoric in prose,
other than what might be called the rhapsodist mode of certain
passages in *Ideas of Good and Evil, Per Amica Silentia Lunae, The
Cutting of an Agate. Hodos Chameliontos.* But the recorded Senate
speeches show little of the orotundity of deliberàte art which we might
have expected. On the contrary; his style is usually crisp, controlled,
and no more than adequate to the understanding of that somewhat
heterogeneous body. His intention was excellent: "I do not like to
speak in this House unless on things I have studied — letters and art".[1]
Exceptions are the coinage and divorce. The latter gave rise to some
passionate writing, in a slightly Burkean mode that employs all the
traditional devices, and is worth quoting. It will be seen that he picks
up, paraphrases, the 'namings' of 'Vacillation' and of the patriotic
songs:

> "I think it tragic that within three years of this country
> gaining its independence we should be discussing a measure
> which a minority of this nation considers to be grossly
> oppressive. I am proud to consider myself a typical man of that
> minority. We against whom you have done this thing are no
> petty people. We are one of the great stocks of Europe. We are
> the people of Burke; we are the people of Grattan; we are the
> people of Swift, the people of Emmet, the people of Parnell.
> We have created the most of the modern literature of this
> country. We have created the best of its political intelligence
> . . ."[2]

1. *The Senate Speeches of W.B. Yeats,* ed. D.R. Pearce, London 1961 (p. 134).
2. *Ibid.* p.99. See 'The Tower' III.

And there is a passage of denunciation which has something of the resonance of *The Drapier's Letters.* He is speaking of a clerical opponent of divorce:

> "I know little or nothing about Father Finlay's career. It may have been eminent and distinguished, but I am sure that very few members of this House will think with pleasure of following the guidance of a man who speaks with such monstrous discourtesy of a practice which has been adopted by the most civilized nations of the modern world — by Germany, England, America, France and Scandinavian countries. He must know by every kind of statistics, by every standard except the narrowest, that those nations, because they so greatly exceed us in works, exceed us in virtue. Father Peter Finlay has been supported by an ecclesiastic of the Church of Ireland, the Bishop of Meath, who has even excelled him in invective. Perceiving, no doubt, that indissoluble marriage, which for the guilty party at least he passionately desires, has in other countries made men and women exceedingly tolerant of certain forms of sexual immorality, he declares that every erring husband or erring wife should be treated as a robber, a forger or a murderer."[1]

There is also the Yeatsian trick of picking up odd fragments of knowledge, and of using them to some effect. This passage concerns the arming of Ulster, but has more modern relevancies:

> " . . . I have found that Edmund Burke in the middle of the eighteenth century drew attention to a very remarkable item in the Estimates of the year. It was an item of so much money for the purchase of five gross of scalping knives, which scalping knives were intended to be given to the American Indians that they might scalp the French."[2]

And there is much that is topically ironic, half a century later, of the independence of the judiciary (much called in question during 1969/72):

> "There is a feeling in this country among a number of people — it may be an unjust feeling — that the judges have hitherto been subservient to an alien Executive." (This view, though popular, was demonstrably untrue.) "Some members of this House have gone to the other end of the balance and thought that they would secure safety by being quite sure that an Irish Executive would have considerable control over judges. Those who take my point of view have done their

---

1. *The Senate Speeches of W.B. Yeats* (p.95).
2. Ibid (p.21). Yeats might have been equally interested in the export, by a Birmingham firm, of a special oil to a South American tribe: designed to keep their spear-heads from rusting.

best to secure that the Irish Judges shall be independent of every Executive whatsoever."[1]

Finally, of the burning of the houses — 'many ingenious lovely things are gone' — of a number of Senators:

"I also suggest that it is very desirable that any clause in this Bill which encourages a man to rebuild should be kept. This Country will not always be an uncomfortable place for a country gentleman to live in, and it is most important that we should keep in this country a certain leisured class. I am afraid that Labour disagrees with me in that. On this matter I am a crusted Tory. I am of the opinion of the ancient Jewish book which says 'there is no wisdom without leisure'."[2]

The burnings of houses 'blacklisted' in 1923 by the I.R.A. included those of the Earl of Mayo, Oliver Gogarty, the Earl of Granard, Sir Thomas Esmonde, Sir John Keane, Col. Moore (Moore Hall), Sir Horace Plunkett. Dr. George Sigerson, the Irish scholar and poet, who was forced to resign under the threat of burning.

$ix

It would be possible to give many instances of these traditional rhetorical devices. The typical Yeatsian 'attack' (common also in Donne) is often the *exclamatio:*

What shall I do with this absurdity . . .

That is no country for old men . . .

O but there is wisdom
In what the sages said . . .

There is the *quaestio,* often gnomic, of which he is fond:

What's water but the generated soul?

— with its reference to Porphyry, or

What theme had Homer but original sin?

Was there another Troy for her to burn?

There is the *amplificatio,* the use of the 'minute particulars' — the use of tropes and figures; the preparation for the dramatic climax, as in 'Easter, 1916' the *sprezzatura* or pride (that often seems insolent, again like Donne's, because it is born of the certainty of high poetic breeding) that Professor Tuve noted.[3] "The audacity of the conception has borne him outside and beyond persuasion."[4]

For a last example we may consider some passages from *Purgatory,* a play which shows an astonishing variety and control; as well as the tact with which the rhythm is adjusted precisely to the speaking voice:

1. *The Senate Speeches of W.B. Yeats* (p.61).
2. *Ibid.* pp.38-9.
3. *op.cit.* 279.
4. 'Longinus', *op.cit.* $xv.

Great people lived and died in this house —
(we remember the remark of the old countryman when he had seen
the pictures at Coole)
        Magistrates, Colonels, members of Parliament,
(the rhythm gathers itself for the momentum of the 'heroic-myth'
names)
        Men that had fought at Aughrim and the Boyne
or
        Had loved the house, had loved all
        The intricate passages of the house,
        But he killed the house; to kill a house
(the repetitions, I think on a rising tone, lengthen the rhythm to
prepare for the climax)
        Where great men grew up, married, died,
then the rhetorical and hieratical condemnation —
        I here declare a capital offence.

But the whole ebb and flow of the dramatic rhythm of the play
repays detailed study. Beside it the *ordonnance* of *The Death of
Cuchulain* is relatively crude. It would not be difficult, as I have
suggested, to list examples of Yeats's achievement under the traditional
divisions, and to refer to Longinus, Dionysus of Halicarnassus and many
others for precedents and *exempla;* to praise his use of the high, middle
and low styles. But this 'eminence and excellence of language' is in
all respects in the main current of Renaissance poetic theory. Its
similarities with the basic techniques of Spenser, King, Donne, can be
shown. But above all it is the product of this traditional reading and
training:

> "No new man has ever plucked that rose, or found that
> trysting-place, for he could but come to the understanding
> of himself, to the mastery of unlocking words, after long
> frequenting of the great Masters, hardly without ancestral
> memory of the like. Even knowledge is not enough, for the
> 'recklessness' that Castiglione thought necessary in good
> manners is necessary in this likewise, and if a man has it not
> he will be gloomy, and had better to his marketing again."[1]

---

1. *Essays and Introductions*, p.255-6.

VII
THE LIGHTER SIDE OF
THE IRISH LITERARY REVIVAL

$i

In a forgotten essay by my friend F. L. Lucas — the essay is actually about Bernard Shaw — he tells the story of a town called Tiryns, not far from Mycenae in ancient Greece. Now the people of Tiryns were, according to Athenaeus, incurably frivolous. Any and every event, however serious, was liable to move them to uncontrollable mirth. This, for some reason that is not clear to me, distressed them; they decided, after considering the matter at the local parish council or its equivalent, that they wished to be cured of their flippancy. So they sent an envoy (just like the one in *A Winter's Tale*) to Delphi, to enquire what they should do to be cured. The Oracle replied that the whole village must dress in their ceremonial robes on the top of the cliff beside the village. They must have ready a pure white bull, and garland it for sacrifice. The bull must then be pushed over the edge of the cliff into the sea as a sacrifice to the sea-god Poseidon: the village keeping perfectly straight faces the while.

Most of this they did. The villagers in their best robes assembled on the cliff-top. The bull, duly washed and decorated with flowers (you can see such bulls in the many paintings of that event so dear to the Renaissance imagination, *The Rape of Europa;* the bull in these always looks to me a little worried) was pushed forward to the edge of the cliff. The village maintained a religious solemnity. But at the critical moment there occurred some event at whose nature we can only guess; a small boy in the congregation burst into an uncontrollable guffaw, and the whole village dissolved in helpless laughter. So the people of Tiryns have remained incurably frivolous to this day. We are not told what happened to the bull; I like to think that it became a village pet.

Now far be it from me to suggest any parallels or parables, though it is possible that there may be a moral concealed somewhere in the story. We should have been spared many literary inanities if all writers had possessed a sense of humour. There is indeed some truth in the French view of English Literature, as being obsessed by an incorrigible gloominess: we remember how Matthew Arnold excluded Chaucer from the Pantheon of poets, and how an over-earnest Cambridge undergraduate attacked my friend C. S. Lewis on the grounds of lack of a moral sense, because he had just said in a public lecture that *The Miller's Tale* was funny. I think, too, of the young lady of thirteen who said coldly to F. L. Lucas: "I don't read poetry to enjoy it; I read it to *criticize* it."

Now I do not suggest that there has ever been any need to deplore a lack of a sense of humour in Sligo; still less that we should make a pilgrimage to Aughris Head, driving before us some choice product of the Cattle Market. What I am suggesting is that Ireland has a most ancient comic and satiric tradition; that the Irish Literary Renaissance lent itself, for a variety of reasons, to healthy satire and parody (it is profitable to read Joyce's *Ulysses* for its superb exercises in this form); and that it may at times — perhaps the end of a Yeats Summer School is one — be appropriate to cease to take ourselves and our heroes quite as seriously as we usually do, and to glance at the lighter side of the movement as Dublin and the world saw it. Parody can be a valuable and relevant form of indirect, or not so direct, criticism.

$ ii

Let us start with what we might call a biographical example: this is by M. J. MacManus in a book called *So this is Dublin* (1927).

"I saw the poet Yeats one time, and he visiting Gort Work- house in company with a noble lady. A grand woman she was with fine pleasant talk. Content to listen all day she would be, and the old people telling her stories or singing her the old songs. A lot of lies we used to be telling her too, God forgive us, and she would write them all down in a little book and have them printed in Dublin, or maybe in London, for to be read by the English. The poet Yeats was a pale dying-looking young man with long black hair and black clothes. Queer dreamy eyes he had, and they never looking at you, but away and beyond you. A great hand he was at making a poem, as great as Raftery himself. He had only to look at a bird or a stone, or maybe a fish itself, and he would put a song on it. Talking to himself he used to be and he going the roads and the mist on the bog, though some would say it was with the leprecauns and fairies he did be talking."

This is passable though not wholly inspired imitation of the style that has come to be known as Kiltartanese. There are various shafts: the Ulster Players did a parody of Synge's *In the Shadow of the Glen* called *The Mist that does be on the Bog*. The Irish have a courteous habit of telling a 'foreigner' (even though me may come from the next parish) what they think it would please him or her to know; and there is more than a suspicion that, in *Visions and Beliefs of the West of Ireland*, what the 'foreigners' were told was adjusted to what it was thought they would like to know.[1] (News travels quickly in North Munster and Connaught). And of course Yeats *did* compose by ceaseless testing upon the tongue, and that in all kinds of public places. And why not?

1. See (e.g.) Austin Clarke, *A Penny in the Clouds* (London, 1968), p.138.

Next come two pieces by J. C. Squire. The first is from a collection called *Solo and Duet*. Innisfree is perhaps the most parody-able of all Yeats's poems.[1] "I think he hated all his early poems, and 'Innisfree' most of all." This was written in the early '20s, and refers to a certain noble war-profiteer:

> I will arise and go now, and go to Inverness,
>   And a sham castle raise there, of stone and concrete built.
> Nine golf-holes will I have there, and wear my native dress,
>   And walk around in a bee-loud kilt.

More to our purpose is J. C. Squire's *Tricks of the Trade* (1925) which has a section called 'How They Would Have Done It'. One of the best is a take-off of Gray's *Elegy*, of which I quote a couple of stanzas: of the population of a particularly criminal village, now in their graves:

> For them no more the whetstone's cheerful noise,
>   No more the sun upon his daily course
> Shall watch them savouring the genial joys,
>   Of murder, bigamy, arson and divorce . . .
>
> Stranger, you quail, and seem inclined to run;
>   But, timid stranger, do not be unnerved;
> I can assure you that there was not one
>   Who got a tithe of what he had deserved.

But under 'How They Do It' there is a poem called 'Numerous Celts':

> There's a grey wind wails on the clover
>   And grey hills, and mist around the hills,
> And a far voice singing a song that is over
>   And my grey heart that a strange longing fills.
>
> A sheen of dead swords that shake upon the wind,
>   And a harp that sleeps though the wind is blowing
> Over the hills and the seas and the great hills behind,
>   The great hills of Kerry, where my heart would be going.
>
> For I would be in Kerry now where quiet is the grass,
>   And the birds are crying in the low light,
> And over the stone hedges the shadows pass,
>   And a fiddle weeps at the shadow of the night.
>
> With Pat Doogan
> Father Murphy
> Brown maidens
> King Cuchulain
> The Kine
> The Sheep
> Some old women
> Some old men
> And Uncle White Sea-gull and all.
> (chorus) And Uncle White Sea-gull and all.

1. And, for the summit of the ridiculous in criticism, we may cite that commentator who holds that the Nine Bean Rows refer to the Nine Months of Pregnancy.

We may pause to pick out the aspects of 'stock' technique, used effectively by Yeats and indifferently by his imitators. *Grey*, for example, is a key-work which, according to the Princeton *Concordance*, comes 102 times in *Collected Poems*. *Far* and *grey* are as frequent as *death* and *heart*. And in three particular groups of 'frequency' words we have in the high thirties *mournful, passion, silence, harp, heaven, hold, tears, faces, shadow, songs*. Again, this is the vocabulary of the early poems, up to 1910; the *Concordance* throws much light upon it.

But there is also the glance at the general Celtic *desiderium*, the longing to be somewhere other than where one is now; a nostalgic but wholly legitimate sentimentality of place, usually connected with boyhood. We can think of a dozen poems from any anthology of Irish verse, and in particular the poems of 'A.E.', Eva Gore-Booth O'Shaughnessy; and match them, without great difficulty, with poems from the Elizabethans (not so many here) and with many from the Romantics and Victorians. 'Innisfree' is not untypical; there are very many poems of exile.

The chorus of the parody, with the rhythm of *Uncle Tom Cobleigh* glances at present drama, Celtic Myth, the 'choruses' of peasant and heroic drama —

> Some old women
> Some old men

While

> Uncle White Sea-gull and all

picks up not only Chekhov and Uncle Vanya but also Yeats's 'The White Birds':

> I would that we were, my beloved, white birds on the foam of
> the sea!

but also the sea-gull that announced death to members of the Pollexfen family, and the sea-gull in that lovely poem on Countess Markiewicz's imprisonment. It is legitimate to emphasize how easily a diction can become stock or staled, how evocative words can be used as counters, how imagery can be deadened by unintelligent use. The best writers, of course, are apt to parody themselves. When old Dan in Synge's *Shadow of the Glen* breaks into The Tramp's great speech beginning

> "Come along now, with me now, lady of the house . . ."

with

> "Get out of that now, and do your blathering below in the glen"

—Synge is puncturing his own lyric outburst. I would give even odds that the same high speech in a company of 'rural people' today would meet with the same sort of reception.

The 'wit' of Dublin conversation has long been famous, and the mantles seem to have descended in a kind of succession: Lever, Oscar Wilde. Mahaffy, Shaw, Moore, Oliver St. John Gogarty; with many lesser lights. There are innumerable diaries, memoirs, biographies. But if we stand back from the painted scenes of those brilliant 'evenings' the talk does not seem to have worn too well. Perhaps they lacked a Boswell. Yeats himself was too profound to take part in invective, in the audacities of rudeness, that are so often quoted; nor did he take part in that mimicry of a just-departed guest which seems to us now in doubtful taste. Yet we may recall with pleasure some of the less familiar incidents: such as Yeats's encounter with the Court Poet of the Shah of Persia, once famous for his impassioned but chaste love-poems, but whose present bardic duty was to report to his master, in verse, on the meetings of the League of Nations.[1] Or the American composer who said to the poet: "I wish you could have heard my setting of your *Innisfree* sung in the open by two thousand Boy Scouts."[2] To which the smiling reply was the quotation "And I shall have some peace there." Lady Gregory could be acidly witty, but not unkind; as in her comment on 'the somewhat warlike English lady' staying at Coole: 'She was civilization in its most violent form'.

No doubt much of the wit, especially in verse, was Rabelaisian, and often in oral circulation only; Gogarty's 'Ode of Welcome to the Returning Troops' — published in *Irish Society* — proved to conceal an acrostic alerting the whores of Dublin,[3] and he was especially fertile in Limericks and the wit of the medical schools.[4]

Among the wittiest (and quietly ironic) comments on the movement are the obiter dicta of Lady Gregory in her long-concealed autobiography, *Seventy Years*.[5] Out of great riches we may select a few.

"Two significant things have happened; last week a priest denounced us from the altar, and Larkin the socialist who is getting up the strikes has praised *The Playboy* in his speech.[6] There is the portrait of a dull M.P. "He is like a hearse-horse at a pauper's funeral." She quotes Yeats's urbane comment on the rebellion: "I admire Pikes and Muskets in the abstract, but to use them would be too sectarian."

And side by side with the popular, sentimental and partly true picture of Blind Raftery holding audiences entranced, of the great Shanachies, the story-tellers, of Kerry, Clare, Aran, there is a healthy brutal disbelief in the Grand Style of which we might well take note. And there is nothing to regret: we may remember Shaw in the Preface to *John Bull's Other Island*:

... When I see the Irishman everywhere standing clear-

1. L.A.G. Strong, *Green Memory*, p.305. (London, 1961).
2. *Ibid.* p.261.
3. Ulick O'Connor, *Oliver St. John Gogarty*, p.23. (London, 1964).
4. *Ibid.* p.113ff.
4. Published, with the dramatic story of its provenance, in 1974. (Colin Smythe Ltd.)
6. Lady Gregory to Yeats. 7 Dec. 1911.

headed, sane, hardily callous to the boyish sentimentalities,
susceptibilities and credulities that make the Englishman the
dupe of every charlatan and the idolater of every numbskull,
I perceive that Ireland is the only spot on earth which still
produces the ideal Englishman of history.

$iii

Probably the wittiest of all those who ragged the Movement was
Susan Mitchell. It was she who knew all the leading personalities and
their weaknesses. Her book — now rare — called *Aids to the Immortality
of Certain Persons in Ireland* — is dated 1908. That is a year before the
death of Synge, a year after the *Playboy* riots. We might say that it
comes just at the end of the first great phase of the Abbey. Yeats was
then forty-three. The centre of the skit is really George Moore, whose
progress is given in a sort of epic, of which I can quote no more than
fragments. The first movement of the saga is when he returns to Dublin;
in an attempt to jump on the bandwaggon of the Irish Literary
Renaissance. (He expected to be welcomed with open arms.)

> We have reformed the Drama, myself and Yeats allied,
> For I took small stock in Martyn, and less in Douglas Hyde:
> To bow the knee to rare A.E. was too much for my pride.

> But W.B. was the boy for me — he of the dim, wan clothes;
> And — don't let on I said it — not above a bit of a pose;
> And they call his writing literature, as everybody knows.

Moore, who came from a Catholic family, had lived long as a professed
atheist and a source of scandal because of his novels, had spread a
rumour that, after his return, he proposed to join the Church of
Ireland; but was bitterly disappointed: first, because the announcement
caused no great sensation, and because the authorities sent a plain
clergyman, not even a bishop, to instruct him in the faith.
Again, I quote in fragments:

> No more in pagan carelessness I skip down Ely Place,
> Softly I glide through Dublin with the convert's timid grace.
> The lamp of Protestant reform lights up my bashful face.

Now George Moore — round, soft and plump — "a man carved out of a
turnip", — as Yeats put it — did move with a peculiar feminine tripping
gait. And at least by his own accounts he was irresistible to women, the
great lover; though the word had gone round that he was impotent,
and this is the point of a famous scandalous passage in Yeats's *The Cat
and the Moon*. And he had evinced a good deal of interest in the
problem of the unmarried mother, particularly of the seduced servant
girl. (It is worth remembering that the *droit de seigneur* appears to have
survived in Mayo and Galway until the 1870s). Hence the point of this
verse with its phrase borrowed from Suckling:

> Ye pretty little Papist maids, whatever your degree,
> Come hither fearlessly and sit on my converted knee,

Bid me to live and I will live your Protestant to be.

A heaven-sent opportunity came when George Moore, whose family place, Moore Hall, was on Lough Carra, became High Sheriff of Mayo. He had had the front door of his house in Ely Place painted green, in defiance of his landlord who wanted uniform colour along that famous terrace; and had kept up a notable quarrel about it, much to the amusement of Dublin:

> O then, Martyn dear, and did ye hear the news that's goin' round,
> Your old friend George will seldomer in Ely Place be found.
> He's left his loving neighbours, he's life his hall-door green
> To execute the English law in Ballaghadereen.

The 'wit', of course, comes in the superb way in which the name of that insignificant little town fits into the tune of *The Wearin' o' the Green* and picks up the colour of the hall-door at Ely Place: which Moore had asserted was necessary to him on purely aesthetic grounds and which brought him into conflict with the uniformity of his neighbours. Both the rhythms and the internal rhymes of the original are caught successfully:

> I met A.E. and W.B., I took them by the hand.
> Says I, "Alas, a soothing glass will either of you stand?
> Moore has left us dry and drouthy and my grief I cannot screen,
> While he's hangin' men and women down in Ballaghadereen."

The point here is that both 'A.E.' and W.B. were virtually teetotallers. W.B., so O'Connor tells us, had been taken to a pub *once*, at his own request — to see what it was like. Susan Mitchell is a superb corrective to pomposity. So is Max Beerbohm: the two most successful cartoons show Edward Martyn, plump, rather grim in pincenez beside an infinitely elongated Yeats,[1] and 'Mr. Yeats introducing George Moore to the Queen of the Fairies'.

It is pleasant to record a story of the impish James Stephens: how at a lecture in America a lady went up to him and said:

> "O, Mr. Stephens, I must tell you how much I enjoyed your masterpiece, *Hard Cash.*"

Stephens kept his face straight and said:

> "Thank you very much, madam, but you know I don't consider that my masterpiece."
> "Really," said the lady: "What do you consider your masterpiece?"
> "Why, of course, *Uncle Tom's Cabin.*"
> "Really, Mr. Stephens! I must get it."

§iv

But it is of course George Moore who remains part-comic historian, part licensed buffoon, of the Irish Literary Renaissance. It would not be

1. The title is 'Celtades Ambo'

impossible to compose a wholly delightful, dramatic and utterly unreliable account of it from the three volumes of the *Hail and Farewell* Trilogy. Here I can do no more ' than choose for our subject a few of the more pleasant incidents.

This is an extract from an account of an early meeting with Yeats in Symons' rooms:

"Rising from the low stool in the chimney-corner, he led me to a long box, and among the manuscript I discovered several packs of cards. As it could not be that Yeats was a clandestine bridge-player, I inquired the use the cards were put to, and learnt they were especially designed for the casting of horoscopes.[1] He spoke of his uncle, a celebrated occultist, whose predictions were always fulfilled, and related some of his own successes. All the same, he had been born under Aquarius,[2] and the calculations of the movements in the stars in that constellation were so elaborate that he had abandoned the task for the moment, and was now seeking the influences of the Pleiades. He showed me some triangles drawn on plain sheets of cardboard, into which I was to look while thinking of some primary colour - red, or blue, or green. His instructions were followed by me — why not? — but nothing came of the experiment; and then he selected a manuscript from the box, which he told me were the new rules of the Order of the Golden Door,[3] written by himself. There was no need to tell me that, for I recognize always his undulating cadences. These rules had become necessary; an Order could not exist without rules, and heresy must be kept within bounds, though for his part he was prepared to grant everyone such freedom of will as would not endanger the existence of the Order. The reading of the manuscript interested me, and I remember that one of its finest passages related to the use of vestments, Yeats maintaining with undeniable logic that the ancient priest put on his priestly robe as a means whereby he might raise himself out of the ordinary into an intenser life, but the Catholic priest puts on an embroidered habit because it is customary. A subtle intelligence which delighted me in times gone by, and I like now to think of the admiration with which I used to listen to Yeats talking in the chimney-corner, myself regretting the many eloquent phrases with floated beyond recall up the chimney, yet unable to banish from my mind the twenty-five men and women collected in the second pair back in West Kensington, engaged in the casting of horoscopes and experimenting in hypnotism."[4]

1. This was the Tarot Pack.
2. Subsequently, an astrologer warned Yeats not to live near water: hence, perhaps, the departure from The Tower.
3. So Moore deliberately misnamed the Order of the Golden Dawn.
4. *Ave* p.51.

Shortly after there is a riotous account of Edward Martyn, who had never produced a play, trying to control the final rehearsals of *The Heather Field*. Equally good is the account of a rehearsal of *The Countess Cathleen* in London:

> . . . we sat down together to listen to *The Countess Cathleen* rehearsed by the lady, who had put her psaltery aside and was going about with a reticule on her arm, rummaging in it from time to time for certain memoranda, which when found seemed only to deepen her difficulty. Her stage management is all right in her notes, Yeats informed me. But she can't transfer it from paper on to the stage, he added, without appearing in the least to wish that the stage management of his play should be taken from her. Would you like to see her notes? At that moment the voice of the experienced actress asking the poor lady how she was to get up the stage drew attention from Yeats to the reticule, which was being searched for the notes. And the actress walked up the stage and stood there looking contemptuously at Miss Vernon, who laid herself down on the floor and began speaking through the chinks. Her dramatic intention was so obscure that perforce I had to ask her what it was, and learnt from her that she was evoking hell.
>
> But the audience will think you are trying to catch cockroaches. Yeats whirled forward in his cloak with the suggestion that she should stand on a chair and wave her hands.
>
> That will never do, Yeats; and the lady interrupted asking me how hell should be evoked, and later begged to be allowed to hand over the rehearsal of *The Countess Cathleen* to the experienced actress's husband, who said he would undertake to get the play on the stage if Mr. Yeats would promise not to interfere with him.[1]

One could go on for ever with the delightful episodes, the scene of chaos at Euston Station when Martyn moved the company to Dublin, and the telegram that Martyn sent to Moore when the company arrived there:

> 'The sceptre of intelligence has passed from London to Dublin.'

There were the famous consultations of theologians in both cities over the possibilities of heresy lurking in the text of *The Countess Cathleen*, the prelude to the anti-Yeats pamphlet *Souls for Gold*. But one of the priests called in a referee,

> . . . "a Jesuit of considerable attainment (who) had pointed out that the language objected to was put into the mouths of demons."[1]

In the briefest of sketches Moore hits off some of the ancillary characters: Plunkett, T.P. Gill, O'Grady, Rolleston. Here, for example, is Rolleston:

1. *Ave* pp.69-70.
2. *Ibid.* p.95.

O'Grady tells me that he found Rolleston a West Briton, but after a few lessons in Irish history Rolleston donned a long black cloak and a slouch hat, and attended meetings, speaking in favour of secret societies, persuading John O'Leary to look upon him as one that might rouse the country, going much further than I had ever dreamed of going, O'Grady said. His extreme views frightened me a little, but when I met him next and began to speak to him about the Holy Protestant Empire, he read me a paper on Imperialism.
And when did that happen?
About ten years ago, a Messiah that punctured while the others were going by on inflated tyres . . . poor Rolleston punctured ten years ago.[1]

And here is part of the description of how Moore volunteered to help Yeats disentangle some of the knots that had appeared in *The Shadowy Waters:*

. . . he eagerly accepted my proposal to go over to Coole to talk out the poem with him, and to redeem it, if possible, from the Fomorians. He would regret their picturesque appearance; but could I get rid of them, without losing the poetical passages? He would not like the words poetical passages — I should have written beautiful verses.
Looking up at the ivied embrasure of the tower (*at Tillyra*) where Edward was undergoing the degradation of fancying himself a lover so that he might write the big scene between Jasper and Millicent at the end of the third act,[2] I said: 'He will not come out of that tower until dinner-time, so I may as well ride over to Coole and see what can be done. But the job Yeats has set me is a difficult one.
Away I went on my bicycle, up and down along the switchback road, trying to arrive at some definite idea regarding Fomorians, and thinking, as I rode up the long drive, that perhaps Yeats might not be at home, and that to return to Tillyra without meeting the Fomorians would be like riding home from hunting after a blank day.
The servant told me that he had gone for one of his constitutionals, and would be found about the lake. The fabled woods of Coole are thick hazel coverts, with tall trees here and there, but the paths are easy to follow, and turning out of one of these into the open, I came upon a tall black figure standing at the edge of the lake, wearing a cloak which fell in straight folds to his knees, looking like a great umbrella forgotten by some picnic-party.
I've come to relieve you of Fomorians, and when they've been flung into the waters we must find some simple and suggestive anecdote. Now, Yeats, I'm listening.

1. *Ave.* pp.109-110.
2. Of *The Tale of a Town*. Martyn was notorious for his celibate views.

As he proceeded to unfold his dreams to me I perceived that we were inside a prison-house with all the doors locked and windows barred."[1]

And for a last vignette - we could go on indefinitely - another, of A.E. Here there is no malice:

"He had refused to dine with us because he did not wish to put on evening clothes, but he had come in afterwards, more attractive than anybody else in the room in his grey tweeds, his wild beard, and shaggy mane of hair. Some friends we seem to have known always, and try as we will we cannot remember the first time we saw them; whereas our first meetings with others are fixed in our mind, and as clearly as if it had happened no later than yesterday I remember A.E. coming forward to meet me, and the sweetness of his long grey eyes . . . his mind embracing the whole universe in one moment, he understood that there is but one life: the dog at his heels and the stars he would soon see (for the dusk was gathering) were not different things, but one thing."[2]

Finally we may recall some of Yeats's descriptions of Moore:

It was Moore's own fault that everybody hated him except a few London painters. In one of Dostoevsky's novels there is a man who proposed that everybody present should tell his worst action. Nobody takes the proposal seriously; everybody is witty or amusing till his turn comes. He confesses that he once stole half-a-crown and left a servant girl to bear the blame.[3] Moore might have so confessed, but his confession would have been a plagiarism or a whole lie. I met a man who hated Moore because Moore told some audience that he had selected a Parisian street-boy, for one day dressed him in good clothes, housed him in an expensive hotel, gave him all that he wanted, then put him back into rags and turned him out to discover what would happen: a plagiarism from a well-known French author. 'Yeats', he said to me once, 'I was sitting here in my room the other night when there was a ring. My servant was out; when I opened the door a woman ran in and threw her arms round my neck. 'At last I have found you. There are thirteen George Moores in the *London Directory*. Your're the ninth I have called on. What? Not recollect me − not recollect the woman you raped in Paris twenty years ago?' She had called about her daughter's musical education, he said . . . He was all self and yet had so little self that he would destroy his reputation, or that of some friend, to make his audience believe that the story running in his head at the moment had happened, had only just happened.[4]

1. *Ave.* pp.186-7.
2. *Ibid.* pp.120-21.
3. The incident occurs in *Esther Waters*.
4. *Autobiographies* 'Dramatis Personae', p.433.

He and I went to the town of Galway for a Gaelic festival that coincided with some assembly of priests . . . A Father Maloney, supposed to know all about Greek Art, caught sight of Moore and introduced himself. He probably knew nothing about Moore, except that he was some kind of critic, so he set out upon his favourite topic with: 'I have always considered it a proof of Greek purity that though they left the male form uncovered, they invariably draped the female.' 'Do you consider, Father Maloney,' said Moore in a voice that rang through the whole room, 'that the female form is inherently more indecent than the male?' Every priest turned a stern and horrified eye upon Father Maloney, who sat hunched up and quivering.[1]

And this also from *Dramatis Personae,* again of Moore:

"Even to conversation and acted plays, he gave an inattentive ear, instincts incapable of clear expression deafened and blinded[2] him; he was like Milton's lion rising up, pawing out of the earth, but, unlike that lion, stuck half-way. He reached to middle life ignorant of even small practical details. He said to a friend:

"How do you keep your pants from falling about your knees?' 'O', said the friend, 'I put my braces through the little tapes that are sewn there for the purpose.' A few days later, he thanked the friend with emotion. Upon a long country bicycle ride with another friend (this was A.E.) he had stopped because his pants were about his knees, had gone behind a hedge, had taken them off, and exchanged them at a cottage for a tumbler of milk. Only at pictures did he look undeafened and unblinded, for they impose their silence upon us.[3]

But surely no fiction or parody is stranger than the truths recorded of the whole movement, of the trap that George Moore set to catch the cat that threatened his blackbird in Ely Place, and that finally caught the blackbird; of the host with attractive daughters who insisted on locking them in their bedrooms at night when George Moore was a guest in the house; of Lady Gregory placing thick layers of rugs along the passage that led to Yeats's room, lest any ill-judged footfall should disturb the poet's meditations; of the rejoicing at Coole when five and a half lines of verse had been completed by lunchtime. Yet let us never underestimate Lady Gregory, her courage and her solid motherly competence; I doubt if we shall ever be able to assess how much we owe to her. The vision of a cultured aristocracy was seen through a glass darkly at Lissadell, but only became clear at Coole and Tillyra.

---

1. *Autobiographies.* p.405.
2. Note the recurrence of the phrase: and *cf.* 'The Cold Heaven' and 'A Dialogue of Self and Soul'.
3. *Autobiographies* pp.405-6.

Was there, indeed, anywhere else till Lady Dorothy Wellesley, enthusiastic and indiscreet, offered him some substitute at Penns-in-the-Rocks?

§ v

But no fiction could provide comedy more outrageous than the account of the *Playboy* Riots of 1907. Fortunately they are now amply documented[1]. We may mention two instances. The first is from 'A Western Girl 2': [2]

> "Nothing redeems the general sordidness of the piece. Every character uses coarse expressions, and Miss Allgood (one of the most charming actresses I have ever seen) is forced, before the most fashionable audience in Dublin, to use a word indicating an essential item of female attire, which the lady would probably never utter in ordinary circumstances, even to herself."

Later, Yeats pointed out that the word 'shift' appeared in Longfellow.

And we might quote with profit some of the remarks by a Mr. Sheahan, allegedly a medical student, at the public discussion at the Abbey, who had

> . . . drawn attention to a particular form of marriage law which though not confined to Ireland, was very common in Ireland (disorder). It was with a fine woman like Pegeen Mike (hisses) and a tubercle Koch's disease man like Shaun Keogh (some laughter, groans, hisses, and noise)—and the point of view was not the murder at all (hisses), but when the artist appears in Ireland who was not afraid of life (laughter) and his nature (boos), the women of Ireland would receive him (cries of 'shame' and great disorder). (At this stage of the speech many ladies, whose countenances plainly indicated intense feelings of astonishment and pain, rose and left the place. Many men also retired.)[3]

It is amusing to see some of the eminent figures of the Renaissance through the eyes of two small girls at Coole; obsessed (very properly) with ponies, donkeys and their own pursuits. Mr. Yeats who, they noted, seemed to stay there almost continuously always had second helpings and never said 'Thank you'. Mr. Bernard Shaw cheated at 'Hunt-the-thimble': Mr. O'Casey arrived from Dublin without collar or tie, to the grave scandal of the coachman and the parlourmaid. Dr. Gogarty's anecdotes did not amuse them, but of Yeats

> He always seemed to be there, leaning back in his chair at table — huge, with (in our eyes) an enormous tummy. He wore a signet ring with an enormous stone in it on his little

1. See the admirable *The Playboy Riots* by James Kilroy (The Irish Theatre, Series 4.) (Dolmen Press, 1971).
2. *Ibid*, p.10.
3. *Ibid*, p.86.

finger, and Nu and I used to giggle like mad, and say he expected everyone to kiss it, like the Pope. She and I used to copy his habit of running his fingers through the great lock of hair that fell forward over his forehead, and then hold out our hand with the imaginary ring, saying: 'This ring is a holy ring; it has been in touch with my holy halo.'

But Jack B. Yeats and Augustus John clearly won their approval.[1]

§vi

No consideration of The Lighter Side could omit some mention of the dealings of the Renaissance with the Supernatural. It would take us into too many by-roads if we were to consider Theosophy and its practices, then and now. But we should certainly glance at Madame Blavatsky, celebrated in verse by both T.S. Eliot and Louis MacNeice. Many, including Yeats sat at her feet. She seemed to him 'to surpass all others in honesty, as she sat there talking, vast and shapeless of body, rolling cigarettes, inconsequent and incomprehensible'. But, clearly, the authoress of Isis Unveiled was a formidable person, capable of controlling her body of earnest disciples. One lady among them complained that decayed corpses were trying to get into bed with her;[2] Madame reproved her with "Very bad taste on both sides." It would be unwise to mock universally the magical practices and rituals which seem to satisfy man's passion for secret societies, esoteric rituals and a Faustian desire for power over the unseen world. I do not, for example, think it improbable that Yeats successfully exorcised a boy-ghost who haunted Gogarty's house at Renvyle. But I do find it difficult to take seriously his story of the ghost of an ancient sea-captain who had long been imprisoned — like Ariel in the oak — in the pillar of a doorway and flew out in the form of a snipe when the house was being demolished. So also with the story of the Sligo lady who sacked her groom on the grounds that he had exiled her husband's ghost to a lonely lighthouse in Sligo Bay. I take pleasure in the account of one of A.E.'s theosophical meetings (with Yeats in the chair) when a heckler, protesting against neo-Druidism, pronounced 'The Trinity is good enough for me', 'That', said Yeats, 'is an interesting suggestion'. So with the account of A.E.'s being knocked up at midnight with the offer of a place in the newly formed Senate of the Free State, and retreating into his bedroom saying that he would have to consult the Elder Gods before deciding. Then there would be the story of George Moore and A.E. bicycling out to a prehistoric

1. *Me and Nu*: Childhood at Coole. By Anne Gregory. (Colin Smythe, 1970) She was acutely embarrassed by the poem to her yellow hair ('For Anne Gregory') which he read to her in his 'humming' voice. But later, when he broadcast it, 'it sounded really rather splendid'.
2. This seems to be an ancient hazard. Perhaps the archetype is in the final movement of the ballad of *Clerk Saunders*.

underground tomb, in which A.E. proposed to invoke the Earth Gods who, he hoped, would appear to him: while Moore kept guard above. But the seance was spoilt by the untimely arrival of two nonconformist clergymen on bicycles, who insisted on going into the tomb: and the gods did not appear.

And from another angle —

> I have just heard a piece of information at which I am not very pleased though I have half expected it. Russell (A.E.) has married Miss North. An aerial Theosophic marriage. It came off a day or two ago and the bride is off to Mullingar by herself. Mrs. Russell is a person who sees visions and is well-bred and pleasant enough; but I suppose I would never think anybody quite good enough for Russell. She has, as I have noticed, been in love with him for years . . . [1]

Theosophy and psychical research were fair game - as always - for the mockers. So A.E. on a picnic at a numinous place, Ballinamantane Castle. A.E. hated to be put to see anyone else's ghosts and wandered, about in a discontented silence. Presently I said "Don't you see anything, Russell?" and he replied "Oh yes I do, but they are a low lot". And in a letter of Lady Gregory's in 1913: "Russell is delighted to hear of Macgregor's downfall." (This was Yeats's great enemy in the complicated quarrels of The Golden Dawn.) "He never could think much of a man who had to look at his watch to know what was going on in the other world."

$ vii

By now it may, I hope, be plain to you what I have been trying to do in this last lecture. In one sense it may have been a sort of satiric Epilogue to the 'tragedies' of this International Summer School. It has turned out a little differently to what I had intended when I planned this course nearly a year ago. But there is, I think, a moral; and the moral is this.

The main warning is of course that we should beware of taking ourselves, the School, the Sligo scene, our pilgrimage, too seriously. It would not have been difficult, six years ago, to allow ourselves to develop attitudes and values to Yeats and his poetry that might, in the course of time have become unduly sentimental, chauvinistic, even bardolatrous. Yeats is not a poet who is notable for a highly-developed sense of humour. (Is there any of the greatest poets, outside Chaucer and Shakespeare, who is?) Yet as one student put it to me last year, we may be in danger of being 'Yeats-sodden' so that

> the appetite may sicken and so die.

We have tried to achieve some balancing correctives: by lectures

1. Wade, *Letters* p.299.

on the other great figures of the Irish Literary Renaissance. We have
had before us, amongst others, Allingham, Synge, Moore, Lady Gregory,
Wilde, Gogarty; and I would hope that we should continue this practice
in a wider setting: not merely of personalities, but of culture, mythology,
history. Yeats is a great Irishman; but he belongs to the literary history
of the world.

Yet in this Epilogue it is well to remember Synge's words in the
Preface to *The Tinker's Wedding:*

> Of the things which nourish the imagination humour is one
> of the most needful, and it is dangerous to limit or destroy it . . .
> where a country loses its humour, as some towns in Ireland are
> doing, there will be morbidity of mind . . .

And to cultivate *selbst-ironie,* as the Germans call it, this power to
laugh at ourselves, to perceive the antinomies and contradictions in
things, to see and ponder upon the discrepancy between the Doer and
the Thing Done. To reflect on the changing perspectives of life, art,
religion, morals (and never in human history have they changed so
rapidly as in the last five decades) - these are qualities which are, I think,
desirable. We are dealing with the personalities not of one but of many
writers who made the Irish Literary Renaissance. These personalities
are - as we all are - noble, ridiculous, exalted, laughable, generous, petty,
by turns; we do well to remember Shakespeare's

> A rarer spirit never
> Did steer humanity; but you, gods, will give us
> Some faults to make us men.

There is, I believe, a balance here. In the nature of this School you
have heard much reminiscence, many anecdotes, from those who knew
Yeats, and the Abbey Theatre, and his friends. It is a very human,
and, on the whole (I think) generous, moving and noble story. When
anecdote or reminiscence illuminates personality or achievement it seems
to me valuable because it may fill out the borders or the background
of our picture. The poet has long had a distinctly ambivalent role in
society. In the history of literature he has seldom been without his
eccentricities of behaviour, dress, manners. They are part of that strong
and serious *persona* which he must have cultivated as the price of
keeping away what distracts him, sometimes even Church and State,

> The mob that howls at the door.

And as any man grows older he is apt to develop a definiteness of
mind, even a mask of aristocracy, that is the reverse side of the authority
with which he has learnt to speak. And if he survived to write great
poetry in his sixties and after - as no English poet had ever done before -
it was in the nature of things that his authority in speaking and his
aristocracy, should increase rather than diminish. All these are aspects
of the human situation; we should recognize them, sympathize, and,
sometimes − smile a little.

But there is a very much wider sense of what I have been trying to say. I believe that there is a danger in taking literature, poetry, *too* seriously. It is the highest achievement, next to religion, of the human spirit: it is, in Wordsworth's phrase,   'the breath and finer spirit of all knowledge'. It is there for our delight, instruction, the enlargement of our minds and souls . But we do ourselves, and it, a grave wrong, if we use it badly, by allowing it to get out of proportion. It is, to use one metaphor, an armour and armoury for living: but it must be tested and re-tested against the three cardinal experiences of love, war and death. If, at any point, we allow ourselves to stop short of living, in the belief that this is the *whole,* failing to see it is no more than a prelude, that whatever its greatness it is only in its full strength when we perceive it as a balance in the totality of living, then we are doing it and ourselves a wrong. The truth is greater than poetry, or living, or ourselves.

I think again of F.L. Lucas:
"And anyhow, who would rather never have read Shakespeare
than never have been in love?"

But there is another and more terrible danger. Much literature today is immersed in a destructive element, even one of anarchy. It cries aloud in the market place that life is not worth living. Novel after novel proclaims this: that love, death, war, are Dead Sea apples, that crumble to dust at a touch. It is something that seems a new phenomenon, for there is nothing of the noble and exalting or of the pessimism that runs through the Western Tradition from Plato to Hardy, from the writer of the Book of Ecclesiastes to Leopardi. Perhaps I can make my point clearer by a quotation from a recent review in *The Atlantic Monthly:*

"Over and over the agonising tunes are played: helplessness, desperation, impotence, the lapse of the present from the promise of the past, flawed vision, the malign dissociation of the self from the senses. They are played so brilliantly that the reader finds himself forgetting that life and poetry have major keys as well as minor, victories as well as defeats."

And the article goes on to quote Robert Lowell on Hawthorne:
The disturbed eyes rise,
furtive, foiled, dissatisfied
from meditation on the true and insignificant.

I have sometimes thought that our approval and even advocacy of literature that is defeatist and anarchical without the redeeming nobility of a Leopardi or a Hardy has involved us — as I think it has involved certain theologians — in a new Treason of the Clerks.

There is nothing of this in Yeats. The epithets which I have used and would use again, in defiance of popular critical usage, are 'wisdom' and 'nobility'. There are faults in plenty, God knows. But — and here one must be subjective — I have tested it on the perimeter of two wars, and in the midst of a third. I have shared, in boyhood, the society, the scenery and the conflicts that his poetry mirrors. I have carried it in my mind - maybe poetry should always be carried there - when there were no books. I have tested it against that supreme touchstone, death and tragedy; and it has worn well. For the young he can give, I think, the elements of an understanding of Love and War - as profanely as any poet has ever done: to the old, a still more vital exhortation:

> No longer in Lethean foliage caught
> Begin the preparation for your death
> And from your fortieth winter, by that thought
> Test every work of intellect or faith,
> And everything that your own hands have wrought,
> And count those works extravagence of breath
> That are not suited for such men as come
> Proud, open-eyed and laughing to the tomb.

VIII
THE SAINTHOOD OF A.E.[1]
$i

The Irish Literary Revival was not, I think, prolific in its production
of saints: the most charitable ecclesiastical commission would hardly
ascribe that condition to George Moore, or to Lady Gregory (however
blameless her life) or even to Bernard Shaw who was expelled for
Atheism by the Wexford Bee-Keepers' Society. Yeats, indeed, selected
as one of the pairs of antinomies that he liked to imagine as components
of his own character The Swordsman and The Saint — the former
repudiating the latter - but it would not be unkind to describe both as
theoretical concepts. And one recalls those lines describing his father
at a public meeting:

-'This land of Saints,' and then as the applause died out,
-'Of plaster Saints'; his beautiful mischievous head thrown
back.[2]

Edward Martyn was too much the victim of his own sensitive conscience,
concerned with his own soul (you may remember how the malicious
Moore wanted to write a pamphlet called 'Edward Martyn and His Soul')
to be a candidate for this particular category. In spite, or because, of all
his eccentricities, his enthusiasm for Theosophy, for strange primitive
or primaeval Druidic and earth-cults, I think I should put my money on
George Russell. May I start by giving you a first-hand impression from
my friend Luba Kaftannikoff, who worked as a girl in his editorial
office. It touches, besides, a great figure of Irish Literature and of our
Sligo School. The time is the spring of 1922:

"I had turned into Plunkett House one spring morning, and
run up to the top of the house, where A.E. and Susan Mitchell
worked." (This was Susan Mithcell. the gifted and wicked
parodist of the whole movement.) "A big sunny room: its
walls decorated by pictures drawn straight on to the walls by
A.E.: a lovely room.

A.E. sitting at his desk, looked across at me, and said -
'Oh, Luba, I'm just reading a poem sent me from Coole by a
new young man. I can't understand it. Sit down and I'll read
it to you.' So I sat, and A.E. read the poem aloud. We looked
at each other. 'I can't understand it either,' I said mournfully,
'But I do think it sounds sincere - as if *he* knew what he was
at, and had something real to say.'

'He sent me a self-portrait, too,' said A.E. rising, and turning towards the fire-place where, fastened up with a drawing
pin, was a pen-and-ink drawing of an attenuated, eager young

1. Sligo, 1964.
2. 'Beautiful Lofty Things'.

face in profile, bearing a head covered with a shock of black hair. (That portrait was there for years.) A.E. looked at it: he said, 'I have a feeling that our young man will go far. His name is Frank O'Connor. I'll print his poem.''

§ii

My subject then, is A.E. and his poetry. He is at once central, and curiously peripheral to the Irish Literary Revival. He was born in 1867, two years younger than Yeats. Both attended the same Art School in Dublin, and Yeats was even then declaiming his poems to any one who would listen. But there their paths diverged: George Russell went, (like H. G. Wells in England) into a draper's shop; Pim's, in Dublin. He continued to paint: but seems to have "feared it as a kind of self-indulgence which, if yielded to, would stunt his life". Art with him was a means rather than an end; it should be sought, for by its help we can live more purely, more intensely, but we must never forget that 'to live as fully as possible' was his main concern. Which is the normal pre-Raphaelite creed. This is what George Moore said of him; and this gives us, in a phrase, the artist's perpetual dilemma:

> The intellect of man is forced to choose
> Perfection of the life, or of the work . . . [1]

Yeats made himself into a dedicated poet: A.E. preferred the multiplicity of a life most strangely divided between immense activity in both the material and spiritual worlds. Like Yeats he came easily under the influence of Indian mysticism; he was a Theosophist (that sect met thrice a week in Dublin) and a contributor to *The Theosophical Review.* His copy of Madame Blavatsky's *The Secret Doctrine* was heavily underlined. More important were the works of Max Müller, Edwin Arnold, Charles Johnston. He knew from a comparatively early age the *Bhagavadgita* and the *Upanishads,* and it is not fantastic to perceive certain similarities with Tagore, perhaps even with Gandhi. And in some curious fashion the concern of the Hindu sacred books with a rural civilization, and the need for its reconstruction as well as the maintenance of its culture, in India and Ireland, gave weight to his unremitting propaganda for the Irish Agricultural Organization, as well as to his concern with the high and sacred places through which divinity might exhale. (We remember Yeats's praise of CrôPatric, of Mount Meru.) He was concerned with Spirtualism, and with psychic experiments as to the means by which visionary experiences may be induced. We may quote from a letter to him from Yeats:

"By the by when Miss Gonne and myself were seeing visions in Dublin we got a message for you which was 'number the people of God'. Does it mean anything to you? Is it an

1. Yeats: 'The Choice'.

appeal to you to help in that systematization which you so
dislike?"[1]

A.E. painted visions: so Yeats writes to him again about them:

"If you can call up the white fool and have the time I wish
you could make a sketch of him, for Dalua seems to be becoming
important among us. Aengus is the most curious of all the
gods. He seems both Hermes and Dionysus. He has some part
perhaps in all enthusiasm."[2]

Like Yeats, the Hindu wisdom developed side by side with a projection
of the Celtic mythology with its euphoneous pantheism, into a kind of
Irish Druidic twilight of the Elder Gods, linked to the very soil and
stone of ancient Ireland: the Indian and the Celtic giving each other
material support as Byzantium had certified Ireland. There is no shadow
of doubt as to his complete sincerity. Standish O'Grady relates how
he visited Bray one fine Sunday, and saw a bearded young man 'evange-
lizing' the crowd of holiday-makers; he was preaching faith in the pagan
gods of Ireland.[3] That is typical of a sort of gentle unselfconscious
fearlessness that followed him throughout his life.

This business of vision is so important, and so often mocked at, that
we should examine it further. The gift is, today, as unfashionable
as it is rare. Yet when we look at A.E.'s paintings, with their ethereal
figures set in a peculiar radiance of light, of spirit or faery children on
open golden sands, among tree shadows, I am reminded irresistibly of
two other poets; Blake, and my friend Walter de la Mare. Of Blake, I
do not think that any scholar would deny the validity of his Four-Fold
Vision, or question the energy and integrity of his spiritual perceptions of colour, light and form. The so called 'Visionary Heads' are
a classic instance, 'The Ghost of a Flea' the most familiar and one of the
most intense in its perceptions.[4] Of de la Mare, I am convinced that
this other world had, at times, a complete reality; and that he was
peculiarly sensitive in his perception of people and above all of places
inhabited by the invisible. All three, Blake, de la Mare, A.E. are
concerned with the idealized feminine form, the *anima* of Jung. A
single short poem will serve to illustrate:

> A shaft of fire that falls like dew,
>   And melts and maddens all my blood,
> From out thy spirit flashes through
>   The burning glass of womanhood.

1. Wade, *Letters*, p.297.
2. *Ibid.* p.324.
3. It is worth noting that A.E. seems to have encountered no opposition
   from the ecclesiastical authorities.
4. See, e.g., Sir Geoffrey Keynes's *Blake Studies.* (1971), p.130ff.

Only so far; here must I stay:
  Nearer I miss the light, the fire;
I must endure the torturing ray,
  And with all beauty, all desire.

Ah, time long must the effort be,
  And far the way that I must go
To bring my spirit unto thee,
  Behind the glass, within the glow.[1]

Like de la Mare he has this delicate sensitivity to natural scenery, and the same sense (like Hardy) of the beauty that passes. L.A.G. Strong quotes from him:

"I think all good poetry is written out of doors. I think in some mysterious way we are lit by *anima mundi* and get more brilliant colours in our minds."[2]

Within or behind nature moves divinity, in many forms:

Those delicate wanderers,
The wind, the star, the cloud,
Ever before mine eyes,
As to an altar bowed,
Light and dew-laden airs
Offer in sacrifice.

The offerings arise:
Hazes of rainbow light,
Pure crystal, blue, and gold,
Through dreamland take their flight;
And 'mid the sacrifice
God moveth as of old.

In miracles of fire
He symbols forth his days;
In gleams of crystal light
Reveals what pure pathways
Lead to the soul's desire,
The silence of the height.[3]

It is the verse of a painter, verse which (perhaps) were better made into a painting in which clichés are unlikely or impossible. But the verse does not wholly obey his call; the evocative words seem to grow a little tired.

§ iii

If we study a bibliography of A.E.'s work, the thing that strikes one first is the multiplicity of his interests and his competence in each:

1. 'The Burning Glass'. As often in his work, one feels that the poem is not sustained after a strong first stanza.
2. *Green Memory*, London, 1961.
3. 'Sacrifice'. It is not irreverent to see echoes of the colours of *Revelations*.

and I do not think it unkind to suggest that the very dispersion (in contrast to the comparatively single-minded Yeats) prevented his work from extending to its full power either as poet or as painter. He was always poor. After the period in Pim's drapery shop Sir Horace Plunkett selected him to be the chief propagandist of the Irish Agricultural Organization Society. We may quote Yeats (on whom, too, some light is here reflected)

> They want a man to organize agricultural banks and I suggested him. He seems to combine the three needful things — business knowledge, power to make a speech, enthusiasm. . . I could not have urged him to give up a certainty like Pim's for an uncertainty like Plunkett's did I not know that he was going to leave Pim's in any case. The American Theosophists have been asking him to give up Pim's and write for them and have promised him a small income.[1]

He was editor of its paper, *The Irish Homestead,* from 1895 to 1923: and (so Moore relates) had refused a salary of more than £3 a week, on the grounds that no man's labours were worth more. (This was rather Shavian. You will remember Shaw's statement that anyone with less than £365 a year should undergo euthanasia.) From 1923 to 1930 he was Editor of *The Irish Statesman,* a journal of great importance in its day, and through it kept before the new Free State the ideal of that sweetness and light, not unmixed with fire, that animated all his being. It is not strange that, in spite of being originally associated with the Abbey Theatre, he found no time to write for it, (though *Deirdre* is his only play), or to take part in that confused warfare of personalities and insults that had driven Yeats to doubt whether the Abbey period had not killed his inspiration as a poet:

> My curse on plays
> That have to be set up in fifty ways,
> On the day's war with every knave and dolt,
> Theatre business, management of men . . . [2]

Even the genesis of his pseudonym is typical of George Russell. We are told that it was originally ÆON, but a compositor could not read it, and left it as A.E., which he always used afterwards; but it was his grief that publishers and others refused to use the diphthong which (he said) 'expressed the mood of his soul'. The term ÆON itself shows the devious workings of his thought: he had made "a drawing of the apparition in the Divine Mind of the idea of Heavenly Man.[3] He lay awake considering what title he should give it. Something whispered to him 'Call it the Birth of Æon'." A fortnight later his eye caught the word Æon in a book in the National Library, and that led him to

1. Wade, *Letters,* p.291
2. 'The Fascination of What's Difficult'.
3. Blake would have understood this.

Neander's 'History of the Gnostic Religion' with its passage on the
Gnostics and the doctrine of the Aeons. He analysed the words into
the components of the 'primal language':

      A — sound for God.
      AE — its first divergence from A.
      AU — sound. continuity for a time.
      N — change;

Thus ÆON represents revolt from God, the passage of the "separated
soul through its successive incarnations in man homeward to God,
and God's consequent amplification".

I take this account from Herbert Howarth,[1] with my own reservation
that there is possibly a further connection with the Jewish Kabbala,
and the five vowels (which must never be spoken) of the Ineffable
Name. What is important for our purpose is this early absorption in
Eastern Literature, the Rosicrucian view that every man is God, and
the belief (shared by Yeats) in the doctrine of reincarnation.

§iv

He and Yeats shared a Protestant tradition; both revolted against
it. But both retained a certain Puritanism that was characteristic. For
A.E. it seems to have taken the form of rejecting his talents as a
painter, precisely because he enjoyed painting so much. Another facet
was a deliberate under-valuation of his own painting.

> "He only paints on the whitewashed wall of his lodgings, as
> he is sure it will be all whitewashed out when he leaves it,
> and to paint anything that lasts would be a 'bond upon his
> soul'."[2]

In his office he kept a number of paintings, casually rolled up — canvas
or drawings — and strewn on the floor, so that when some caller came,
perhaps a farmer in search of agricultural advice, he would say: 'Would
you like a picture? Here, take this!" Yeats wrote to him:

> "I am nothing but an artist and my life is in written words
> and they get the most of my loves and hates, and so too I am
> reckless in mere speech that is not written. You are the other
> side of the penny, for you are admirably careful in speech,
> having set life before art, too much before it as I think for
> one who is, in spite of himself perhaps, an artist . . . "[3]

This was written in 1904; and is so important that I must continue to
quote fragments of it:

> "My own early subjectiveness rises at rare moments and

1. *The Irish Writers.* (London, 1958) pp.169-70.
2. From a letter of Yeats's to Lady Gregory. But happily a number of murals,
   painted on wall-paper are now (1973) being salvaged by The National Gallery
   of Ireland.
3. Wade, *Letters,* p.433.

yours nearly always rises above sentiment to a union with a pure energy of the spirit, *but between this energy of the spirit and the energy of the will"* (this last phrase is very Nietzschean) "out of which epic and dramatic poetry comes there is a region of brooding emotions full of fleshly waters and vapours which kill the spirit and the will, ecstasy and joy equally."[1]

And again, of The Decadence generally:

. . . "I cannot probably be quite just to any poetry that speaks to me with the sweet insinuating feminine voice of the dwellers in that country of shadows and hollow images . . . We possess nothing but the will and we must never let the children of vague desires breathe upon it nor the waters of sentiment rust the terrible mirror of its blade."[2]

He goes on to reprove A.E. for his exploration of the 'dim shadowy region'; though the reproof is ostensibly for A.E.'s championing of the younger poets of the early 1900's. "Let us have no emotions, however abstract, in which there is not an athletic joy."[3]

We must face the facts: it was precisely this dim shadowy world which Yeats had explored in the '90s, and rejected when he hurled — laughing and weeping —

helmets, crowns, and swords into the pit.[4]

The elder gods, the lost druid faiths, the mysterious earth deities might, as A.E. thought, bind Ireland in a new and pagan sainthood. Yeats held different views. He wrote to A.E. when he first engaged in the work of preparing the spirit that was to revolutionize Irish agricultural cooperation:

"Absorb Ireland and her tragedy and you will be the poet of the people, perhaps the poet of a new insurrection."[5]

But he wasn't, and he never would be: A.E.'s vision was the Shelleyan, the cosmic, the aerial. We are reminded continually of his own paintings, now scattered and difficult of access; the spiritual vision of Blake without Blake's training in the 'hard and wiry line'. To obtain effects of translucent light he often used *pointillisme.* He owes much both to Corot and to Puris de Chavannes (whom Yeats admired); but I find the symbolic content often confused and unsatisfactory. And one might dare say of his visions as Rodin said of Blake's:

"Yes, he saw them once. He should have seen them three or four times."

$v

Next year, for the Centenary Celebrations, we shall have Kathleen Raine with us. She is not only a poet, but an authority on Yeats.

1. Wade, *Letters,* p.434. Presumably the allusion is to Porphyry.
2. *Ibid.* p.434-5.
3. *Ibid.* p.435.
4. 'Reconciliation'
5. Wade, *Letters,* p.295.

She is also one of the most important of Blake scholars. Some time ago she gave me a treasured and rare copy of A.E.'s little book *Song and its Fountains*, saying, "It's all there — everything you and I believe in." And it is about this book that I want to talk to you next: for it is a kind of confession or an apology or justification of a poet as to *how* his mind and meditations grew out of his poetry; what he calls a 'partial discovery: in that region of our being was the foundry where poetry was fashioned."

'Sometimes it seems that there was a 'fiery rushing out of words from within me'; and he wrote them down as quickly as possible. At others the verses . . . 'seemed to float about the brain like a swarm of bees trying to enter a hive . . . I did not know what idea was in the poem until it was written down'. (That is of course a common experience.) But A.E.'s theory of poetry seems to depend first on meditation. We are to train ourselves by thinking *backwards:* first of all through the day that has just passed, then through months, years, till we are as it were practised in recollection. (We remember Wordsworth's 'emotion recollected in tranquility'.) In such meditation the past surrenders its secrets to us. We begin to have memories of two lives, those of the body and of the psyche or spirit, as well as intuitions of many other lives. (This is very much the Yeatsian 'Great Memory', the Jungian 'collective unconscious', which Yeats thought could be 'tapped' as it were by means of image and symbol.) Both Yeats and A.E. believed, at least at moments, in reincarnation.

When A.E. was young he was in passionate revolt against 'accepted faiths' and against orthodox Christianity. (So were Blake, Shelley, Swinburne, Yeats, Shaw, Joyce.) This spirit of revolt is later transmitted into mysticism; in the eternal quest for the Unknown God:

> When defiance fierce is thrown
> At the god to whom you bow,
> Rest the lips of the Unknown
> Tenderest upon my brow.[1]

In all this there is a strong kinship with earth-worship. He tells how in boyhood he lay on the hill at Kilmasheogue and 'earth revealed itself to me as a living being, and rock and clay were made transparent *so that I saw lovelier and lordlier than I had ever known before, and was made partner in memory of mighty things, happenings in ages long sunken behind time.*'[2] This is normal Romantic thinking, but we

1. 'The Man to the Angel': *Song and Its Fountains*, p.7.
2. This is confirmed by Yeats in a letter to Lady Gregory: 'On Saturday afternoon and Sunday, his only holidays, he goes to the Wicklow Hills and wanders there, sometimes lying down and seeing visions of the old Celtic gods of which he has done some beautiful pastel drawings: the first afternoon I took the two poets across the lake to the cromlech, and there they sat till A.E. saw a purple druid appear.'

immediately remember Traherne. As he grows older "the walls about the psyche have thickened": this is the Wordsworthian "shades of the prison house", or Blake's transition from Innocence to Experience. Personality is born out of a duality between inner and outer aspects of being. He tells how Yeats was much absorbed by one of his (A.E.'s) paintings of a man on a hill top amazed at his own shadow cast gigantically on a mountain crest (was this something like The Spectre of the Brocken?) – and he goes on to show, in Yeats's early poetry, this obsession with the dualism of Being and Shadow: linking it with the self consciousness of Yeats's *A Vision,* 'a gigantic philosophy of self and anti-self'.

It is, I think, true that the experiences of our childhood are the well-springs of our poetry, just as they are the well-springs of so many verses:

> All the strong powers of Dante were bowed
> To a child's mild eyes,
> That wrought within him that travail
> From depths up to skies,
> Inferno, Purgatorio,
> And Paradise . . .
>
> Let thy young wanderer dream on,
> Call him not home.
> A door opens, a breath, a voice
> From the ancient room,
> Speaks to him now. Be it dark or bright,
> He is knit with his doom.[1]

So the poet speaks of the imaginations that visited him, seeking entrance (as it were) from the outside. "It was no angelic thing, pure and new from a foundry of souls, which sought embodiment, *but a being stained with the dust and the conflict of a long travel through time,* carrying with it unsated desires, base and august, and, as I divined it, myriads of memories and a secret wisdom". This is in part the doctrine of Plotinus, of souls awaiting reincarnation into body; and something of Wordsworth's children 'Trailing clouds of glory', from their experiences of the divine; it is a perennial image, this of the Traveller on his journey, and I think again of de la Mare:

> Earth's thronging beauties may beguile
> Thy longing lovesick heart awhile;
> And pride, like clouds of sunset spread
> A changing glory round they head;
> But fade will all; and thou must come,
> Hating thy journey, homeless, home.[2]

---

1. *Song and its Fountains,* pp.13-14.
2. 'Haunted'.

But this psyche is complex, dual in nature; one part 'avidly desirous
of life, while another part was cold to this, but was endlessly seeking
for the spirit'.

These mysterious workings of the psyche are, at least in part, made
known in the exploration and analysis of dream. This dream is either
sleeping or waking; more often the latter. The dream-state is one in
which he experiences the most intense emotions. In it there is a conflict
between light and darkness, between the gross and the spiritual, between
the sensual and the psyche. But I think that A.E. feared this sensual
component, whereas Yeats accepted it, sought it by various devices,
fused it with his poetry: notably in the poems of *A Woman Old and
Young*. Neither the Saint nor the Swordsman subscribed to that ancient
asceticism which feared and rejected the body: perhaps because Yeats
had learnt his lesson from Blake. "Those who restrain desire do so because
their desires are weak enough to be restrained". We cut ourselves off
from the source of wisdom when we forget our intimacy with nature,
with country:

"But I was shut out, exiled from intimacy with that myriad
beauty, the life which breathed everywhere subtle and penetrating, which brought all but the gazer into unity with itself".

That might have come from the great and joyful source of so much
nature-mysticism, Traherne's *Centuries of Meditation*. And we remember
George Herbert's

Sweet rose, whose hue angrie and brave
Bids the rash gazer wipe his eye . . .

and Hopkins's sense of unity with God in the acute perception of
'country' that was eternal, tender, vulnerable, to man's cruelty.

And here is another resemblance to Yeats, who doubted, in 1910,
whether his genius would ever revive again after his years of drudgery
at the Abbey Theatre. So A.E. goes on:

. . . I was shut out, for I had been traitor to earth and had forgotten it, having been long at other labours. Then a yearning
had arisen in me to revisit the places of childhood, but the
doors were closed to me. Earth denied me her blessing. I was
no longer one of her children . . . The things I had laboured
at in the city, which there seemed so mighty, here dwindled
to the insignificance of dust beside the miracle of pure life I
had lost, having fallen outside the circle of spirit.[1]

You will have recognized a similar theme in Yeats, this benediction
(like that which came to Coleridge's Ancient Mariner) that issues from
unity with the living earth; and of this the most notable expression
is in 'Stream and Sun at Glendalough'; when the sudden sense of union
with eternity is given by the image of the arrow and the ray of light
in classic pictures of the Annunciation:

1. *Song and its Fountains*, p.37.

> What motion of the sun or stream
> Or eyelid shot the gleam
> That pierced my body through?
> What made me live like those that seem
> Self-born, born anew?

$vi

Of A.E.'s poetry it is not easy to speak without seeming pompous or affected. Within the limits of a single sheet I have set out for you a number of poems and single verses that are perhaps worth your attention; more particularly because the poems themselves, in the collected volume, are hardly worth the purchase for the permanent library of most of us, and there is not, I think, any good cheap selection.

I am left with the impression of a vast mass of competent, worthy, even 'noble' work, most of it irredeemably in the middle of the second rank; where, in the Nineteenth Century, we should put Coventry Patmore, Stephen Phillips, a little below Dowson, Lionel Johnson, Francis Thompson. Yet we should recall that Symons and Gosse admired the collection called *The Earth Breath*, and in 1898 Yeats praised his style as resembling that of a Jacobean writer of lyrics. (I cannot, I confess, see the resemblance.) Philosophically, in the broadest sense, it is 'worthy' and 'noble': I have chosen these two words, and I repeat them, deliberately. There are, I think, four 'centres' in A.E.'s mind.

First, there is a layer of Celtic legend, and you will be familiar with most of it through Yeats. There is Angus or Aengus, the Celtic Eros or Orpheus, the tall golden-haired youth who plays upon a harp and is surrounded by singing birds. There is Balor, the Prince of Darkness, a sort of Medusa-figure, whose eye turns everything to stone; he was killed at the Battle of Moytura by Lu or Lugh the Sun-God, the God of Light, with a sling. For at this battle the Tuatha de Danaan, led by Lugh, defeated the Fomorians. Then there are several poems about the sacred hazel, the Celtic Tree of Life, whose leaves are bitter wisdom. So this verse:

> The wonder of the world is o'er:
>   The magic from the sea is gone:
> There is no unimagined shore,
>   No islet yet to venture on.
> The Sacred Hazels' blooms are shed,
> The Nuts of Knowledge harvested.[1]

It grew over Conla's well, and from its branches the nuts of knowledge fell with the water, and were eaten by the Salmon that came up there; who in his turn went out into the rivers and spread this wisdom abroad. There is Mananan Mac Lir, the sea-god, the Irish Neptune who ruled

---

1. 'The Twilight of Earth'.

the Irish seas, and sent out the three mystical waves which celebrate the life or death or Irish heroes. (These come in the original Deirdre story). Lir also had children who were changed magically into swans; A.E. considers this 'a very theological account of the descent of the spirit from the Heaven-World to the earth and its final redemption'. Yeats saw other and varying significances in his swans; as did Oliver St. John Gogarty. Finally, there is a reference to 'The Feast of Age', 'the Druidic form of the mysteries'. Whoever ate of this became immortal.

The second group, and by far the largest, is something that we might call, rather vaguely, 'mystical nature poetry'. These poems seem to be written to a kind of formula. There is a description of some kind of natural scene: written often with great skill, great sensitivity to light, colour, the moods of the countryside. They are clearly what we might call 'painter's pieces' in their first conception. After the description comes, almost uniformly, the gathering-up (as it were) of the description into an assertion of the unity of the natural elements of the scene with the Infinite, the earth-spirit, the Eternal. Typical of these are two of the pieces I have set out on your broad-sheet,[1] in two moods, those called 'Winter' and 'Answer'. Sometimes the statement is pessimistic, the romantic's longing for the past: sometimes the reverse. Behind both, and in the Love Poems, there is a strong flavour of neo-Platonism, which A.E. shared with Yeats: both owing much, I think, to Stephen Mackenna's great translation: which still remains in its revised form[2] the best, and certainly the most poetical, version that has yet been made. And in this, of course, his thought is in direct conflict to the ascetic Christian view: as in this, called 'Dust':

> I heard them in their sadness say
> "The earth rebukes the thought of God;
> We are but embers wrapped in clay
> A little nobler than the sod."

— which has a Tennysonian flavour, and the eternal banality of the God-rhyme, which has bedevilled so many poets and hymn-writers. He goes on, addressing Dana, or the Earth-Mother:

> But I have touched the lips of clay,
> Mother, thy rudest sod to me
> Is thrilled with fire of hidden day,
> And haunted by all mystery.

These two quotations illustrate, I think, A.E.'s chief weakness. It is what Yeats, with detestation, called 'abstraction': generalized and vague. In the lines

> . . . Is thrilled with fire of hidden day,
> And haunted by all mystery

he cannot convince us of the connection between 'lips of clay' and

---

1. These poems were taken from the *Collected Poems* (Macmillan, 1913)
2. Revision of B.S. Page, Preface by E.R. Dodds. (London 1956).

'rudest sod'. I think, indeed, that this obsession with the sacred character
of a literal earth is responsible for much of A.E.'s weakest verse.

§vii

Then there is a group of Love Poems: of which I have chosen 'Pity'
(to the girl called Olive). Here there is a note of tenderness, of pity, of
the *suffering* of love, of the coming of old age: that theme so often
handled by Ronsard, Villon, Shakespeare, Yeats, Synge. It is not untypical
that one of the poems should be called 'The Grey Eros':

> We are desert leagues apart;
> Time is misty ages now
> Since the warmth of heart to heart
> Chased the shadows from my brow.

> Oh, I am so old, meseems
> I am next of kin to Time,
> The historian of her dreams
> From the long-forgotten prime.

We are now, I think, in a position to suggest comparisons and contrasts
with Yeats: and to ask ourselves 'What is it that makes this poetry, in
spite of its nobility, its tenderness, the essential and apparent *goodness*
of the poet, so irredeemably of the second rank?'

As always, there is no one answer. The first, I think, is A.E.'s
commitment to an extraordinarily narrow technical range. His favourite
metre is the conventional four-foot iambic couplet, fully rhymed, a b a b.
Quite often he varies this with a final three-stress line, also fully rhymed,
to give the effect of a falling close. Sometimes there is a long rather
dragging many-stressed metre, in the line of descent from Swinburne,
Morris, not unlike parts of *The Wanderings of Oisin*. Yeats discarded
those long metres, with their inevitable redundancy and padding, at a
very early stage. But let us not be intolerant, many young poets are
(or were) attracted to them, for the sake of the sonority, the sheer drive
of the rhythm: and I think they are perhaps less pernicious for the
young poet as initial models than the deceptive facile slackness of free
verse.

One trouble with A.E. is the monotony of his rhymes. You remember how this monotony has been 'ragged' since Shakespeare's time:
from *Romeo and Juliet*:

> Cry but Ay, me! couple but 'love' and 'dove';
> Speak to my gossip Venus one fair word.

and Pope's 'Essay on Criticism':

> Where'er you find 'the cooling western breeze'
> In the next line, it 'whispers through the trees';
> If crystal streams 'with pleasing murmurs creep'
> The reader's threatened (not in vain) with 'sleep' . . .

That is one trouble; the monotony of the rhythms, the banality of the rhymes. But more important is the diffuseness, the lack of 'edge' or 'attack' in most of A.E.'s poems. One reason may well be that he never gave himself wholly to poetry; having (in his view) more important things to do to secure his world. There is little energy from the verbs: the adjectives (often chosen with the sensibility with which a painter chooses colour) seem over-prominent. This is because there is, as a rule, to be no genuine fusion, as it were, between image and idea. His natural scenery, the actual living world of his poems, seems continually to be subordinated to the *idea:* itself so vague, so diffuse, that it is seldom or never integrated with the image. In an earlier lecture on Yeats's 'world' I suggested this close and intricate fusion of image and thought, the art that he had learnt (as I think) from Donne. And this fusion is in turn evidenced by the strong unique and personal rhythms and the characteristic resonances in which Yeats's poems are set, the power of the lines to live by their individual weight and strength. The energy of the syntax reveals, as always, the energy behind it.

Perhaps the failure is in sheer craftsmanship. Many of the poems are in the long dragging metres that Yeats abandoned after *Oisin*. The stanzaic forms quickly grew monotonous; and there is a certain sameness of subject, a re-handling of basic themes, which leave an impression of weakness. For all the invocation of the divine fire there does not appear to be sufficient power to over-ride the impression of a diction that is largely spent. Perhaps there has been no true mystical poetry since the Seventeenth Century, when language was still fresh enough to match the strength of the Christian conflict or certainty in the individual soul.

Yeats wrote a study of A.E. called *An Irish Visionary*,[1] and described his early poems as "exceedingly wonderful".[2] He was liable to overestimate the work of his friends, as *The Oxford Book of Modern Verse*, and its *Preface*, bear witness. Later he described *Songs by the Way* as "a very notable book, but not especially Irish in subject".[3] Like many others he came under the full attack of the journalists; but, rather strangely, his heretical pantheistic teachings, openly preached, do not seem to have attracted opposition of any kind on this matter. He fought passionately for what he believed in - the integrity of the nation, the labour movement of 1913; above all, for a sense of *caritas* in Ireland. But the 'battle-joy' never touched him, and he had no illusions about warfare whether in fact or fantasy.

§ vi

It may seem a strange opinion; but it is as a prose writer that I

1. Wade, *Letters*, p.179.
2. *Ibid*, p.231.
3. Ibid. p.250.

would chiefly praise A.E.: the more so, indeed, since his books have for long been inaccessible and little appreciated. The prose can afford to pass by those elements of poetic technique that seem to me lacking. It is a gracious and generous kind of writing. *Song and Its Fountains* contains his theory of poetry. It seems to me by far the most penetrating account — always excepting that of Coleridge — of the workings of the creative mind. Poetry is born of meditation and sacrifice, out of some commerce (which is not conflict) between the outer and inner being. "Our meditation is sacrifice, and some one of its tongues of intellectual fire descends upon us."[1] This has a long history, starting perhaps from the Bible:

> My heart was hot within me, while I was musing the fire
> burned: then spake I with my tongue.[2]

So too in the neo-Platonism of Henry More, whose *Psychozoia* Yeats admired. It is an ascent of the spirits towards the divine. "The words often would rush swiftly from hidden depths of consciousness and be fashioned by an art with which the working brain had but little to do."[3] This is surely a Jungian view. All great poets have known that their art demands solitude; and in that solitude the poet wrestles with opposing forces, and the perpetually unsatisfied desire of the creative act (and of lassitude and depression when it is finished). Here are four stanzas from a strange poem called 'Resurrection'.[4]

> . . . Let the dragons of the past
> In their caverns sleeping lie.
> I am dream-betrayed, and cast
> Into that old agony.
>
> And an anguish of desire
> Burns as in the sunken years,
> And the soul sheds drops of fire
> All unquenchable by tears.
>
> I, who sought on high for calm,
> In the Ever-living find
> All I was in what I am,
> Fierce with gentle intertwined,
>
> Hearts that I had crucified,
> With my heart that tortured them —
> Penitence, unfallen pride,
> These my thorny diadem.

One more quotation:

> How can we explain the mystery of imagination, the power

1. *Songs and Its Fountains*, p.23.
2. *Psalms* 39:3.
3. p.24.
4. *Song and Its Fountains*. p.46.

we discover in ourselves which leaps upon us, becoming
master of ideas, images and words, taking control of these from
the reasoning mind, giving to them symbolic meanings, until
ideas, images and words, swept together, become an intellectual
organization by some transcendental power superior to all
reasoning? It is as mysterious as the growth of an organism
in nature which draws from earth by some alchemy the essences
it transmutes and makes subservient to itself."[1]

This owes much to Coleridge; but it leaves out of the statement the need,
which Yeats realized so profoundly, for the prolonged and arduous
cultivation of sheer poetic technique. It is perhaps because of their
violence that A.E. seems, so often, unable to impose a satisfactory
pattern upon the poems; there is a sudden flash, and then the poem
subsides upon cliches that obey only the tyranny of rhyme. "No sooner
does there come illumination than it is gone."[2]

$vii

The second book to which I invite your attention is called *The
Interpreters*. It was published in 1922. Its theme is of special interest
to us today. The form is that of a discussion among a group of men
condemned to death for their part in some Rising, talking freely to each
other of their hopes and dreams in what one of them calls "the ante-
chamber of death". Each man declares what is in his mind, and I do
not doubt that we have A.E.'s political and poetic thinking (one of the
characters recites a longish 'poem of pilgrimage') at its most mature:

After centuries of frustrated effort the nation, long dominat-
ed by an alien power which seemed immutable, had a resurrection. It would join the great procession of states, of beings
mightier than man created by man. It would become like
Egypt, Assyria, Greece or Rome. The genius of multitudes
would unite to give it spiritual greatness.[3]

But the rising fails. The historian among the group comments on the
nature of violence: in reply to the question

"But when did our nation win anything save when it stood
armed and ready for the last sacrifice?"

"You will find" answered the historian "that every great
conflict has been followed by an era of materialism in which
the ideals for which the conflict ostensibly was waged were
submerged. The gain if any was material. The loss was spiritual.
That was so inevitably because warfare implies a descent of the
soul to the plane where it is waged, and on that plane it cannot
act in fulness, or bring with it love, pity, or forgiveness, or

1. *Song and Its Fountains,* p.51.
2. *Ibid.* p.83.
3. *The Interpreters* p.5. For this, and for what follows, consider the opening
   Chapter of this book.

any of its diviner elements . . . : Love and hate have a magical transforming power; they are the great soul changers . . . By intensity of hatred nations create in themselves the character they imagine in their enemies' . . . [1]
Now the historian has been writing a history of 'our nation'. His earlier nationalism fades: . . . " the lure of national ideals began to be superseded by imaginations of a world state . . ."[2] The end is to be a conquest of "that vast life which is normally subconscious to us". "The solitary or captive can by intensity of imagination and feeling affect myriads so that he can act through many men and speak with many voices".[3] Lavelle, one of the characters, accuses the speaker of transcendentalism, which of course this is. But the nobility of A.E.'s vision is not diminished. Men are the children of deity. Their duty is, first to realize the nature of man's kinship with the earth; to purge themselves of all grossness, whatever the pain of that sacrifice. For man is spiritual at the root; however imperfectly he must seek to cherish the spark of divinity: "Be ye perfect even as the Father in Heaven is also perfect."[4]

This is the way of the saint. I do not know of any other poetic voice in our time that has used these terms.

§ viii

What, then, are we to say of A.E.? I think of him as a man of the utmost integrity, of genuine vision, of a moderate poetic gift; whose circumstances, a sense of duty, the perception of a significance in his own childhood experiences, combined to produce a body of work in which the prose is more significant than the poetry, and the life's work than either.

Unlike Yeats he was never a single-minded, dedicated professional poet. His gifts were diffused in the Civil Service, organization, theosophy, the agricultural cooperative movement, editorial work. He shared the genius of the great literary figures of Dublin, during the first quarter of this century, for friendship, for strong quarrels, for good talk, and better letter-writing. All who knew him speak well of him; his immense kindness, a massive homespun integrity: such diverse figures as Lennox Robinson and L.A.G. Strong bear ample witness.

A.E. found and mined his own vein of poetry: traditional in its return to the innocence and ecstasy of childhood, traditional and certified by so many noble names. (We think of Herbert, Traherne, Vaughan, Smart, Wordsworth, Blake, de la Mare.) This perception of the glory, this sensitivity to the minute particulars of the sensuous world

1. *The Interpreters* p.136.
2. *Ibid.* p.138.
3. *Ibid.* p.140.
4. *Ibid.* p.152.

is, first, to be apprehended, then drawn into a unity of the whole poetic
statement. Above and behind the world of the senses A.E. is conscious
of the powers which offer to him the prospect of this unity. But those
powers are many and diffuse; like the vague capitalizations which the
early Yeats used and then abandoned. 'The Poet Speaks with the
Elemental Powers', 'The Mystic Rose', and others. In A.E.'s pantheon
there is not only the awareness of the praeter-natural world (he
quotes Kant in support) but awareness of a multiplex world of the Irish
countryside, both historical and actual, in which an unorthodox God,
the Earth Mother, the Celtic heroes, together with some of the Vedic
deities, move uneasily together. His intention is to communicate his
sense of unity with the whole created world; and, through that unity,
to reach towards the love of God.

But there are two difficulties for him and for us. Firstly, he is
striving towards too many and too diffuse objects: so that we seem to
move in a vague cloud of these concepts. I doubt very much whether
this tissue of allusions to past mythologies, whether Hindu or Druid
or Celtic, can have validity today. It is, as Yeats called it, 'a dusty dream'.
The vocabulary of classical and Biblical mythology and allusions were
poetic tools only for as long as an educational system, and life-long
habits of reading, burnt them into the consciousness of Western
Europe. Lir, Lugh, Dana, the Morrigu, Kali, Shiva, have to be re-evoked
or recovered by sheer labour. They can never have the familiarity of the
gods of Greek and Rome; whose names live at least in the stars. Yeats
solved the problem by abandoning all the 'heroic' images except that
of Cuchulain; and he established his validity by repeated and many-
sided re-alignments and linkages with Irish history in the present. The
Yeatsian synthesis works in a wholly different manner. It is ultimately
concerned with the same problem of unity of being, the conveyance
of the One and the Many, but with a concreteness of living imagery, a
tautness of control, a rhythmical attack that is foreign to A.E. We
may think of the last stanza of 'Stream and Sun at Glendalough' which
I have already quoted. A.E. could never have achieved the simplicity,
or the audacious colloquialisms, of the stanzas that lead up to that; nor
could he have achieved the rich complexity of the imagery of those first
three lines.

And this brings me to my next point. Yeats writes out of an incredibly
rich poetical tradition, and a tenacious and dramatic memory. Three
times in his life-time he had proceeded to 'make his soul', or his
intellect:

> —compelling it to study
> In a learned school.

He has served his apprenticeship on Spenser and Blake, on 'Davis,
Mangan, Ferguson', on Shakespeare, Shelley, Tennyson. Grierson's

Donne had revealed a new world to him: Ezra Pound had re-educated him; no one knows as yet what came out of those years of reading in the Bodleian in the early 'Twenties. The hints of it are mysterious and tantalizing.

A.E. had no such fortune as liberty to read, to travel, to enrich his verse. His life was full, busy with friendship, even a little chaotic because of that very richness and its talk. When he relinquished his editorship of *The Irish Statesman* Yeats quoted from Thomas Davis:
'it leaves us
Sheep without a shepherd when the snow shuts out the day'.
He foresaw something like a European Community as an alternative to 'the ancient fetters of frontiers, tariffs and languages which hindered Europe from a realization of its myriad unity'. This was in 1922. In Dublin he held open house without regard to social rank. His parties were unpretentious, and people went to them for the sheer joy of hearing poets and artists talk about their trades. He could write about Irish finance; he lectured on agricultural matters, of every kind. Yeats wished that he would write an essay 'laying down a cultural economic political policy of economic unity'.

It was inevitable that he should be reflected in 'the mirror of malicious eyes':

"I have just heard from Ezra from Rome, 500 copies of *Ulysses* confiscated in the English customs, and he would like to import into this country. I have promised enquiries but no one dare wake an ecclesiastical terrier, which is at present only hunting in its dreams. George Russell and I and the head of the Education Board are accused, by the by, of being in a conspiracy to destroy the Catholic faith through free education ...
The Head of the Board tells me that objection is made to 'The Lady of Shalott' because "Tennyson is a poet of Revolt". It must not be permitted in the school books. But *Ulysses* - that would wake the terrier in earnest."[1]

Yeats was fortunate in the events of Choice and Chance that enabled him to renew repeatedly his poetic vitality: A.E. seems to have suffered only the wounding crises appropriate to a kind of divine simplicity, and to a country which did not recognize his great services to Ireland.

A.E. died in Bournemouth; one of the many expatriates of his time. The body was brought back to Dublin for burial, as Parnell's had been; and later, Casement's bones. We may quote for an epitaph from a letter of Yeats's in July 1935:

1. Wade, *Letters*, p.705. The whole episode recalls Moore and Martyn's project for publishing *The Arabian Nights* (in Irish) (*Salve* p.108-9): eventually refracted by the journalists into the proposition: 'Mr. George Moore has selected *The Arabian Nights* because he wishes an indecent book to be put into the hands of every Irish peasant.'

"I am suffering at present from A.E.'s funeral. I had to use all my powers of intrigue and self-assertion to prevent a fanatical woman from making it a political demonstration by draping the coffin with the tricolour . . . All is well with A.E. His ghost will not walk. He had no passionate human relationships to draw him back. My wife said the other night, 'A.E. was the nearest to a saint you or I will ever meet. You are a better poet but no saint. I suppose one has to choose' . . . A.E. was my oldest friend — we began our work together. I constantly quarrelled with him but he never bore malice and in his last letter, a month before his death, he said that generally when he differed from me it was that he feared to be absorbed by my own personality. He had no passions, but as a young man had to struggle against his senses. He gave up writing poetry for a time because it stirred his senses. He always wanted to be free."[1]

1. Wade, *Letters* p.838.

IX

YEATS AND THE PICTURE GALLERIES[1]

What, precisely, is thinking? When, at the reception of
sense-impressions, memory-pictures emerge, this is not yet
"thinking". And when such pictures form series, each member
of which calls forth another, this too is not yet "thinking".
When, however, a certain picture turns up in many such
series, then — precisely through such return — it becomes an
ordering element for such series, in that it connects series which
are themselves unconnected. Such an element becomes an
instrument, a concept.

Albert Einstein, *Philosopher and Scientist.*

Yeats was the son of a pre-Raphaelite painter; he himself had some
training in pastel work. He was the friend of contemporary artists of
importance: Ellis, J.T. Nettleship, Shannon, Ricketts, 'A.E.', Dulac
among them. In his poetry and prose he mentions some fifty artists
and sculptors, who sometimes serve as type-figures of *A Vision.* Among
the stranger conjunctions are Blake and Aretino (with Rabelais and
Paracelsus), Baudelaire and Beardsley; Keats and Giorgione, Rembrandt
and Synge, are more understandable. He was an admirer of Wilde's
Salome, illustrated by Beardsley and by Ricketts. Certain reproductions
were constantly beside him, and appear to have been objects of meditation; with such objects as Sato's sword, the sculptured stone of 'Lapis
Lazuli'. 'My table here (at the Bodleian) is covered with such things as
the etchings and wood-cuts of Palmer and Calvert," he wrote to Lady
Gregory in 1918. In the 'Nineties he had planned to write a book on
Calvert, and in old age the memory of that strange company of pastoral
poet-painters at Shoreham, with the venerable Blake in their midst,
returned to his mind in 'Under Ben Bulben':

> Calvert and Wilson, Blake and Claude,
> Prepared a rest for the people of God,
> Palmer's phrase, but after that
> Confusion fell upon our thought.

And that rich simplicity of labour, the herdsmen's cottages that seem
to grow into the trees, impressed him with their tender security as he
wrote in a letter to Olivia Shakespeare in 1932: "This little creeper-
covered farm-house might be in a Calvert woodcut, and what could be
more suitable for one's last decade?"

And we might recall an extract from his Introduction to his selections
from Spenser:

> I got up from reading the 'Faerie Queen' . . . and wandered

---

1. I am indebted to the Editors of *The Southern Review* for permission to
reprint parts of an essay (Vol. I, Nol. N.S., Winter 1965).

into another room. It was in a friendly house, and I came of a
sudden to the ancient poetry and to our poetry side by side - an
engraving of Claude's 'Mill' hung under an engraving of Turner's
'Temple of Jupiter'. Those dancing country people, those cow-
herds, resting after the day's work, and that quiet mill-race
made one think of Merry England with its glad Latin heart, of a
time when men in every land found poetry and imagination
in one another's company and in the day's labour. Those
stately goddesses, moving in slow procession towards that
marble architrave among mysterious trees, belong to Shelley's
thought, and to the religion of the wilderness - the only religion
possible to poetry today . . . It may be that those goddesses,
moving with a majesty like a procession of the stars, mean
something to the soul of man that those kindly women of the
old poets did not mean, for all the fulness of their breasts and
the joyous gravity of their eyes. Has not the wilderness been
at all times a place of prophecy?[1]

The hand of Morris, and of Victorian neo-medievalism, is all too
clear, but there are other matters of interest besides the emphasis
on loneliness and the oft-repeated quotation from Proclus[2]. I had once
thought that the lines from 'Her Vision in the Wood' referred to a
painting:

> All stately women moving to a song
> With loosened hair or foreheads grief-distraught,
> It seemed a Quattrocento painter's throng,
> A thoughtless image of Mantegna's thought −

were related to a picture. But the roots may be in Spenser. He explains
how he chose processional episodes - provided that they were symbolical,
not allegorical - for his selection. It has been suggested to me - I am
indebted to Edward Malins - that the passage may be a reminiscence
of Mantegna's 'The Enchantment', in the British Museum. Here Christ is
carried in a sort of litter: his blood-bedabbled breast faces one of the
women who is singing. Another has loosened hair, but this hardly fits the
rest of the poem. Perhaps we are dealing with some sort of visual and
aural 'overlay': Mantegna's 'Parnasso' in the Louvre, the death of Venus
in the *Faerie Queen* (III.1.38) or Shakespeare's *Venus and Adonis,*
(1015 ff.)

A special interest, for obvious reasons, was in Blake and his illustrations. "The Ancient of Days" hung on his staircase in Bloomsbury;
and while he disapproved of the illustrations to Young's *Night Thoughts,*
he collected for an American lecture tour the slides of all the illustrations
to *Job.*

During his lifetime he neglected no opportunity to visit galleries,

1. Introduction to the 1893 Edition: pp. XXXIX-XL.
2. 'The lonely returns to the lonely, the divine to the divinity.'

sculptures, mosaics. It is said that his first reaction on receiving the
Nobel Prize was gratitude for the financial freedom it would give him
to take frequent taxis to visit the National Gallery of Dublin. We know
the titles of a number of the books on art which he consulted. We may
quote at this stage two important statements, the first from his preface
to W.T. Horton's *A Book of Images:*[1]

> All art that is not mere story-telling, or mere portraiture, is
> symbolic, and has the purpose of those symbolic talismans
> which medieval magicians made with complex colours and
> forms, and bade their patients ponder over daily, and guard
> with holy secrecy; for it entangles, in complex colours and
> forms, a part of the Divine Essence. A person or a landscape
> that is part of a story or a portrait, evokes but so much
> emotion   as   the   story   or   the   portrait   can   permit
> without loosening the bonds that make it a story or a portrait;
> but if you liberate a person or a portrait from the bonds of
> motives and their actions, causes and their effects, and from all
> bonds but the bonds of your love, it will change under your
> eyes, and become a symbol of an infinite emotion, a perfected
> emotion, a part of the Divine Essence; for we love nothing but
> the perfect, and our dreams make all things perfect that we
> may love them.

This is vague and loose writing, with a strong tincture of the neo-
Platonism that he may have learnt from Pater; later (for he modifies
somewhat the 1908 Horton Preface) Yeats becomes more concrete in
his approach, as in his 'Symbolism and Painting':[2]

> Wagner's dramas, Keats' Odes, Blake's pictures and poems,
> Calvert's pictures, Rossetti's pictures, Villiers de l'Isle-Adam's
> plays, and the black-and-white art of Mr. Beardsley and Mr.
> Ricketts, and the lithographs of Mr. Shannon, and the pictures
> of Mr. Whistler, and the plays of M. Maeterlinck, and the poetry
> of Verlaine, in our own day, but differ from the religious art of
> Giotto and his disciples in having accepted all symbolisms, the
> symbolism of the ancient shepherds and star-gazers, that sym-
> bolism of bodily beauty that seemed a wicked thing to Fra
> Angelico, the symbolism in day and night,[3] and winter and
> summer, spring and autumn, once so great a part of an older
> religion than Christianity; and in having accepted all the Divine
> Intellect, its anger and its pity, its waking and its sleep, its
> love and its lust, for the substance of their art.

We may glance at Yeats's exegetical method in an almost forgotten
article on the work of Althea Gyles:

> I have described this drawing because one must understand
> Miss Gyles' central symbol, the Rose, before one can under-

---

1. London, 1898.
2. *Essays and Introductions,* p. 149.
3. See 'Michael Robartes and the Dancer.' He is referring to Michelangelo's Medici
   Tombs.

stand her dreamy and intricate *Noah's Raven*. The ark floats
upon a grey sea under a grey sky, and the raven flutters above
the sea. A sea-nymph, whose slender swaying body drifting
among the grey waters is the perfect symbol of a soul untouched by God or by passion, coils the fingers of one hand
about his feet and offers him a ring, while her other hand
holds a shining rose under the sea. Grotesque shapes of little
fishes flit about the rose, and grotesque shapes of larger fishes
swim hither and thicker. Sea-nymphs swim through the
windows of a sunken town and reach towards the rose, hands
covered with rings, and a vague twilight hangs over all . . . The
raven, who is, as I understand him, the desire and will of man,
has come out of the ark, the personality of man, to find if the
Rose is anywhere above the flood, which is here, as always, the
flesh, "the flood of the five senses".[1] He has found it and is returning with it to the ark, that the soul of man may sink into
the ideal and pass away; but the sea-nymphs, the spirts of the
senses, have bribed him with a ring, taken from the treasures
of the kings of the world,[2] a ring that gives the mastery of the
world, and he has given them the Rose. Henceforth man will
seek for the ideal in the flesh,[3] and the flesh will be full of
illusive beauty, and the spiritual beauty will be far away.[4]

§ii

But beyond and perhaps above such symbolic content the painters
and sculptors were of immense significance. He said in 'To a Shade'
that the Lane Pictures would (in 1910) have given to the grandchildren
of those who rejected them

loftier thought,
Sweeter emotion, working in their veins.

Michelangelo had given in the Adam of the Sistine Chapel the perfection of the male form so that "instinct might find its lamp". "The
plummet-measured face" based on mathematical proportion stood for
a more austere but 'profane' perfection. In 'The Statues' the sculptures
of Phidias

Gave women dreams, and dreams their looking glass[5]

and

. . . put down
All Asiatic vague immensities

to be transformed, at the last, to Buddha with its "empty eyeballs".

1. See 'Byzantium': "Spirit after spirit, the smithies break the flood . . . "
2. See Wagner; in particular, Arthur Symons's essay, 'The Ideas of Richard Wagner'.
3. Consider the dialogue of 'Michael Robartes and the Dancer'.
4. 'A Symbolic Artist and the Coming of Symbolic Art', *The Dome*, 1 (December 1898), 235-6.
5. "We lose all in the pursuit of ourselves – a thing which does not exist. Tell Miss White to double the size of every girl's looking glass, and Dublin will put on joy once more." (To Miss Dickenson, from Coole, 10 August 1908).

The significance of the artist might indeed be historical, sociological, archetypal; as well as giving "images for poetry", as did the Instructors of *A Vision.*

§iii

Some years ago I found it possible to visit, in America, France and Italy, most of the galleries, pictures, sculptures and mosaics that Yeats saw or is likely to have seen. This followed on some minor discoveries in Dublin, which were noted in the first edition of *The Lonely Tower.* Since then Professor Melchiori has carried the whole subject further, the University of Reading has collected a notable exhibition under the title *Images of a Poet,* and Edgar Wind in *Pagan Mysteries of the Renaissance* has opened up a new and important area of iconographical investigation. Originals for 'Leda and the Swan' have been put forward to augment those listed by Melchiori in his *The Whole Mystery of Art,* and the famous Raphael, "Do you know Raphael's statue of the Dolphin carrying one of the Holy Innocents to heaven?"[1] appears to have been identified by Wind.[2] In this last instance we may draw attention to the meanings-in-depth revealed by Wind's admirable analysis, and the light thrown on 'News for the Delphic Oracle' as well as 'Byzantium'. "With his unfailing instinct for Renaissance imagery, Yeats interpreted the statue exactly as Raphael's contemporaries treated that kind of subject - as an example of the 'Bitter-sweet union of Love and Death'." Of 'Leda and the Swan' I am not so certain, and inclined to suggest a source from Athens; though Charles Madge has made out a convincing case.[3] Since then I have seen a marble Leda in the garden of a Sligo house; it once stood in the garden of Markree Castle in Co. Sligo, one of Yeats's legendary 'great houses'.

At this point it may be well to draw attention to some of the dangers and uncertainties of this kind of study. There are relatively few instances in which we can be certain, whether by the closeness of the observed correspondences or from other sources, that Yeats found a special significance in any one picture or image, or drew upon it. Among the few certainties are, in Dublin, the Poussin for 'News for the Delphic Oracle'[4], the 'Virgin Enthroned and Sewing' and the 'St. George and the Dragon' attributed to Paris Bordone. As regards the manifold Ledas, for example, we might be persuaded that the lines

>   . . . her thighs caressed
> By the dark webs, her nape caught in his bill,
> He holds her helpless breast upon his breast.

1. Ursula Bridge, *W.B. Yeats and T. Sturge Moore* (N.Y., 1953), p.165.
2. *Times Lit. Suppl.* October 25, 1963.
3. *Ibid.,* July 20, 1962, Melchiori agreed, in a letter dated August 3.
4. Then known as 'The Marriage of Peleus and Thetis'; now entitled 'Acis and Galatea'. See *The Lonely Tower,* Ch. XIII.

have their genesis in some particular ikon, but might then reflect whether they are not merely the imagined probabilities of Leda's physical situation. In the same way it is sometimes helpful to have in mind the first drafts, and remember for the Dolphin the magnificence (and the verisimilitude for the joyous movement of a school of porpoises or dolphins) of the discarded couplet to be found in Jon Stallworthy's *Between the Lines:*

> Where the great drowsy fins a moment rise
> Of fish that carry souls to Paradise.

And in any event the value of the ikon may well be marginal, doing no more than throw a momentary light on Yeats's concerns or moods at a particular time.

There remains, however, a strong serial or total impression from the American and European galleries; and that is why I have begun this essay with the quotation from Einstein. One feels this immensely strong collective character in the dominant symbols on which Yeats's imagination seized. There is a preference (as we should expect) for pictures embodying the dramatic moment (as in the pre-Raphaelite tradition); a restless search for material which would support the validity or enlarge the significance of symbols on which he had already meditated. It may seem a little strange that Yeats did not make more use of the Tarot Pack and its symbols;[1] though the 'magical pack' is important in *The Stories of Red Hanrahan.* The simplest explanation is probably the best; the Tarot, and the Rituals of the Golden Dawn[2] were too complicated to lend themselves to 'metaphors for poetry'. There was no lack of more traditional esoteric material —

> Truths without father came, truths that no book
> Of all the uncounted books that I have read . . .
> Self-born, high-born and solitary truths,
> Those terrible implacable straight lines
> Drawn through the wandering vegetative dream . . . [3]

Their dispersion in time and history may have suggested a steady convergence towards his desired perception of unity in multiplicity.

And if those symbols had a direct physical correlative in his own experience, and were not "mere images" sought in books, then the link between objective and subjective, between the inner and outer worlds, closed and tightened. The wild swans at Coole are known in their physical presence, their integrity as birds. They carry their traditional references to fidelity and to death, their overtones in classical and

---

1. See Kathleen Raine: *Yeats, the Tarot and the Golden Dawn.*, Dolmen Press, 1972.
2. Israel Regardie, *The Golden Dawn:*. Chicago, 1937. There are four volumes.
3. 'The Gift of Harun Al-Rashid'. For the first line, see Chapman's projection of Marlowe's *Hero and Leander,* Sestiad III. I do not think that Yeatsian scholars have paid enough attention to this metaphysical poem.

Celtic myth, and these references are modified from poem to poem. But this fusion of the physical presence, and the symbolism, can be illustrated by a comparison of the swans of 1903, in 'Baile and Aillinn', with those of 1919:

> They know undying things, for they
> Wander where earth withers away,
> Though nothing troubles the great streams
> But light from the pale stars, and gleams
> From the holy orchards, where there is none
> But fruit that is of precious stone,
> Or apples of the sun and moon.

The "wavering meditative rhythms," the lack of syntactical energy, prepare us for the decorative embroidery, as of a Jessie King illustration,[1] of the last three lines and their dispersed images. So it continues:

> What were our praise to them? They eat
> Quiet's wild heart, like daily meat;
> Who when night thickens are afloat,
> On dappled skins in a glass boat,
> Far out under a windless sky.

These are echoes, perhaps of Tennyson, Shakespeare, Marvell and there are resemblances to A.E.'s poetic style: but it is the rhythm that has failed. Compare these lines from 'The Wild Swans at Coole':

> I have looked upon those brilliant creatures,
> And now my heart is sore,
> All's changed, since I, hearing at twilight,
> The first time on this shore,
> The bell-beat of their wings above my head,
> Trod with a lighter tread.

The movement is easy yet tense with the perceived relationships of Yeats's own thought:

> Unwearied still, lover by lover,
> They paddle in the cold
> Companionable streams or climb the air;
> Their hearts have not grown old;
> Passion or conquest, wander where they will,
> Attend upon them still.

So the white heron fishing in a dome mosaic in the church of San Vitale at Ravenna or in Binyon's *Eastern Painting*, might be lonely subjective man, or an aspect of the multiplex image of The Fisherman, himself, or perhaps John Synge; but it was also "the old crane of Gort", and the white heron, for whom God had not died, of *Calvary*. In Piero di Cosimo's mysterious painting 'The Death of Procris', (now known as 'Mythological Subject') there is a white heron fishing on the

---

1. She illustrated his *Poems of Spenser.* But I cannot discover any significance either in the choice of subjects or in their treatment; there is a decadent elaboration in the manner of Burne-Jones.

margin of the lake. 'The Great Herne' is perhaps the most obvious (of the symbols). For he is simply the repository of Yeats's most cherished values and longed-for ideals. He is the fountain-head of spirituality, subjectivity and loneliness. He is also a male principle, capable, like the Old Yeats, of violent rage. He is, in fact, the God of Yeatsism, the final flower of Yeats's deeply ingrained paganism, and the only such figure in all the plays.[1] And we remember the heron that excited him whenever it flew over the house at Riversdale. When such similitudes seemed to repeat themselves in different and often widely separated contexts, they acquired as it were a special poetic energy, certified by the perennial endurance of their cyclic emergence in history; serving both to stabilize and extend the cosmic sweep of his imagination.

Let us consider some examples. In the market-place at Ravenna he could have seen the cherub riding the dolphin; he might have seen it also in the Ostia mosaic,[2] or in any of a multitude of Renaissance pictures. In the yard of the Museum behind the Archbishop's Palace at Ravenna there are fragments of carven masonry which might have come from some ancient Irish churchyard. But it was in the Dublin Poussin, and in the Titian (and he had discovered a profound significance in that painter) in the Isabella Stuart Gardner Museum at Boston; one of the few galleries, incidentally, where we can be sure that the pictures are still in the position in which he saw them. The gracious setting, a certain fantastic quality in the whole collection, would not, I think, have been inimical to Yeats's instinct for collecting *miscellanea* of every kind. The Titian is that of 'Europa and the Bull'. The bull is just coming to land, with Europa poised at a most undignified angle on his back. In the far background, across the strait, Europa's attendants make gestures of dismay. On the left, a cherub riding a dolphin is escorting the pair; he is parodying Europa's attitude. All unions of the divine and human intrigued Yeats; they appealed perhaps, to the heretical Anglo-Irish Protestant, and, at greater depth, embodied speculations — like those of Milton and Boehme — on the nature of Godhead and the sexual behaviour of angels, as well as (in the Ribh poems) unorthodox views on the doctrine of the Trinity. It is sufficient to quote from *The Player Queen:*

> Shall I fancy beast or fowl?
> Queen Pasiphae chose a bull,
> While a passion for a swan
> Made Queen Leda stretch and yawn . . .

As one looks at the Titian one recalls that song of Crazy Jane (for there are elements of comedy in the thought as well as in the picture),

---

1. William Becker, *Yeats as Playwright.* It is in the background, in the margin of the lake, in Piero di Cosimo, and occurs in at least two of Bellini's paintings.
2. Reproduced in *The Lonely Tower* (First Edition, London 1950), p.225.

> Great Europa played the fool
> That changed a lover for a bull.

Einstein's "series" is, I think, perceptible; we might add, as terms in it, the Francesco Giorgio 'Rape', also with dolphins in the Louvre, or Tiepolo's in Florence.

An image that presents some interesting features is the famous one from *The Countess Cathleen:*

> The years like great black oxen tread the world,
> And God the herdsman goads them on behind,
> And I am broken by their passing feet.

There are no oxen in the West of Ireland, nor do they tread kelp, as I had once been told. In the Isabella Stuart Gardner Museum there are two Pesellinos, tempera on panel: respectively the 'Triumphs' of 'Love, Chastity and Death' and of 'Fame, Time and Eternity'. Both illustrated the 'Triumphs' of Petrarch. They were exhibited in London in 1893-4. Yeats could have seen them before they went to America; I do not know whether he did. Until Sir Philip Hendy catalogued the Collection they were attributed to Piero di Cosimo, in whom Yeats was interested. The references to Petrarch are familiar. I quote from Hendy's account in the Catalogue of Paintings (Boston, 1931). The italics are mine:

> Upon a car driven by four white horses Love, with his feet on a ball of fire tended by cherubs with bowls of flame, *menaces with taut bow*[1] amid a throng of willing victims. Chastity then has him bound and weaponless at her feet while she sits erect, laurel in hand, *her car drawn by two unicorns,*[2] symbolic of purity . . . Against them death advances with shouldered scythe and the black banner with the white cross of the Misericordia, *upon a hearse drawn by a yoke of starved black buffaloes, slow symbols of the inevitable.*[3]

There is, I repeat, no evidence that Yeats saw this, or the equally magnificent example of the School of Mantegna, in Washington, of the car driven by two black oxen, with the same corpses under foot. He could have read the description in Vasari's *Lives,* or in Crowe and Cavalcassanti. But this quotation from Fulke Greville's *Life of Sir Philip Sidney* may be relevant, and (in any event) illustrates Yeats's desire for 'the images of life':

> 'For mine own part, I found my creeping genius more fixed upon the images of life, than the images of wit, and therefore chose not to write to them *on whose foot the black ox had not already trod'.*

1. See 'No Second Troy'.
2. Supporting the image from Puvis de Chavannes. See 'The Tower', vii.
3. . . . "and march on as oxen move over young grass", 'The Wanderings of Oisin', III.

Again it is this concatenation of the images that is so striking: we
remember Maud Gonne's alignment with Laura, and her
                    Beauty like a tightened bow . . .,
the magical unicorns that bear ladies on their backs, the unicorns of
Where There is Nothing, the Unicorn from the Stars; which is ultimately
the emblem of the soul, though it can also be seen as the destroyer of
the lion, the British imperial power. But the total impression, from many
galleries, was precisely that of the universality as well as the "serial
conjunctions" of the images presented in pictures and sculpture. In the
courtyard of the Archbishop's Palace at Ravenna are many architectural
fragments, stonework so strongly Celtic that one stood amazed,
wondering whether some broken High Cross had been transported there
from Glendalough or Clonmacnoise; serving to solidify a little the
imagination that linked Ireland with Byzantium or Egypt. The "sages
standing in God's holy fire" might be taken from the mosaic of the
Saints in the church of San Apollinare Nuovo at Ravenna; some slight
support might be perceived in an early draft of "Sailing to Byzantium",
where Yeats thinks of himself as prostrate on the steps before them: San
Prassede, and the Battistero Delgi Ortodossi have also been suggested
in *Images of a Poet.* But they, and the "staring Virgin" also meet in the
apse mosaic of the Basillica at Torcello.

Sometimes we come across paintings that throw light upon an obscure
passage' "Did da Vinci, when he painted a St. John that seemed a
Dionysus, know that St. John's father begot him when the grape was
ripe, and that his mother bore him at the ripening of the corn?"

I think it is clear that Yeats had in mind the two pictures in the
Grande Galerie of the Louvre,[1] which are, or were, separated by 'The
Virgin of the Rocks'. Not far off is 'La Gioconda', the subject of Pater's
lyric description, which Yeats printed as the first poem of *The Oxford
Book of Modern Verse;* chosen, I suspect, because Pater saw in the
picture just the foreshortening of history that appealed to Yeats:

> She is older than the rocks among which she sits; *like the
> Vampire,*[2] she has been dead many times, and *learned the
> secrets of the grave;*[3] and has been a diver in deep seas, and
> keeps their fallen day about her; and trafficked for strange webs
> with Eastern merchants and, *as Leda, was the mother of Helen*

1. It was curious to find, in a corner of the Louvre, in an obscurity which was
   perhaps intentional, a bust of a girl suckling snakes. I had previously thought
   of Swinburne's lines as related to the famous 'Simonetta Vespucci' of
   Piero di Cosimo; but this seemed a far better ikon for
        O lips full of lust and of laughter,
        Curled snakes that are fed from my breast . . . 'Dolores'.
2. See 'Oil and Blood'.
3. See 'Byzantium', 'A Bronze Head', 'The Gyres', and perhaps the fifth line
   of 'Death'.

of Troy,[1] and, as St. Anne, was the mother of Mary . . .

Seldom can a single passage have contained more of the symbols on which Yeats was to meditate so deeply. But in the two da Vincis that flank 'The Virgin of the Rocks' we have John the Baptist and the so-called Bacchus/Dionysus which the Louvre Catalogue tells us "used to be St. John the Baptist, transformed at the time of Louis XIV, attributed to da Vinci". The same model has served for both: and in this strange super-positioning of pagan and Christian we can find, if we wish, another dimension for *The Resurrection.* Among the "serial" pictures those that left the strongest impression were those of the innumerable San Sebastians and the Severed Heads. Both are archetypal. I have no doubt but that Yeats's interest began with Wilde's *Salome* and Beardsley's illustrations, those astonishing productions which begin with the sensuality of the Victorian demi-monde, and pass to the horrifying ending of 'The Dancer's Reward' and 'J'ai baisé ta bouche, Jokanaan'. In the last all evil seems to have been distilled. Salome's hair is twined into the bristling arms of some octopus-like plant, her face twisted by lust into a male mask of the utmost cruelty.

The severed head may be woman's revenge on man, or man's on woman.[2] The singing or speaking head is age-old. Yeats used it to proclaim the poet's revenge on woman, perhaps against the background of his own personal mythologem. But the second Beardsley drawing with the blood on the floor and the phallic emblems rising from it, suggests sharply the lines:

> A severed head! She took it in her hands;
> She stood all bathed in blood; the blood begat,
> O foul, foul, foul!

The Queen's Song –

> Child and darling, hear my song,
> Never cry I did you wrong;
> Cry that wrong came not from me
> But my virgin cruelty.

recalls Salome's terrible last speech; with rhythms which sometimes seem to suggest, most curiously, those of *The Resurrection.* A mysterious feature of many pictures – 'Agonies', 'Nativties', 'Crucifixions' – is the black bird that so often seems to be watching them; sometimes as if it were a malignant spirit, sometimes in response to a mere counter-pointing convention. In Mantegna's 'Agony in the Garden' it appears as a sort of vulture, on a dead tree, or perhaps the "portly green-pated bird"[3] that watches Christ on the Mount of Olives; it is also in Bellini's

---

1. See the whole group of Helen of Troy poems.
2. See 'Demon and Beast'; and *'The Harvest of Tragedy'*, Ch X.
3. 'Demon and Beast'. Possibly a cormorant: but note the line Being no more demoniac, and the black birds that fought with St. Patrick. (See p.169 infra)

'Agony', as the Morrigu or Crow watches Cuchulain in the Oliver
Sheppard statue in the Post Office. And it seems to be used as a
contrasting agent, or that which releases or terminates the lover's
delight. So in 'A Memory of Youth':

> (We) had been savagely undone
> Were it not that Love upon the cry
> Of a most ridiculous little bird
> Tore from the clouds his marvellous moon.

And in 'Her Triumph':

> And now we stare astonished at the sea,
> And a miraculous strange bird shrieks at us.

Also in 'A Last Confession':

> There's not a bird of day that dare
> Extinguish that delight.

§iv

Yeats does not often mention his brother's painting; one was aware,
I think, of a certain coldness. Jack Yeats has few direct illustrations: an
exception is the illustration to 'Come Gather Round Me Parnellites' for
the 1937 Cuala volume of Broadsheets, which the poet mentions with
approval in a letter to Dorothy Wellesley dated February 8, 1937. But
the little-known 1913 volume of Cuala Broadsheets offers two suggestive
parallels. One is called 'Two Tinkers': the date is close to that of 'The
Hour Before Dawn'. It shows a cairn of stones on a mountain-top - it
might well be Knocknarea or Cruachan. White clouds are sailing by; it
is "a windy place" with a suggestion of spring-time. A young man in
rags sits on a stone looking out over the landscape; his face is vacantly
cheerful. Beside him, sitting in a kind of hollow among the stones, sits
another man clasping his knees; a broad-brimmed hat half conceals a
melancholy sardonic face, with piercing eyes. The lines that suggest the
similarity are scattered throughout the poem; as samples

> When close to his right hand a heap
> Of grey stones and a rocky ledge
> Reminded him that he could make,
> If he but shifted a few stones,
> A shelter till the daylight broke.

and

> "My sleep were now nine centuries
> But for those mornings when I find
> The lapwing at their foolish cries
> And the sheep bleating at the wind
> As when I also played the fool."

In the same volume is an illustration called 'The Circus Wagon'; a
two horsed van, the driver whipping up as he leaves the circus pitch. On
the panels of the wagon are painted, garishly, two lions, a tiger, a
leopard. One thinks of 'The Circus Animals' Desertion':

> ... although
> Winter and summer till old age began
> My circus animals were all on show,
> Those stilted boys, that burnished chariot,
> Lion and woman and the Lord knows what

The phrase from 'The Mother of God'

> Wings beating about the room

is aligned naturally, in the fashion of Yeats's laminations of history, with

> A sudden blow: the great wings beating still
> Above the staggering girl . . .

of 'Leda and the Swan'. There are several possible sources (even if we suppose a pictorial one to be probable). There is Rembrandt's cartoon: Titian's tumultuous 'Annunciation' in the Church of San Salvatore in Venice. But there is a Ricketts which was nearer home, and which has the additional advantage of a pagan-Christian 'convergence'. This is the 'Eros Leaving Psyche', a woodcut enlarged from 'De Cupidinis et Psyches Amoribus'. Eros, with strong heavy wings — a single feather is falling from them — strives to break free from Psyche who is clutching his feet. In the same volume 'Don Juan and the Statue' seems relevant not only to the epigram 'On Those That Hated *The Playboy of the Western World*' but perhaps to 'The Statues' and to 'Horseman, pass by!'. Of the Annunciations proper, the line

> Another star has shot an ear

might have any one of many originals, in which the Logos appears as a dove, or a ray of light, piercing the ear of the Virgin. There are two excellent examples in the National Gallery at Washington: by Van Eyck and The Master of the Berberini respectively. This coalesces, perhaps, with the arrow - or spear - imagery of 'Stream and Sun at Glendalough', with all its religious overtones.

§v

The Municipal Gallery, and the poem on its revisitation, I find a little disappointing. I cannot think that Yeats was right when he called it "perhaps the best poem I have written for years, unless 'The Curse of Cromwell' is". It seems too much of an 'artefacted' poem, built around a catalogue, the emotions limited too much to the surface content and context of the pictures. Are not the interwoven stanzas a little clumsy, as superficial as 'Blessing the Tricolour', the rhythms commonplace and lacking in energy?

> . . . Hugh Lane, 'onlie begetter' of all these;
> Hazel Lavery living and dying, that tale
> As though some ballad-singer had sung it all.

As one enters the Gallery, the Bronze Head of Maud Gonne (which is plaster painted bronze) is a competent but not exciting piece of

sculpture, its artistic merits perhaps magnified unduly as the pretext
of a complex and considerable poem. Strangely, there is no mention
in the poem of the portrait of Constance Markiewicz, by Szankowski.
Mancini's 'Lady Gregory', painted through the netting that still shows
its faint rectangles, has certainly no claim to be called "Greatest since
Rembrandt", (I cannot believe that Synge made this remark); Yeats's
more cautious praise "A great ebullient portrait certainly" seems less
than meaningful. Robert Gregory's 'Coole Lake' is competent, with a
pleasant sense of depth, but a certain amateurishness of technique (in
this and in other landscapes) is apparent, so that the lines in the 'Elegy':

> We dreamed that a great painter had been born
> To cold Clare rock and Galway rock and thorn,
> To that stern colour and that delicate line
> That are our secret discipline
> Wherein the gazing heart doubles her might.

seem qualified only by Yeats's *pietas*. The Gallery is used rather as
a pretext for recollection, for a processional celebration; the imagination
is scarcely stirred. Nor does the Collection include any paintings
embodying the kind of symbols which fascinated him. I found only
one, and he did not write of that, which suggests the kind of antinomy -
an opposition between saint and the black bird - such as we find
in 'The Pilgrim'[1] The picture is by Margaret Kennedy. St. Patrick is on
the path leading to the summit of Cro-Patrick which, with Lough Derg,
is one of the great places of pilgrimage. Round the feet of the Saint, in
postures which seem to menace him, are large black birds; in form a
little like black-backed gulls, or albatrosses or cormorants. (All such
birds are connected with evil spirits.) The symbolism, is presumably that
of St. Patrick's struggle with the demons: but there is also the third
stanza of 'The Pilgrim':

> A great black ragged bird appeared when I was in the boat;
> Some twenty feet from tip to tip had it stretched rightly out,
> With flopping and with flapping it made a great display,
> But I never stopped to question, what could the boatman say
> *But fol de rol de rolly O.*

$vi

It is well to admit to disappointments and failures. Urbino itself
suggested nothing of any consequence; there was the steep street, the
room with "the high window looking on the dawn" of *Il Cortegiano* and
Coole. Michelangelo's tombs in the Medici Chapel (so closely linked,
as Wind· has shown, to 'Leda') threw no light, so far as I can see, on the
lines from 'Michael Robartes and the Dancer':

1. Lavery's 'St. Patrick's Purgatory', the scene of the Lough Derg landing place,
   is striking but perhaps hardly relevant.

His "Morning" and his "Night" disclose
How sinew that has been pulled tight,
Or it may be loosened in repose,
Can rule by supernatural right
Yet be but sinew.

- unless the statues embodied for him the antinomies that Pater had
seen in Michelangelo: "He secured for his work individuality and intensity of expression, while he avoided a too heavy realism".[1] According
to Pater the sculptor's incompleteness "is his way of etherealizing pure
form, of relieving its stiff realism . . .." "In this way he combines the
utmost amount of passion and intensity with the sense of a yielding and
flexible life . . . " But perhaps it is no more than an alignment with 'The
Creation of Adam' (as in 'Long-Legged Fly' and 'Under Ben Bulben')
of the thesis

That all must come to sight and touch
denying the neo-platonic proposition of Donne's 'Valediction'

Care lesse, eyes, lips, and hands to misse
(and of Shakespeare's Sonnets), and perhaps of his own 'Ribh at the
Tomb of Baile and Aillinn'. Nor did there seem any painting in Venice
that could be referred to the Veronese quotation, with

all his sacred company,
though S. Sebastiano at Venice was filled with 'exquisite bodies.'
Grose's Catalogue of Greek Coins in the Fitzwilliam Museum at Cambridge (see 'Parnell's Funeral') was used for the 'Cretan Coin';
and Euripides' *Bacchae*, which is as it were a backcloth to *The Resurrection*.

I do not know which of the paintings he had in mind (there were
many possibles in the Louvre) for

What made the drapery glisten so?
Not a man but Delacroix.
Nor have I found anything in Dulac, especially in his illustrations to
the *Arabian Nights:* though the 'Black Centaur' is of course familiar.

And at the end one can do no more than speculate, though with
ever-growing fascination. Is there some connection with that great
Bellini of 'St. Francis in Ecstasy' in the Denver Museum where, on the
plateau on the right of the Saint's Cave, a donkey and a grey heron
wait together? Are they related to the symbols of *The Herne's Egg?*
Why did he choose, among his Calverts for the American lecture tour,
that picture in which a figure comes riding on a donkey, with a crook
over His shoulder, along a path on the edge of a woodland, towards a
forest hut, where a stately woman seems to await Him? ("Ribh, but
for his views on the Trinity, would be considered an orthodox man.")
What did Yeats find that was of such profound interest in the tombs

1. *The Renaissance,* "Luca della Robbia".

of 'Morning and Night' in the Medici Chapel? Is there any significance in that drawing of Ricketts's in the Fogg Museum at Boston in which cherubs float upon a grey green sea, which is covered with red roses that look like wounds? Do Plotinus and Thomas Taylor converge perhaps with Ricketts? — to illuminate the second stanza of 'News for the Delphic Oracle'? And what impact had the Egyptian Rooms of the British Museum upon his early meditations there? Did the great hawk that floats above the sarcophagus, with outspread wings, lead him to choose the hawk for his own private symbol? — so that it seemed to converge, at *The Hawk's Well*, with Aoife and Maud Gonne, and with that metempsychosis in which men had the throats of birds? Was this metempsychosis confirmed, as it was for Cuchulain in the Dantesque underworld of 'Cuchulain Comforted', by the thought of that astonishing vault mosaic in the Cathedral of Cefalu, where those strange beings seem to rise above the angels as their hair and bodies are transfigured to great pinions barred with white and blue, black and gold? Is there anything new to be found among those strange pictures, many "of supernatural beings" by A.E., now largely dispersed and inaccessible? What of the Gozzoli prints that hung at Coole? Did the Blake woodcut of 'When Shall I see My Hut, That Small Abode' which he set beside Calvert's 'The Sheep of His Pasture' — and which are among the collection of slides for the American lecture tour, suggest, however faintly, the Tower with its "storm-beaten cottages" and the river beneath his window-ledge? Above all, what of that strange working of the poet's mind by which a picture, singly, or self-begotten or projected into a series, seemed to act so often as a trigger for his imagination; so that images could beget fresh and ever more vital images?

X
GEORGE MOORE[1]

It is the policy of The Yeats Society that we should have every year one or more lectures on the ancillary figures of the Irish Literary Revival. We have recently had Allingham and Synge; and for the future there are likely to be all sorts of notable figures, greater and lesser. There are Lady Gregory, Edward Martyn; that strange figure the Count de Basterot; the inscrutable and bad-tempered benefactress of the early Abbey, Miss Horniman; Maud Gonne, Eva Gore-Booth, Katharine Tynan Hinkson; Mabel Beardsley; Althea Gyles; that fierce poet, Wilfrid Scawen Blunt (much neglected) and the members of the Rhymers' Club, in particular Johnson, Dowson, Wilde. This morning I want to speak of George Moore, very great in his time. Perhaps the peak of his reputation was in the early 1920's. I doubt if there are many in this room who read him regularly. Yet, in order to show something of his stature then, I quote a tribute to him signed by most of the great writers of England to celebrate his eightieth birthday. They described him as

". . . an artist who, since he came to London from Paris many years ago, has not ceased to labour with a single mind in the perfecting of his craft, who has written in *Daphnis and Chloe* a flawless translation, in *Esther Waters* a tale that marks a period in our literature, in *Hail and Farewell* an autobiography that has ranked with Rousseau's, in *Heloise and Abelard* a philosophical romance of supreme beauty, and in *The Brook Kerith* a prose epic unique in the English language. The uses of that language have been changed by your influence, as though in an ancient music you had discovered new melodies and rhythms that shall be in the air when young men in future time have stories to tell. You have taught narrative to flow again and anecdote to illumine it as the sun a stream. You have persuaded words and invention to sing new songs together that would have been heard, as those of an equal, by the masters upon whom the tradition of our literature relies, and on your eightieth birthday your pen is still unfailing in your hand. For these reasons we salute you, and for our friendship's sake. – SALVE."

Now when we have made every allowance for the flattery due to an octogenarian, there must be something of importance to consider; even if we do no more than wonder at this strange reversal of the wheel of fame. Let us take stock of Moore's position.

From the historical point of view he is a highly individual yet characteristic figure of his time. In the pattern of Anglo-Irish literature

1. Sligo, 1963.

he is the expatriate, yet who is drawn irresistibly to return; the would-be cosmopolitan of Paris, the ambivalent lover and hater of Ireland (so were Swift, Yeats, Joyce, Beckett and, I think, Synge); the leader who returns in enthusiasm and haste to further the new causes of Home Rule, of the Irish Language, even of agricultural cooperation: and to mock at all of them. It is too easy a solution to suggest that he and Yeats were incompatible through rivalry as returning leaders, or as opposing types with the same self-dramatizing instinct. Both wore masks: but, while Yeats wore his with a remarkable consistency through-out his life — perhaps with a few carefully designed modifications, as the stage-lighting altered — Moore was deliberately parading his own changes. From a boyhood episode he cherished the nickname of 'Mr. Perpetual'. because he had confessed even then that he was continuously in love. The great lover, promiscuous but exquisitely fastidious, (even to the cleanliness of his mistresses) squared well enough with his picture of himself as the very flower of virility, combined with a connoisseurship that oscillated pleasantly between women, food, and pictures. But with all this there went a commendable self-awareness:

'To be ridiculous has always been *ma petite luxe,* but can anyone be said to be ridiculous if he knows he is ridiculous?'[1]

We may go a stage further. As a young man he was a poet, rather in the manner of Baudelaire. The titles of his poems are characteristic: *Flowers of Passion* (Fleurs du Mal?) 1878, *Pagan Poems,* 1881. He is rather more than a decade ahead of the Rhymers' Club, and closer to Swinburne than they. His great passions, next to painting, were for Zola and Balzac. There was to be realistic documentation on the one hand, and on the other the aestheticism of Pater, half-parodied by Wilde, and brought to its *reductio ad absurdum* in Huysman's *A Rebours.* His essential feminine sensitivity, together with an assumed arrogance and need for re-assurance, led him to explore with considerable skill the psychology of women in love. His first important work was *A Modern Lover* in 1885; then *A Mummer's Wife in* 1885, followed by his *Confessions* in 1888. His best early work is *Esther Waters* (1894) which is the story of a servant-girl who has been seduced, and of her brave struggles to bring up her son. Moore had been brought up in the Black Country, and in his realistic approach to its landscape and ethos anticipated to some extent Arnold and Lawrence. He is interested in the problems of abnegation, and of celibacy, particularly in the Short Stories. In *A Drama in Muslin* he handles the double theme of the marriage-market and the tenant-landlord relationship in Ireland.

In the 'Twenties he was widely read and known: today he is even less read, I suspect, than Meredith. We may suggest some possible reasons.

1. *Vale,* p.40. (The references are to the Heinemann edition of 1947).

$ ii

The exploration of women in love was one peculiar phenomenon of the complicated and ambivalent pre-Raphaelite legacy. "Woman herself was still in our eyes, for all that, romantic and mysterious, still the priestess of her shrine, our emotions remembering the *Lilith* and the *Sybilla Palmifera* of Rossetti . . . It could not be otherwise, for Johnson's favourite phrase, that life is ritual, expressed something that was in some degree in all our thoughts, and how could life be ritual if woman had not her symbolical place?"[1] Across this pseudo-medieval tapestry are many threads, patches of colour. Worship of women can co-exist with Swinburne's 'Dolores', with Baudelaire's thorny ravines down which lovers roll in ecstasy. "Woman's virtue is man's greatest invention"; so he quotes from Balzac. The realism would rival that of Zola and is linked with a desire to *'épater le bourgeois'*. So Moore: "A wonderful thing is the race of woman, entirely misunderstood by men. So much more emotional than we are - lovely animal natures!"

There was indeed at the time much clinical material in two million surplus women, not yet educated or enfranchised. The humanitarian movement of the century was gradually extending its interest towards servant girls and prostitutes. Mr. Gladstone's explorations of that sociological field are familiar. The *droit de seigneur* was apparently a feature of life in the West until the 1870s, at the price of some scandal and some enrichment of both peasant and aristocratic stock. As to the seduction of the servant girl, and of the artists' models, conduct in Ireland strongly contrasted with that in France and Italy. These, with the problems of the 'arranged' marriages in small Mayo parishes, the market in the marriageable debutante *(A Drama in Muslin)* are constant themes.

In these amorous imaginings there is a paradoxical element. Moore can treat women with delicacy, sympathy and compassion. He can also posture ridiculously as the great lover, the connoisseur, the great seducer:

"In those days I prefaced my love affairs with a copy of Mlle. de Maupin[1]." The discussions of the lines and curves of beauty are prolonged, elaborate and rather ridiculous. Here he has just missed seducing the girl-friend of his painter-friend, Jim Browne: . . . "and I walked down the paved alley meditating that once again I had missed the prey for the shadow. And, as if my punishment were not enough, Jim continued to talk of her beauty, telling that her legs were shapelier than Mademoiselle d'Anka's; they did not go in at the knee, and this great beauty, or this great fault, formed the theme of many conversations in the studio at Prince's Gardens; Boucher's

1. *Vale*, p.67.

women did not go in at the knee, but Rubens's did . . . ."[1]

Here the affected sensuality converges with the aestheticism which is another feature of Moore's writing. There are many references to, analogies from, painting. Yet I find in his writing on women a constant under-current, as it were, of cruelty. Perhaps it arises from his own uncertainties, perhaps from a cynicism over the whole problem of the duration of love after marriage as seen by the celibate observer. This is evident in *The |Untilled Field*.

There is also the constant impression that he is hunting for epigrams that are nearly always witty, often sacrificing a proportion at any rate of the truth to this desire. As example:

> "Manet is an instinct, Degas an intellectuality."[2] (This means little or nothing.)

> "One felt on entering his room that his dinner was not a sexual one."[3]

> (Of Sir Horace Plunkett, the great figure in the agricultural reorganization of Ireland.)

Or

> "Maupassant . . . seemed to me too much like an intrigue with a housemaid."[4]

$ iii

Perhaps he is now read in the main for his short stories, for the *Hail and Farewell* trilogy which is supremely witty, malicious, and — as the history of the Irish Literary Renaissance — wholly unreliable. Add *The Brook Kerith* for some of the most perfect prose of the century; and the long-banned play *The Apostle*. Both book and play rest on the assumed truth of the legend that Christ did not in fact die on the cross; he was taken down in a coma, smuggled across to the monastery of the Essenes, and slowly nursed back to health. And Christ confronts St. Paul, back from his missionary journeys, preaching the Risen Lord. Moore's reading of the Bible which came late, and therefore with a fresh impact, coincides with his conversion from Catholicism, and his violent attacks (once he had assumed the position that the evils of the country, as well as its literary and artistic deficiencies, were due to that religion) were directed against his friends and enemies. The chief targets weie his brother, 'the Colonel', and his own collaborator Edward Martyn of Tillyra. He and Yeats kept up a ceaseless and corrosive warfare, which had its origins in the theatre, and one may question the propriety, as well as the good taste, of the mass of personal description on either side.

1. *Vale.* p.46.
2. *Ibid.* p.105.
3. *Ibid.* p.149.
4. *Ibid.* p.2.

The storms raised by Moore's anti-clericalism were wholly deliberate, planned. He gives the impression of perpetually trying to shock his English audiences by his sexual adventures, to which — for Dublin consumption — was added his attack on the priests and the Catholic hierarchy. In both he goes far beyond the anti-clericalism that was one of the consequences of the French Revolution, and the permissive society of Paris that had become a legend. "In order to preserve the purity of his home the Englishman invented the continental excursion". But in addition there was the Paris of myth and of reality. Whistler, Roger Fry, Sickert, and lesser men beyond number, went to France and returned with the praises of the Nouvelle Athènes and of the great men who congregated there. Free thought and free love were perhaps compensations for the defeats of 1870. There was talk unlimited, in Dublin and in the Temple. The subjects have a certain monotony: women, painters, theology, the Irish language, the obsolescence of the English language (which had lost its verbs); but notably, when his egotisms are submerged for a moment, there are the most delicate and sensitive descriptions of the Irish landscape.

§iv

George Moore was half a generation older than Yeats. He was born in 1852 and died in 1933, and it is well to remember that he was nearly forty at the time of 'The Tragic Generation'. He was an Irish landlord, of a once important Mayo family, and you can still see the ruins of Moore Hall, on the West side of Lough Carra, which lies just north of Lough Mask. Like so many of his class he was, in theory, comfortably off, with a substantial rent-roll; in practice the estate was intermittently shaken by successive waves of the Irish Land Agitation, at its height, perhaps, from 1881-1902. I am half-paraphrasing the title of Yeats's poem on that subject, 'How should the world be luckier if this house . . .'

Moore liked to allude to Turgenev (together with Balzac) as his master: particularly to Turgenev's stories in *Tales of a Sportsman*. But I find in *The Untilled Field*, and elsewhere, none of Turgenev's understanding of the peasantry and his serfs, on his own estates and on those of his neighbours; and none of the intimacy with the Russian countryside which he describes so exquisitely when on his shooting expeditions. Nor is Moore capable of Turgenev's near-mystical experiences of waiting at twilight and dawn for woodcock-flighting, or that strange encounter with the group of boys, herding horses, round their camp-fire at night. Moore's father (there is, rather unexpectedly, no criticism of him) was a noted horseman, who bred horses, made bad paintings of them, lost heavily on them. The visit to Colonel Moore described in *Vale* is tinged with memories of the stables. The admiration for horses and horsemen was, perhaps is, a quality of the Irish aristocracy and near-aristocracy. Yeats eulogizes their feats of horsemanship, and in 'The Gyres' mentions, as inhabitants of the ideal messianic state, 'Lovers of horses and of women'. Sir Jonah Barrington in his *Memoirs* divides the gentry into 'mounted' and 'half mounted' men, according to the horseflesh they could afford. Moore's description of a boy sitting a wildly-bucking horse seems to refer to himself; he might, he says, with luck have ridden a Grand National winner, and describes how he *nearly* rode as an amateur jockey in a race at Croydon. There is no description of a hunt; but there is a highly objectionable episode in childhood in which he set the dogs on a tame white cat belonging to the laundrymaids, climbed a tree to shake her from the branches, and finally 'broke up' the beast before the weeping girls. He does not appear to have been a fisherman (we remember Yeats's aspirations here), and his one attempt to explore Lough Mask (linked to Lough Carra by a stream) was abandoned because that great and dangerous lake was 'gloomy'.

Of shooting there is little mention though he alludes to himself as a good shot: but there is an enlightening episode of a visit as a guest to a Scottish shooting-lodge. His mother had offered him as a present the choice between a fitted dressing-case and a new gun. Typically, he chose the dressing-case, and sent to Moore Hall for a pair of his father's ancient muzzle loaders, then long obsolete. Even these were rusted up. Someone in the shooting party lent him a modern weapon. Then his boots disintegrated on the Scottish heather, for he had bought a ladies' pair in London. To these, he explains, he was attracted by the decorative buckles, and out of pride at the smallness of his feet which made the choice possible. But he did hold the opinion that the purity of his English style owed much to his boyhood in Mayo, among grooms, woodmen, gamekeepers: for gamekeepers, he believed, spoke the best and purest English. *Lady Chatterley's Lover* is of interest here.

§v

The family once Protestant, and turned Catholic — hence the association with the devout 'holy man', Edward Martyn. George was educated at a Catholic Seminary near Manchester, revolted violently against that faith, toyed with the idea of becoming a Protestant, and finally died an agnostic. 'Youth is a very unhappy time, Art and sex driving us mad, and our parents looking upon us with stupid unconscious eyes.'[1]

He was sent to a hated school, learnt nothing, and was then sent to an army crammer. (There is a brilliant description of his life at 'Jurle's' in *Vale*.) His brother, of whom he writes much, ended as a

1. *Vale*, p.22.

Colonel in the Connaught Rangers. But when his father's death provided him with a competence, he took up painting, first in London, and then in Paris. We may recall that W.B. Yeats, whose father was a Pre-Raphaelite painter, took up painting before he found his trade, and remember Jack Yeats's meteoric career in old age as a painter; as well as the fortune that Lady Gregory's nephew, Hugh Lane, made as a dealer and connoisseur of pictures.

Fortunately, Moore discovered in time that he had no talent as a painter, but made himself an admirable and sensitive critic, of French painting in particular. There are many descriptions, and perhaps some names-dropping, of the writers and artists who met as the Nouvelle Athènes. Monet was his real love, but he was 'in' on the great period of the Impressionists, Manet, Sisley, Pisarro, Degas, and he wrote a goodish book on *Modern Painters*. The novels are filled with descriptions of artists; whose reputation as romantics and non-conformists (see *Patience*) was at its height in the last two decades of the century. Even Yeats paid tribute to his knowledge. He was particularly interested in Degas (whom he knew in Paris) and his studies of ballet-dancers, and at this point we may draw attention to a minor skirmish in the long war between Moore and Yeats.

In Yeats's late play *The Death of Cuchulain*, in the Prologue spoken by the Old Man, you will remember this:

> . . . "I spit upon the dancers painted by Degas. I spit upon their short bodices, their stiff stays, their toes whereon they spin like peg-tops, above all upon that chambermaid face. They might have looked timeless, Rameses the Great, but not the chambermaid, that old maid history. I spit! I spit! I spit!"

And we then remember with some amusement that the very fine Degas pictures in the Municipal Gallery of Dublin were presented by George Moore, and reflect on the recent astronomical growth in Degas's reputation.

So far the pattern is fairly clear. The young man mildly rebelling against the family tradition, background and career, rejecting the religion of his birth, as did Yeats and others; with a personal income that was just enough to keep him if things went well, but which had a habit of ebbing mysteriously away and forcing him to write; turning from the almost incredible backwoods existence of a Connaught country mansion in the 70's (it was only tolerable if one hunted, fished, shot and drank heavily, in due season) to the romance and glitter of Paris. For Paris from 1875, after the scars of the Prussian Wars had grown a kind of unhealthy scab, gave itself up to an almost hysterical gaiety and the licence of real or imagined genius. The glitter of the boulevards, the society of the Nouvelle Athènes, music halls and cafés, had their somewhat sordid counterpart in the Strand by gaslight, the hordes of prostitutes that descended from the little streets each evening,[1] and the chambers in the Inns of Court that provided such pleasant bachelor quarters. We may thus discern in Moore a complicated and ambivalent tissue of impulses: the break-away from the feudal life of his Irish home, yet writing nostalgically about it; the rebellion against religious orthodoxy; a break with his father and the Victorian tradition, and the perpetual desire to *épater le bourgeois* by the sexual romances which he built about his somewhat feminine personality.

Let us recall his portraits: the plump, soft-looking, intelligent, rather effeminate face, the sensual lips, the eyes deep set and a little too small, the flattened thinning hair, the rimless pince-nez. 'A man carved out of a turnip, looking out of astonished eyes'.[2] thus Yeats.

We are familiar, too, with the wicked epigram by Humbert Wolfe:

> Women he loved, and next to women, art.
> Good friends he had, and sold them all for copy.
> Had but his greatness matched as great a heart
> Time had not mixed his laurels with the poppy.

And we remember the passage in Yeats's *The Cat and the Moon* — surely the most slanderous passage ever acted in the theatre since the Tudor stage — about Edward Martyn and George Moore, sometime Yeats's co-directors of the Abbey:

Blind Beggar: Do you mind what the beggar told you about the holy man in the big house at Laban?

Lame Beggar: Nothing stays in my head, Blind Man.

Blind Beggar: What does he do but go knocking about the roads with an old lecher from the county of Mayo, and he a woman-hater from the day of his birth! And what do they talk of by candle-light and by day-light? The old lecher does be telling over all the sins he committed, or maybe never committed at all, and the man of Laban does be trying to head him off and quiet him down that he may quit telling them.

Lame Beggar: Maybe it is converting him he is.

Even if we did not remember that Laban is the name of Edward Martyn's townland at Tillyra, and Martyn's perpetual trouble with his sensitive conscience that had to be consulted so frequently over the Abbey plays (and other matters), we have Yeats's own assurance of the identification, as well as his naïve instructions that the speeches might be omitted for an audience that would not understand the references:

> "The Holy man in the big house' . . . and his friend from
> Mayo were meant for Edward Martyn and George Moore, both
> of whom were living when the play was written."

1. See Kipling's story, 'One View of the Matter'.
2. Autobiographies, p. 405.

And Yeats proceeds to give directions for a textual cut 'when the play is performed where the reference is not understood'. The sting of the remark is the knowledge - where the reference would be understood - of contemporary gossip to the effect that Moore was impotent. Nothing fills one with astonishment more than the extent to which one could get away with the most vituperative personal attacks, even in the 'blind bitter town' that was Dublin. But Yeats is not content with one, for

'Old lecher with a love in every wind'

also refers to Moore. We may recall without malice that Yeats recalls, continually, the same epithet in relation to Dante:

'Being mocked by Guido for his lecherous life,'

and Guido's phrase, of Dante, which Yeats was fond of quoting – perhaps as a precedent for many great writers –

'He found room among his virtues for lechery.'

$vi

Dublin Society, particularly that of the theatre, the writers and the public houses they frequent, has always been remarkable for its output of witty malicious gossip, for a boastfulness that does not always find itself transformed into action, and for an anti-clericalism which, outside the brave and kindly hot-house of the pub, often adopts a cloak of sanctimonious conformity. It was and is a somewhat narrow world, and we may suggest some comparisons with Restoration and early Eighteenth Century London. There are many reasons: the closeness of the society, the interlocking gossip, a common source of wit in the criticisms of religion and government (both highly ambivalent), of personal idiosyncracies and appearances, of the eccentricities which so often breed in a society in which time and its associated virtues are largely irrelevant. A convenient illustration of all this may be found in the relationships between Moore and Yeats. It is certain that each was prepared, at any moment, to sacrifice any pretension to truth to the needs of a good story, a dramatic situation, a specially barbed piece of malice. And yet this conflict, this exchange of maliciousness, is worth recalling, for it throws a great deal of light on both Moore and Yeats, as well as Dublin Society.

We may think first of some of Moore's descriptions of Yeats. The first is in the woods at Coole:

'I came upon a tall black figure standing at the edge of the lake, wearing a cloak which fell in straight folds to his knees, looking like a great umbrella forgotten by some picnic party[1]'.

Yeats had visited Aran, and as a consequence sent Synge there.

When the hooker that was taking Yeats over to Aran or

1. *Ave,* p. 186.

taking him back to Galway was caught in a storm Yeats fell
upon his knees and tried to say a prayer; but the nearest thing
to one he could think of was 'Of Man's first disobedience and
the fruit' . . . and he spoke as much of *Paradise Lost* as he
could remember.[1]

Of Yeats's assumption of an ancestry which he did not possess
Moore has a shrewd comment which confirms for ever the bitterness
between the two men:

> ' . . . We asked ourselves why Willie Yeats should feel himself
> called upon to denounce the class to which he belonged essen-
> tially —'

(Moore has in mind the line in the prefatory verses to *Responsibilities*,
where Yeats speaks of his blood 'that has not passed through any
huckster's loin')

> . . . millers and ship-owners on one side, and on the other a
> portrait-painter of distinction; and we laughed, remembering
> A.E.'s story, that one day whilst Yeats was crooning over his
> fire Yeats had said that if he had his rights he would be Duke
> of Ormonde. A.E.'s answer was: I am afraid, Willie, you are
> overlooking your father — a detestable remark to make to a
> poet in search of an ancestry; and the addition: We both belong
> to the lower-middle classes, was in equally bad taste.
> . . . He should have remembered that all the romantic poets
> have sought illustrious ancestry, and rightly, since romantic
> poetry is concerned only with nobles and castles, gonfalons and
> oriflammes.[2]

Blow and cross-counter: the fight went on. Now we can quote Yeats:

> Moore and Martyn were indeed in certain characteristics
> typical peasants, the peasant sinner, the peasant saint. Moore's
> grandfather or great-grandfather had been a convert, but there
> were Catholic marriages. Catholic families, beaten down by the
> Penal Laws, despised by Irish Protestants, by the few English
> Catholics they met, had but little choice as to where they picked
> their brides; boys on one side of old family, grew up, squireens,
> half-sirs, peasants who had lost their tradition, gentlemen who
> had lost theirs. Lady Gregory once told me what marriage
> coarsened the Moore blood, but I have forgotten.[3]

Edward Martyn shares with Moore some of Yeats's obloquy: for
Martyn, the author of *The Heather Field*, had brought Moore into the
affairs of the Abbey when Martyn asked him to find a cast for that
play.

> They were cousins and inseparable friends, bound one to the
> other by mutual contempt. When I told Martyn that Moore

1. *Salve*, p.26.
2. *Vale*, p.114.
3. 'Dramatis Personae', *Autobiographies*, p.402.

had good points, he replied: "I know Moore a great deal longer than you do. He has no good points." And a week or two later Moore said: "That man Martyn is the most selfish man alive. He thinks I am damned and he doesn't care."

Martyn was implicated in the first of the Abbey's censorship troubles. The story of the conflict of ecclesiastical authorities, some condemning *The Countess Cathleen* as heretical and some approving it, is well known. But Martyn withdrew his financial support - he was a wealthy man — relented, and then threatened to withdraw again. According to Yeats, Moore openly lamented the chance of a witty row:

> He had meant to write an article called 'Edward Martyn and His Soul'. He said: "It was the best opportunity I ever had. What a sensation it would have made! Nobody has ever written that way about his most intimate friend. What a chance! It would have been heard of everywhere[1] . . . '

Sometimes Moore, instead of asking us to accept for true some monstrous invention, would press a spontaneous action into deliberate comedy; starting in bad blood or blind passion, he would all in a moment see himself as others saw him. When he arrived in Dublin all the doors in Upper Ely Place had been painted white by an agreement between the landlord and the tenants. Moore had his door painted green, and three Miss Beams — no, I have not got the name quite right — who lived next door protested to the landlord. Then began a correspondence between Moore and the landlord wherein Moore insisted on his position as an art critic, that the whole decoration of his house required a green door — I imagine that he had but wrapped the green flag around him — then the indignant young women bought a copy of *Esther Waters,* tore it up, put the fragments into a large envelope, wrote thereon: 'Too filthy to keep in the house', dropped it into his letter-box. I was staying with Moore, I let myself in with a latch-key some night after twelve, and found a note on the hall table asking me to put the door on the chain. As I was undressing, I heard Moore trying to get in. When I had opened the door and pointed to the note, he said: "Oh, I forgot. Every night I go out at eleven, at twelve, at one, and rattle my stick on the railing to make the Miss Beams' dogs bark". Then I saw in the Newspaper that the Miss Beams had hired organ-grinders to play under Moore's window while he was writing; that he had prosecuted the organ-grinders. Moore had a large garden on the other side of the street, a blackbird sang there; he received his friends upon Saturday evening and made a moving speech upon the bird. "I enjoy its song. If I were the bad man people say I am, how could I enjoy its song?" He wrote every morning at an open window on the ground floor, and one morning saw the

1. 'Dramatis Personae', *Autobiographies*, p. 415.

Miss Beams' cat cross the street and thought, "That cat will get my bird." He went out and filled his pocket with stones, and whenever he saw the cat, threw a stone. Someone, perhaps the typist, must have laughed, for the rest of the tale fills me with doubt. I was passing through Dublin just on my way to Coole: he came to my hotel. "I remembered how early that cat got up. I thought it might get the black-bird if I was not there to protect it, so I set a trap. The Miss Beams wrote to the Society for the Prevention of Cruelty to Animals, and I am carrying on a correspondence with its secretary, cat versus bird." '(Perhaps after all, the archives of the Society do contain that correspondence. The tale is not yet incredible.) 'I passed through Dublin again, perhaps on my way back. Moore came to see me in seeming great depression. "Remember that trap?" "Yes." "Remember that bird?" "Yes." "I have caught the bird."[1]

$vii

Moore was, throughout his life, subject to violent enthusiasms: and in the late 'Nineties he became involved in the Irish Literary Revival: largely, I believe, through his friend Edward Martyn, partly through a wave of Anglophobia arising out of the Boer War, which he loathed and which was attacked in different ways by such varied personalities as Chesterton and Lionel Johnson. It is a fair indication of his state of mind, and of a certain naiveté, that he boasted openly of having frustrated a British Army attack by sending a telegram to the Boer leaders telling them about it. The period 1897 (Victoria's Jubilee), '98 (the centenary of the French-assisted rebellion) and the Boer War itself started a wave of sympathy with Ireland. There was, in fact, something of a rush to jump on the Irish band-wagon; Moore expected to be welcomed with open arms as its returning Lost Leader (the Parnell affair was in everyone's mouth) and his vanity was shocked because he was received coldly. He had been refused membership of the London Irish Literary Society even though proposed by Yeats; and both Moore and Yeats were both, I believe, under suspicion as emigrés at this time. It is evident that the Moore-Yeats quarrel was in part a clash of personalities, but partly because each saw himself as the leader of the literary-political wing of the Irish *risorgimento*. But the quarrels of the Irish Literary Revival are so complicated that we must try to disentangle some of the threads.

As Moore saw it, it was a movement for the revival of the Irish Language; which he did not know, and for a time attempted to learn with enthusiasm. It is recorded that he even wrote (with some assistance) a short story in Irish. The primary grounds seem to have been his assumption that the English language was exhausted, dead; having been used

1. *Autobiographies*, 'Dramatis Personae', p.444ff.

far too long. This was a not uncommon complaint, and is still a pretext for various typographical and other eccentricities in modern
verse.[1]

But in 1898, with Home Rule an apparent certainty, language
revival seemed an essential ingredient of the united Ireland that was to
be: and it was thought that the new literature to be written in it would
be of immense importance in its civilizing effect. In 1898 Lionel
Johnson had offered a £5 prize for an Essay Competition: "How
much Ireland may learn from Wales as to how to preserve her national
language."

The most amusing instance is given in Moore's *Salve.*[2] Yeats
proposed to write a play *Diarmid and Grania;* (Yeats woke Moore up in
the middle of the night, much to his annoyance, to tell him about it):
then —

> Moore was to write the play in *French*
> Lady Gregory was then to translate into *English.*
> Taidgh O'Donohue was to translate this into *Irish.*
> Lady Gregory was to translate the Irish back into *English.*
> — the play by then having acquired a 'flavour' from the Irish
> idiom, like peat-smoke in whiskey. And finally, Yeats was 'to
> put style upon it'.

(It is, however, noteworthy that Moore's collection of short stories,
The Untilled Field, was translated into Irish by Taidgh O'Donohue,
and translated back for Moore's benefit.)

Our second strand is that of Celtic mythology and folk-lore: through
the revival of which Ireland was to be awakened to her consciousness
of nationality and nationalism. Here, I think, there are two minor
threads.

(a)   the 'poetical' and romantic view of Yeats, that through the
poetic *image* the people should be induced to draw upon their
Jungian 'collective unconscious' or 'Great Memory' as he called it, and,
through that knowledge, achieve a mystical unity, as well as a common
mythology.

(b)   the "old gods" view of A.E. in which ancient Irish mythology
was seen (through Theosophy, for A.E. was leader of the Dublin
Theosophical Society) to have much in common with Hinduism,
Christianity being rather an inferior religion. Ireland had once been
a pagan country, and, in A.E.'s vision, should be so again. Both
views were, of course, looked upon with suspicion by the Roman
Catholic hierarchy: though I believe that A.E., who sometimes
drew pictures of the supernatural beings he had seen, was not
considered to have a detrimental influence, being, literally, out of
this world.

1. Hence the 'revolution' of *The Waste Land.*
2. *Salve,* p.101.

There is a vivid account in *Salve*[1] of A.E. and Moore going off on a bicycling trip to Meath to visit an underground Druid chamber; of Moore leaving A.E. in prayer and meditation underground in the hope that the elder gods would appear; but how, just as the gods were on the point of appearing, A.E.'s invocations were brought to nothing by the appearance of two Presbyterian clergymen, who insisted on going down into the tomb and breaking up the party.

A portion of Moore's reverie on the bicycle ride is worth quoting, for it bears on another aspect of the Irish Literary Revival that both he and Yeats believed in; remembering the analogies of England as Rome, Ireland as Byzantium in Yeats's mind:

> . . . 'the art of ancient Ireland must have been considerable, since a little handful has come down to us, despite the ravening Dane, and the Norman, worse than the Dane; for the Dane only destroyed, whereas the Norman came with a new culture, when Ireland was beginning to realize herself. If he had come a few centuries later, we should have had an art as original as the Chinese.'

And the perennial question of the Revival:

> 'Can the dreams, the aspirations and traditions of the ancient Gael be translated into English? And being easily cast down, I asked if the beliefs of the ancient Gael were not a part of his civilization and have lost all meaning for us?
>
> That would be so, A.E. answered, if truth were a casual thing of today and tomorrow, but men knew the great truths thousands of years ago, and it seems to me that these truths are returning, and that we shall soon possess them, not perhaps exactly as the ancient Gael —
>
> I hope that you are right, for all my life is engaged in this adventure, and I think you are right, and that the ancient Gael was nearer to nature than we have ever been since we turned for inspiration to Galilee.'

Our third strand, which involves us with A.E. is, curiously enough, economic, and to explain it we must go back a little into history. The disastrous famine of 1847-8 had resulted in an enormous death roll, infinite distress, and wholesale emigration: but even these factors were insufficient to diminish the teeming population, living perpetually on the edge of hunger; the background against which Swift's *Modest Proposal* must be read and considered. Many efforts (on the whole ineffectual) were made by the Government to mitigate distress: such as road works, harbours, piers, and so on. You can see a score of small harbours and piers on the West Coast, with beautiful and costly stone piers and docks of the finest masonry: and they are for the most part

---

1. p.44ff.

deserted: for one of the dreams of the philanthropists in the Government was to establish a fishing industry, not foreseeing the complicated matters such as dredging, the capital needed for fishing boats, the foreign trawlers and lobster boats that were one day to exploit the Irish shores. Another dream was to reform the system of agriculture; then, as now, wasteful and inefficient, except in the larger farms of the south and south midland areas. For the rest, the tiny fields, divided and re-divided by a land-hungry people, the heavy rainfall, the acid soil always ready to go back to rushes and bog, and the indolence of the peasantry, made the standard of living one of the lowest in Europe.

But Ireland, since Spenser made his famous survey as 'personal assistant' to Lord Grey, has always been an abundant though inefficient exporter of butter, eggs, poultry, cattle, bacon: and the Government of the '80s, noting the enormous success of Denmark as an agricultural country, set about reforming the agriculture: mainly through the agency of Sir Horace Plunkett. (It is at this point that literature converges, first of all, with agriculture, and with politics.) I will give you something of it in Moore's own words:

Years ago the idea of co-operation overtook Plunkett in America. It is unnecessary to inquire out whether he had seen co-operation at work in America, or had read a book in America, or had spoken to somebody in America, or had dreamed a dream in America. Suffice it to say that he hurried home, certain of himself as the redeemer that Ireland was waiting for, and at more than a hundred meetings he told the farmers that through co-operation they would be able to get unadulterated manure at forty percent less than they were paying the gombeen man for rubbish. At more than a hundred meetings he told the farmers that a foreign country was exploiting the dairy industry that rightly belonged to Ireland, and that the Dane was doing this successfully because he had learnt to do his own business for himself - a very simple idea, almost a platitude, but Plunkett had the courage of his platitudes, and preached them in and out of season, without, however, making a single convert. Sometime after he chanced however on Anderson, a man with a gift of organization and an exact knowledge of Irish rural life, two things Plunkett did not possess, but which he knew were necessary for his enterprise. Away they went together, and they preached, and they preached, and back they came together to Dublin, feeling that something was wanting, something which they had not gotten.[1]

The sequel is quite charming: and of some interest in relation to the eternal problem of the incursion of the poet into the world of action. (We may think, at random, of Sophocles, Chaucer, Surrey,

1. *Salve,* p. 60.

Raleigh, Milton, Pryor, Coleridge, Shelley; and, of course, Yeats himself
as Senator of the Irish Free State in 1926.) Anyway –

> 'Plunkett chanted the litany of the economic men and the
> uneconomic holding, and when he had finished Anderson
> chanted the litany of the uneconomic men and the economic
> holding, and this continued until their chants brought out of
> the brushwood a tall figure, wearing a long black cloak, with a
> manuscript sticking out of the pocket. He asked them what
> they were trying to do, and they said, "Trying to revive
> Ireland." "But Ireland is deaf," he answered, "She is deaf to
> your economics, for you do not know her folk-tales, and can-
> not croon them by the firesides."[1]

So Yeats went off as the poet who could sell co-operatives to the
peasantry, and spoke with Plunkett and Anderson at their agricultural
meetings: not, according to Moore's wicked wit, too successfully: for
in a certain speech he alluded to the 'boar without bristles that . . .
went away into the East, rooting the sun and the moon out of the sky';
and this did not go down too well because some of the audience had
lost heavily through selling their pigs co-operatively. Anyway, the Irish
Agriculture Organization Society decided that Yeats wasn't their man;
and on Yeats's recommendation they got hold of the poet-accountant
A.E.:

> . . . They saw a tall, thin man, overflowing with wild humour;
> the ends of his eyes went up and he seemed to them like a
> kindly satyr, something that had not yet experienced civiliza-
> tion, for the first stipulation was that he should not receive
> more than three pounds a week. No man's work, according to
> him, was worth more.'[2]

§viii

What remains? a brilliant mind, and a wasted life: perhaps, as Yeats said
of Edward Martyn, the 'sketch of a great man'. His reputation is, or
was, greater on the continent than in England or in Ireland. He had
shrewdness, wit and a measure of taste, but he could never resist the
chance of dramatizing himself, on every occasion; even to the point of
vulgarity and embarrassment. The delicately-textured prose does not
remain for long without its paradoxes, more subtly concealed than
Shaw's, more profound than that of Wilde. *Hail and Farewell* was
intended to be a sort of epitome of himself, his friends, Ireland, his
enemies, seen through a sharply-defining lens; but it is a book that is
essentially lacking in discipline. Yeats tells how the age was waiting for
'a sacred book'; of which the pallid shadows might have been *Axel,* or
Pater's *Marius,* or his own Order of the Golden Dawn. No

1. *Salve,* pp.60-61.
2. *Ibid.* p.63.

one could describe Moore as a prophet. Together with Yeats's *Dramatis Personae, Hail and Farewell* provides an indispensable background for the study of the time: a background (for both) full of inaccuracies, distortions, and of the malice that bred 'in his blind bitter town'.

Today one wonders why personal invective should have sunk so low, and what useful purpose it served when it outran so far the bounds of literary decorum. Yeats described Moore's body as 'insinuating, unflowing, circulative, curricular, pop-eyed': a covey of very ill-assorted epithets. Moore described his cousin Martyn on the train to Bayreuth:

> There he was − huge and puffy, his back to the engine, his belly curling splendidly between his short fat thighs, his straw hat perched on the top of his head, broader at the base than at the crown, a string dangling from it.[1]

Of Bernard de Lopez:

> . . . 'anything less literary than his appearance it is impossible to imagine: two piggy eyes set on either side of a large well shaped nose; two little stunted legs that toddled forward quickly to meet me, and two little warm fat hands that often held mine too long for comfort.'[2]

The accounts of his love-affairs are almost invariably embarrassing:

> . . .'It was not till several months after parting with Doris that I began to reconsider the important question − important, for no man lives who can say he is not interested in the question when a man should begin to try − how shall I put it? Well, to avoid unplatonic love encounters. But is an encounter ever platonic? A question for grammarians, for me it is to tell that a few months after my return to Dublin a lady called to see my pictures, and that the encounter of our lips sent the blood rushing to my head, and so violently that for ten minutes I lay where I had fallen on the sofa, holding my splitting temples. My time for love encounters is over, I said, reaching out my hand to her sadly . . . She was too frightened to answer, and after proposing a glass of water was glad to get away out of the house'.[3]

What, one wonders, went wrong? Was there some basic vulgarity in Moore which produced this zest for malice, even malice towards his own brother? Was it an overweening desire for the limelight − in the accounts of his amours, even at his own dinner-parties − which went back to an unhappy childhood? and that made him change his religion and attack his own tradition with all the repetitive indignation of the convert? What made the oval pallid face, with the protuberant pale blue eyes, so attractive to women? How many of his mistresses were carried

1. *Ave*, p.128.
2. *Vale*, p.77.
3. *Ibid*, p.207.

in his brain? Yet against all this we must set the birthday message with which I began this lecture; the tenderness of *A Drama in Muslin*, the compassion of many of the short stories, the courage of *Esther Waters*, the noble and translucent atmosphere of the New Testament and of Palestine in *The Brook Kerith*.

XI

J. M. SYNGE: A RECONSIDERATION

§i

I am very conscious of the honour you have done me in inviting me to give this Trinity Monday Discourse;[1] in the University with which my own family connections go back to the later years of the Seventeenth Century, and of which I have for six years been a member, however unworthy, by adoption and grace. You have asked that the Discourse should concern one of your many distinguished alumni, whose centenary is now being celebrated. A little more than a month ago there was indeed the official celebration here: at which again I had the honour to deliver a paper; by request, and a little against my inclinations, upon Synge's Prose Writings. We should perhaps pause for a moment to consider the nature of literary centenaries. In the last few years there have been many of them: Yeats, Wordsworth, Synge, Dickens. No scholar would refuse to attribute to them much that is of value even in these gatherings of the critical eagles. New facts are brought to light; new scholars make or mar their reputations; biographers beat once again the bones of the buried, with results that are not always decorous or good-mannered. One who has taught literary history for a good many years may perhaps be forgiven some measure of cynicism; for it is not easy to predict (whatever one's own certainties and loyalties) the vagaries of literary reputation a century or so hence.

But in our own time there seems to be some sort of pattern that we may discern. A great man dies. At once there is a host of telegrams to the Sorbonne, for that University has a rule that candidates for doctoral theses may not write of the still-living, only of the dead. (We are told that these have no rights). The long-prepared obituary notices are brought out from the files. A hundred journals and magazines print their stored articles on the victor-victim. Rumours, not all credible or creditable, assume their many tongues. Not infrequently these are substantiated by discoveries; of letters, juvenilia, sometimes of the work which a writer wished to conceal but which he had not been wise enough to destroy utterly. The grim evaluation and revaluation begins. And we remember Pope:

> If time improve our wit as well as wine,
> Say at what age a poet grows divine?
> Shall we, or shall we not, account him so
> Who died perhaps, an hundred years ago?
> End all dispute; and fix the year precise
> When British bards begin t' immortalize?

1. 7 June 1971.

"Who lasts a century can have no flaw,
I hold that wit a Classic, good in law" ... [1]

John Synge, who died young, has been in his grave for half a
century. The Irish Literary Renaissance, in which he is one of the
four great figures, has long passed over us. Perhaps, as I think, we
are now aware of its

melancholy long withdrawing roar

or, perhaps more accurately — there is now much economic or fiscal
poetry in this City —

The rattle of pebbles on the shore
Under the receding wave.

Which terminal dates should we fix for its ending? His death in 1909, or
Yeats's thirty years later? The Easter Rising, or the death of Lady
Gregory, and the end of that 'grammar school of courtesies' at Coole?
That is the business, in a multitude of Universities, of what James
Stephens called 'the professors whose mouths are gorged with sawdust';
for whatever dates we give to our period it is rich, varied, and deceptively
simple to teach and to examine at undergraduate levels. But surely there
was never a 'period' when politics, religion, national and sociological
ideals intertwined with such complexity. For evidence we need go no further than the Yeats International Summer School of 1970; where Yeats,
Synge and Lady Gregory were stigmatized by a group interested in
disruption of more academic deliberations as 'the unholy trinity', and
your own most important living poet[2] was dismissed as a Fascist and
Ireland's Public Enemy No. 1. And as the semi-literate propaganda was
handed out on the steps of the Town Hall one was reminded irresistibly
of the notorious counterblast to The Countess Cathleen, 'Souls for Gold'.
Then as now one was doubtful how much of the offending literature
the protesters had actually read. It is perhaps fortunate for my purpose
this morning that this complexity is less significant in the work of
Synge that in that of Yeats, Joyce and Shaw. And I remind myself that
this (by your invitation) is a *discourse,* a rare and to me a noble word,
with strong Eighteenth Century and even ecclesiastical overtones. My
task, as I see it, is to offer you some sort of perspective.

§ii

Let us begin with what Yeats called 'detractions'. Synge was at best a
very minor poet. Much of his work is influenced by Wordsworth,
both in technique, subject, spirit; and it is suffused with a Wordsorthian
melancholy that often becomes morbid. Out of the mass of the poems
we might pause on three of four ballad-like pieces, notable for a
fierce energy, written in conformity with his theory set out in the *Preface.*

1. 'Epistle to Augustus'
2. Brendan Kennelly

It is a challenge to Victorian sentimentality, a plea for a return to realism, even brutaility: "but it is the timber of poetry that wears most surely, and there is no timber that has not strong roots among the clay and worms".[1] Here his allegiance is not to Wordsworth, but to Villon, Shakespeare, Nash, Ben Jonson, Donne; we may remember that Yeats, in a famous letter to Grierson, speaks of the revelation of the primitive Eden that Donne had shown to him.[2]. His aesthetic (which, perhaps fortunately, is not strongly obtrusive) seems to be conditioned largely by Pater, and by Symbolist and Decadent doctrine:

When this atmosphere of humanity is felt in the place where it has been evolved, one's whole being seems to be surrounded by a scheme of exquisitely arranged sensations that have no analogue except in some services of religion or in certain projects of art we owe to Wagner and Mallarmé.[3]

Synge's prose rests mainly in two reflective books of travel and observation: *The Aran Islands* and *In Wicklow, West Kerry and Connemara*. They are of considerable personal interest, and they remain indispensable as setting out for us the sources of thought, plot, even the phraseology of many of the plays. The 'occasional' articles, commissioned by *The Manchester Guardian* and illustrated by his travelling-companion Jack B. Yeats, are competent and interesting journalism. But much of the prose-writing is, to use the term C.S. Lewis used of the Sixteenth Century, 'drab'; it avoids any suggestion of virtuosity, and only occasionally shows the patient, acute and dramatic powers of observation that are apparent in the plays. Synge did not do for Aran what Maurice O'Sullivan or Tomás O'Croghan did in *Twenty Years A-Growing* and in *The Islandman:* and one could name several contemporary books of travel that remain longer in the memory.

And I think that in any event Synge owed more to his boyhood in Wicklow and south Dublin than to the Aran experience; just as the often-quoted debt to Pierre Loti seems likely to have been a less seminal influence than Anatole Le Braz and his Breton folklore.

Nor can Synge's critical writing compare, in scope and in depth, with that of his major contemporaries. It is confined to two slight *Prefaces* to *The Playboy* and *The Tinker's Wedding*. One of these contains the famous pleas for an anti-Ibsen drama that is to mirror what is 'superb and wild in reality' and for the speech out of wild places that was to be 'as fully flavoured as a nut or an apple'. The second plea, less effective, was for a sense of humour in a people, and in a town; the ability to laugh at themselves, in the traditional

1. Preface to *Poems*.
2. "His pendantry and his obscenity - the rock and the loam of his Eden - but make me the more certain that one who is but a man like us all has seen God." (To H.J.C. Grierson; Wade, *Letters*, p. 570).
3. *Prose*, p.102, n.1.

manner, when they were satirized. It was not a fruitful plea; many
years were to pass before *The Tinker's Wedding* could be performed in
Dublin. Perhaps it would have been better if a portion of the Dublin
audiences had shown themselves to be, like the people of Tiryns,[1]
incurably flippant.

$iii

It is on the plays that his reputation must rest. We have to consider
one tragedy, two near-tragedies, and two 'critical' comedies. In comparison with the output of Lady Gregory, the bulk is slight. But most
of it is work of astonishing quality and depth, as Lady Gregory's plays
are not. I am not aware of any adverse criticism of *Riders to the Sea*,
the only perfect 'miniature' tragedy in our language. It is a remarkable
example of sheer purity and economy of dramatic technique. It
exhibits, perhaps strangely, all the structural and traditional features of
great drama, and I need not labour the 'recognition' the 'reversal', the
choric elegy at the ending; whose qualities are enhanced by Vaughan
Williams's music. This purity is made possible by the integrity and universality of the theme of the Drowned Sailor, the Quiet and the Unquiet
Grave,[2] the certainty of the eventual sacrifice demanded by the Sea in
all parts of the world where men use it. The plot is too well known to
need rehearsal here. Only I ask your attention to the fidelity of observation, and the dramatic economy: which is indeed so compressed that
in the hurry and imprecision of a stage performance we may easily pass
it by. It is as if mysterious threads of meaning are being woven about
us. Why are the two horses red and grey, and why does the phantasm of
Michael ride the grey, and what is the connection (if there is any) with
the horses of *Ezekiel, Daniel, The Apocalypse?* How is this colour-con-
trast related to the red and grey cocks, the cock being linked to Theo-
pompus, the Herald of the Dead, that recur in certain of the Scottish
Ballads? Why does the phantasm of Michael have new clothes, new shoes
on his feet? Is this yet another instance of the 'quick' coming for the
dead, as in *Clerk Saunders?* By what craftsmanship are we confronted
(as in *Christ in the Carpenter's Shop,* for which Millais' sketch was on
Yeats's mantlepiece) with the 'fine white boards' for the coffin; and yet
Maurya, who has seen many coffins made, has forgotten the nails (with
all their assocciations) for this, the last of them? The rope that hangs on
the wall will serve as a bridle to take the horses to the fair; or in an island
funeral to lower the coffin 'into some wet crevice in the rocks', or even to
hold its frail sides together. The two girls find difficulty in undoing the
knot of the bundle of Michael's clothes. Synge had noted how quickly
cloth or fibre rotted in the Islands because of the salt-laden air, and it was
to be expected that the shrunken cord should be drawn tight; but in some

1. See Chapter VII
2. Horace, *Odes* 7: 28; and many of the Scottish Ballads.

corner of our minds we may be aware of this perennial imagery of 'that subtle knot, which makes us man'.[1] More obvious (but not less disturbing) is the imagery of the cake baked for the journey, that should be given to Bartley beside the spring well; and — this is an additional touch in the best production I have seen — one of the girls hastily wipes down with a cloth a table on which the cake has been baked, and on which the body of Bartley is to be laid.

It is never Synge's method to make this kind of imagery explicit; I am aware of it rather as a grey mist swirling about the borders of consciousness. Behind his technique there is, I believe, a profundity of reading and reference in a limited but well-meditated area of the classics: and that these authors are largely what I.A. Richards once selected for his great course at Harvard which some called 'the roots of the mountains'. We may rehearse them briefly: the Bible and the Liturgy; Shakespeare; Cervantes; Petrarch; Villon and Ronsard; Montaigne and Molière; Wordsworth, Shelley. And unlike Yeats, whose agile and voracious mind ranged so widely but I think superficially, Synge lived with his chosen authors; so that the references (shaded with subtlety in all kinds of ways) are yet integral with the dramatic statement.

Beyond most of the plays there is what I would call an epic perspective, hinted at rather than stated at a number of levels. Sometimes this quality is perceived in terms of a Homeric or Horatian simplicity. Maurya's
    No man at all can be living for ever, and we must be satisfied.
has resonances too familiar to need quotation. Men's conflict with the sea and with the hills is perennial. Behind Synge's sheep farmer is Wordsworth's *Michael,* and that climax of defeat:
    And never lifted up a single stone.
The shade of that heroic 'half-legendary' man, Patch Darcy, moves in the background of *The Shadow* as an example of magnificence of strength and wisdom, and perhaps of heroic love, and certainly of the macabre of death: he is
    eaten by crows . . . the Lord have mercy on him — in the year
    that's gone.
Once again we are reminded of Villon and the Scottish Ballads, and especially 'The Twa Corbies'.

I have referred to two of the plays as semi-tragedies. Like *Troilus and Cressida, Measure for Measure,* perhaps *A Winter's Tale* they are plays which include in themselves situations and characters which would not be out of place in a normal tragedy, but which are manipulated by the dramatist to provide an ending which leaves our judgements ambivalent or confused. At the end of *Troilus* heroics and anti-heroics

1. Donne: 'The Ecstasy'.

dissolve into bad and bawdy verse by Pandarus. At the end of *Measure for Measure* some 'judicial' remarks are made, but we wonder whether they do not leave the permissive society of Vienna much as it was before. And in *A Winter's Tale,* for all the critics' high talk — valid enough in certain contexts — of regenerative symbolism, we wonder whether the price of a dead son, an old courtier torn to pieces by a bear, a lady immured for sixteen years to provide a dramatic dénouement — where have the 'values' gone?

So, I imagine, of *In the Shadow of the Glen.* A corpse on a table, the horror of a woman's loneliness in the farm at the head of Glenmalure; a picture of greed and cowardice on the part of a would-be seducer, the small farmer of the plains (for the wooing of Nora is little short of that) and we end with the Tramp and Nora going out to the life of tramps or tinkers: she, clear-eyed, bitter, her heart cleft by the Tramp's words

> . . . But you've a fine bit of talk, stranger, and it's with
> yourself I'll go.

We can, I think, isolate the causes of offence to the moderately-riotous audiences of 1905, and we do well to remember Clement Scott's attack when Ibsen first came to London. Some are clear enough. Nora — I have seen her prototype in the West, as the Victorians saw Hedda Gabler and Nora Helmer in London — is the Irish 'unwomanly woman' unable to bear the situation which romantic Ireland, and perhaps her religious tradition, expected her to tolerate. There, too she revolts against her circumstances which arise primarily out of economic causes, of the marriage to the old man, who was always 'cold'. His very appearance is unpleasant. It is an archetypal situation, the January-May marriage. Restoration Comedy indeed attempts to right the balance by making seduction by a younger man tolerated, if not actually meritorious.[1] But to the Ireland of 1905 the thought of rebellion against the loveless marriage, loneliness, the unremitting tasks of the small farm, was, in this social class, inconceivable. And the wind, fog and rain, which acquire in the play mythical and malignant proportions, enhance the horror. Glenmalure offers none of the companionship of the clusters of houses, the visiting at night, that Synge noted on Aran.

There were other causes of offence: a woman left alone with a man, (this is to recur in *The Playboy)* the faint suggestion of a flighty woman who has already had clandestine meetings with Michael Dara, may even have had an intrigue with Patch Darcy — all these were repugnant to the Peasant Image which idealists from Goldsmith onwards had put forward; and which had been reinforced by the contemporary mythology of the absolute chastity and obedience of the women of the Isle of

---

1. Consider Dryden's eulogy of the profligate 'young monarchs' of the Stuart line.

Saints. But the springs of action were neither so complex nor so powerful as those which produced the *Playboy* riots.

§iv

Because protests, demonstrations, mob violence are of particular
interest today, even in most ancient universities, we may examine the
Playboy happenings in some detail. In general terms we are familiar with
what psychologists, anthropologists and zoologists call 'displacement activities'.[1] Acts of racial or political violence become the channels
for some more profound malaise. The wife (we are told) who smashes a
vase to pieces in a tantrum perceives in it the shattering of her husband's
skull. The undergraduate who riots on the grounds of 'idealism' may be
'displacing' his dislike of examinations, or of his teachers, or of whatever government is in power, in his own country or elsewhere. If
he riots in the name of morality or convention the pretext may be of
the most ridiculous; such as the repeated anarchy in the theatre over the
run-on Alexandrine of Victor Hugo's *Hernani*.[2]

The *Playboy* riots took place in the week following 24 January 1907.
They are of immense importance in the history of the Irish Theatre. I
myself believe that they accelerated Synge's death, as did the notorious
review in the *Quarterly* for Keats. They are, perhaps, the first cloudings
that herald the dark night of Yeats, and of the Abbey: the period that
begins with 1909 and comes to its fruitful dawn in Yeats's bitter volume,
Responsibilities. They were projected into the Abbey Players' visit to
America, but here they were more organized and political, and even more
aimless. We may remember that two telegrams were sent that first night;
the first that all was well, no morality outraged; the second —
     Audience broke up in disorder at the word shift.
We may consider the whole phrase. Christy Mahon is wooing Pegeen. He
speaks of "a drift of chosen females, standing in their shifts itself, maybe from this point to the Eastern world". It is worth attempting a
little exegesis. We may first note, but discard, George Moore's ingenious
suggestion that the real cause of offence was the bloody bandage round
Old Mahon's head; the response to this would be no more than an
Aristotelian 'recognition' — 'Ah, that is he.' Some of the audience might
have known that the word 'drift' was applicable to a collection of heifers.
The woman-cow comparison is an image of abuse in many languages. To
a Mayo man the Eastern world may have been Dublin, but more likely
there were some vague associations with *The Arabian Nights Entertain-
ments;* it is not impossible that some of the Dublin audience were familiar
with that widely-circulated piece of Victorian pornography, *The Lust-*

1. See *e.g.*, Morris, *The Naked Ape.*
2. 'Sera-ce déjà lui? C'est bien à l'escalier
   Dérobé.'

ful Turk. 'Shift' was in any event a key-word to the improprieties; we remember Bloom of Ulysses, and perhaps Synge's letter to Stephen McKenna: "I have as you know perambulated a good deal of Ireland in my thirty years and if I were to tell, which Heaven forbid, all the sex horrors I have seen I could a tale unfold that would wither up your blood."[1] Some of the apologetics were ingenious. Pegeen was being forced to marry Shawn Keogh because there was no one better left in the district (this was the fault of emigration, and hence of the government); alternatively, Shawn Keogh was 'a tubercle Koch's disease man'. Yet again, Christy Mahon was a sexual melancholic.[2]

But the phrase was surely no more than a catalyst or point of discharge for a cumulative uneasiness that must have been building up throughout the play: and memories of the immorality of *The Shadow,* and a phrase that might have seemed to reflect upon the infallibility of the priesthood[3] from *Riders to the Sea:*

Didn't the young priest say the Almighty God won't leave her destitute with no son living?

. . . It's little the like of him knows of the sea . . .

And as if to emphasize the point this is the phrase that Nora has quoted from her brother at the onset of the play;

"Herself does be saying prayers half through the night, and the Almighty God won't leave her destitute," says he, "with no son living".

But in *The Playboy* the goading phrases start early in the play, and they continue throughout. I want this morning to gesture towards my own view of Synge as the anti-clerical; the agnostic, of a long lineage of churchmen, turned quasi-pantheist; the critical intelligence of the 1890s as developed in France directed, in the fashion of Shakespeare and Molière, against certain practices of the Church. It is common knowledge that he rejected the tradition of his family: that his reading of the Saints (which led him momentarily to the verge of faith)[4] was rejected in Brittany; and that, in Dublin and in America, he was widely accused of blasphemy. From the standpoint of an Irish audience of the first decade of our century, without a tradition in drama of licensed satire of the church and it ministries, there was much justification. (We may imagine the comments of Irish journalism of the 1900s on *The Tale of a Tub.)* But Synge's satire is mild, even benign, compared with that of George Moore and his successor, Joyce. In the *Preface* to *The Tinker's Wedding* Synge had pleaded for a sense of humour, of proportion, that belongs

1. *Letters,* Synge to McKenna, ed. A.Saddlemyer
   Massachusetts Review, Vol. V, p.281.

2. James Kilroy, *The Playboy Riots,* (Dolmen, 1971).

3. Lady Gregory asserted that "the Irish newspapers were like truffle dogs in their hunt for heresy".

4. *Prose,* p.31.

more to the Fifteenth and Sixteenth Centuries. It seems likely that such
attitudes are predominantly southern — witness Chaucer — and European,
and did not appeal to an Ireland that was still provincial and acutely self-
conscious.

We may recall what seems to me one probable cause of offence. Pious
expletives and invocations are common in the talk of our people in the
West:

> "Where now will you meet the like of . . . or Marcus Quin,
> God rest him, got six months for maiming ewes, and he a great
> warrant to tell stories of holy Ireland till he'd have the old-
> women shedding down tears about their feet."

Shawn Keogh is enjoined to remain in the shebeen to guard the chastity
of Pegeen:

> Don't stop me, Michael James. Let me out of that door, I'm
> saying, for the love of the Almighty God. Let me out. Let me out
> of it, and may God grant you His indulgence in the hour of
> need.
> Is it killed your father?
> With the help of God I did, surely, and that the Holy Immac-
> ulate Mother may intercede for his soul.

More subtly, perhaps (for the Widow has been herself rejected).

> Aid me for to win Pegeen . . . Aid me for to win her, and I'll
> be asking God to stretch a hand to you in the hour of death,
> and lead you short cuts through the Meadows of Ease, and up
> the floor of Heaven to the Footstool of the Virgin's son.
> *Widow Quin:* There's praying!

We might multiply these instances: Shawn's collocation "Oh, Father
Reilly and the Saints of God!"; the parodied benediction that the
drunken Michael pronounces over his daughter and the Playboy. There
is hardly an aspect of the play that was not denounced: and yet there
was some praise for Synge's insight. But the sense of outraged nationalism
was apparent everywhere. Clearly there were political factors of some
complexity. One member of the audience objected that he was not
allowed to speak 'although I am a labour member'.[1] Patriotic songs and
'Vociferations in Gaelic' vied with counter-efforts by the Trinity students,
to some of whom Yeats had given free tickets. 'A low-sized Englishman
in the stalls, who was an upholder of the play, got into an altercation with
a young gentleman in the pit who entertained diametrically opposite
views'.[2] But at least one of the Dublin critics, Patrick Kenny, had
something vital to say:

> . . . "I cannot but admire the moral courage of the man who
> has shot *(sic)* his dreadful searchlight into our cherished

1. *Kilroy op. cit.* p.27.
2. *Ibid.* p.44.

accumulation of social skeletons . . . It is the revolt of Human
Nature against the terrors ever inflicted on it in Connacht,
and in some subtle way of his own the dramatist has succeeded
in realizing the distinction; so that even when the guilt is
confessed, we cannot accept 'The Playboy' quite as a murderer,
and we are driven back to the influences of his environment, for
the origin of his responsibility . . . "[1]

It is clear that national susceptibilities were ready to be exacerbated, not
only by the play itself but by questions of religion, politics, and alarm
over the state of the rural population. The rumour had gone round
of a general immorality in the play. There was no need, therefore, to
have read it. The patriotic songs, and the pleasantly-termed 'vociferations
in Gaelic' are classic instances of the familiar displacement activity,
wholly oblique to the ostensible subject. Moralists have observed that
each age selects a specific vice against which to crusade. We may quote
Yeats's epigram 'On Hearing that the Students of our New University have
joined the Agitation against immoral literature.' (This must be among the
longest poetic titles on record: it is pleasant to see that in the Princeton
Concordance, for which the computer would accept no title of more
than fourteen letters, it becomes *'Students Agit'*.)

> Where, where but here have Pride and Truth,
> That long to give themselves for wage,
> To shake their wicked sides at youth
> Restraining reckless middle-age?

Violent preoccupations have seldom been conducive, in history, to a
sense of humour.

I have mentioned the European background and, as I see it, its
effect in liberating a national literature from undue self-conscious-
ness. Synge himself said, "It may be hinted . . . that there are several
sides to *The Playboy.*" There are. One possible perspective is — following,
perhaps, the example of James Joyce — to regard it as a kind of comic
Odyssey transplanted to Connaught: in which Pegeen is Nausicaa, the
bevy of giggling girls her maidens, and Michael is the king her father.
There is the hospitality to the wandering travel-stained hero, the open
wooing of him, the triumphant games on the strand, and the archetypal
conflict of two women competing for one man; there is the departure of
the hero, and the woman's utter despair. ('Dido and her Aeneas' may
also be relevant in the pattern):

> Oh, my grief, I've lost him surely. I've lost the only Playboy
> of the Western World.

Turn this many-faceted crystal again, and it becomes a semi-parody of
the Celtic heroic cycles: of the violent hero who attains his stature by
giving good blows, and is diminished when it is proved that the blow

1. *Kilroy*, pp.37-39.

is a poor one. And as the epic narrative becomes subject to improvement the violence increases in those primary virtues of epic ferocity, courage and strength.

"There are several sides to *The Playboy*." It is a satire, an expression of a fierce Dionysiac gaiety; it is at times brutal and cruel; it can rise to lyric heights. But it is, like *The Shadow* and *The Well of the Saints* and perhaps *The Tinker's Wedding*, 'free' comedy that verges upon, and retreats from, in its own intrinsic rhythms, 'great' comedy. (I use the terms of Bonamy Dobrée.) It is 'free' because the problems which it raises are left in balance or tension when the curtain falls; it can be 'great' because it seems, in some indefinable manner, to be a significant mirror of a world. It is 'free' as *Measure for Measure* and *A Winter's Tale* are free.

And here we may have in part the reason for the rejection in Dublin and in America. The history of the Irish theatre of the Nineteenth Century is very largely that of melodrama, of closed-circuit comedy, of standard character-types, of predictable moralized endings. Synge is perpetually raising problems — not what he calls (no doubt referring to Ibsen) "the dregs of many seedy problems", but with issues which are of such importance that their resolution lies only in their total statement. If an audience has grown accustomed to a drama in which the intellectual pattern is tied up, neatly and finally, it will not tolerate with any patience a so-called comedy in which the crooked questions are left open. Is Oswald in *Ghosts* given the poison by his mother? Does Nora Helmer return to the Doll's House after that final slam of the door? (The German producer found it intolerable that a good bourgeois wife should not, and altered the ending accordingly.) Are blindness and illusion preferable to sight and disillusion? Under what circumstances may a young wife desert an aged husband? What would a lesser dramatist have made of an act showing Nora and her Tramp, a year later, after walking the roads?

$v

There remains the question of Synge's language, so frequently and so bitterly attacked. The criticisms range between St. John Ervine's description of him as 'a faker of peasant speech' and the qualified praise of T.S. Eliot; whose reservation was that his language was useful only for Synge's type of drama, and that the mine was narrow-veined and easily worked out. I think this is true; but is it not true also of any innovation? And to say that he 'invented it' is nonsense.

Here I can only record my own opinion

Synge's dramatic language is subject to the eternal dramatic laws. It is based on the idiom and rhythms of the speech that he had known in his boyhood in Dublin and Wicklow. On these Gaelic constructions, and more subtle intonations, float (as it were) the waves of Tudor English, reinforced by his own reading in Marlowe, Shakespeare, Ben Jonson, Nashe. Dr. Nicholas Grene[1] has demonstrated the ease with which passages can be translated into Irish. There seems to be room for investigation of the rhythmic qualities involved; in particular, the use of the cadence. I believe that we can also discern, though faintly, traces of French constructions. Like all dramatic speech it is heightened, intensified, compressed. We may discern in it Biblical usages and cadences, as in Shakespeare's prose. It is not universally adaptable: in *Deirdre*, except for those speeches which reflect and maintain moments of high emotion, it seems to me to fail. It is fatally easy to parody, as in *The Mist that does be on the Bog*. It can degenerate into the manière dictum known as 'Kiltartanese'. We need not take seriously George Moore's suggestion, in the Preface to *The Untilled Field*, that his own prose provided the seminal model for Synge. Its failure in that mode can be seen at its worst in Lady Gregory's use of her idiom to write religious drama, notably the plays on the Captivity in Egypt[2] and on the Crucifixion.[3] (Yeats was wiser in *Calvary* and *The Resurrection*.)

In Synge himself it is, I think, variable in quality; and this quality is probably related to the care with which he revised his work. There are touches of *opus alexandrinum* which I myself could wish away, in some of *The Playboy* speeches. I find the first act of *Deirdre* flat and contrived. It is when the emotion rises under the pressures of approaching despair that he seems to me sure-footed, moving, with a lyric integrity, drawing upon 'the masterful images' that rise from a poet's imagination — and that imagination much possessed by death — to serve him. For it is the images that are rooted in the rich simplicity of the countryside, and whose rhythms stand comparison with those of the King James Bible, that achieve greatness. It is never very easy to speak of matters like these, isolated from their settings in the plays, but I am going to ask you to consider two contrasting passages. They are, very roughly, comparable in tone and intention. The first is from Lady Gregory's *Kincora:* [4]

> It is not to banishment they will be sent. I will go meet my
> own death with them, with Sitric and Maelmora. I will not go
> on living after them. My heart will break in me, and I will
> die! I is soon we will all be in the ground together.

This is adequate but wholly commonplace; we could have done without the exclamation mark (however a producer might interpret it) after "and I will die!". Some of the phrases are nearly if not quite exhausted.

1. In a yet unpublished thesis. (1972).
2. *The Deliverer.*
3. *The Story brought by Brigit.*
4. *Collected Plays,* Vol. II, p.68.

By contrast, this:

> I have put away sorrow like a shoe that is worn out and muddy, for it is I have had a life that will be envied by great companies. It was not by a low birth I made kings uneasy, and they sitting in the halls of Emain. It was not a low thing to be chosen by Conchubor, who was wise, and Naishi had no match for bravery. It is not a small thing to be rid of grey hairs, and the loosening of the teeth. It was the choice of lives we had in the clear woods, and in the grave we're safe, surely . . .

We may look at this more closely.

"Sorrow like a shoe that is worn out and muddy" — there are reverberations (rather than echoes) from the *Psalms*[1] as well as *Deuteronomy;*[2] for the shoe is the base thing, worthless ('Over Edom have I cast out my shoe'); but also that which is removed when one enters a holy place. 'Muddy' is both of travel, the long journey from Alban, and perhaps the earthly garment, the 'muddy vesture of decay'[3]. Deirdre's life will be 'envied by great companies': royal courts and gatherings, but with the subsidiary sense of 'companies', married companionship. Her beauty has made kings 'uneasy': we are brought up sharply by the deliberate understatement. The next two sentences take on an incantatory tone. They are sanctioned by medieval rhetorical devices. Then the vivid 'grey hairs' (also with Biblical overtones), and, if we accept the Rabbinic exegis, of *Ecclesiastes* 12:4.[4] We may remember the less effective adaptation by Yeats:

> What made us dream that he could comb grey hair?[5]

And with the last phrase we have shifted from the 'classical' cadences[6] of the first four chapters of the speech, cadences which depend on the light final syllable, and change to the so-called 'English' type.

The diction, as I have suggested, seems to me uneven. I find the language of *Riders* flawless, restrained, and employed with the tact and dignity that reminds us of plainsong. I could, I think, do without the much-praised passage in *The Playboy:*

> If the mitred bishops seen you that time, they'd be the like of the holy prophets, I'm thinking, do be straining the bars of Paradise to lay eyes on the Lady Helen of Troy, and she abroad, pacing backwards and forwards, with a nosegay on her golden shawl.

1. *e.g.* 60:8, 109:8.
2. *e.g.* 25:10
3. *e,g. The Merchant of Venice,* V.1.64.
4. 'And the doors shall be shut in the streets, when the sound of the grinding is low.'
5. *In Memory of Major Robert Gregory.*
6. For a more general discussion, see my Introduction to the *Collected Works* (1963) pp.16ff.

This seems to me at once contrived and derivative; whereas the passage that immediately precedes it seems to work:

> It's little you'll think if my love's a poacher's, or an earl's itself, when you'll feel my two hands stretched around you, and and I squeezing kisses on your puckered lips, till I'd feel a kind of pity for the Lord God is all ages sitting lonesome in His golden chair.

because behind there is Synge's own poem,[1] and behind that the Greek. Again, the diction seems supremely effective in vituperation, and in speeches which are not developed at any great length; and in which Synge's talent for the pregnant word or phrase has full scope –

> – where you'd hear a voice kissing and talking deep love in every shadow of the ditch.

> – dreading that young gaffer who'd capsize the stars.

(Compare Roy Campbell's *The Flaming Terrapin:*

> Her shadow smeared the white moon black: her spars Round wild horizons buffeted the stars.)

> – You'd a right to throw him on the crupper of a Kerry mule and drive him westwards, like holy Joseph,[2] in the days gone by.

The confused memory of an icon of the Flight into Egypt? He did, as T.S. Eliot said, create a new diction that was an adequate vehicle only for his subject matter.

It has, in the hands of his imitators, grave disadvantages. It is fatally easy to write without distinction. The inversions, the excessive use of present participles, and, even worse, the attempts to suggest accent by spelling, can easily become irritating and ineffective. The truth is, I believe, that Synge deliberately created a poetic diction that was based on what he had heard; in conformity with his own desire for wildness, energy, and Marlovian 'high astounding terms'. I believe it to be most effective in crisp simple dialogue and, above all, in passages where the prevalent tone is elegiac or defiant. A great playwright has his ear attuned to the histrionic or metaphysical phrases that may still be heard; but whose incidence, for obvious reasons, is much less now than it was in the early 1900s.

§vi

My real theme this morning is the ambivalence of Synge's outlook; which I see as being the force behind his irony and his anticlericalism, his understanding and compassion and intense apprehension of place. One of the heaviest stones thrown at him is the accusation of being Anglo-Irish, and no true Irishman. He did not mirror the true Ireland (who has ever dared to do this?). He maligned her peasantry. He should have

1. 'Dread'.
2. I do not think the potential blasphemy is often noticed.

written in Irish (can we name a play that has achieved an international reputation in that medium?) And this, and the journalism of the 1905-9 period, (and even later), adds up to the accusation of some kind of betrayal. We recall the attacks made on Yeats, Lady Gregory, Lutyens, Lane, on similar but more complex indictments; and even the widely circulated lie that Synge's death was due, not to cancer, but to a disease resulting from an immoral life.[1] Lady Gregory was, as so often, prophetic: "We shall see Synge accepted as a wicked immortal, an invulnerable spirit who cannot be shot even with a silver bullet."

For we who are Anglo-Irish have faced both inwards and outwards. I do not mean that we have faced both ways. I do mean that we were committed, by birth, tradition, religion and perhaps politics, to a view of Ireland and her people that is necessarily distanced, selective, ambivalent; and this seems to be supported by the views, and even the conduct, of the writers themselves. We were, perhaps are, also committed to a distrust of and contempt for English stupidity and incompetence while admiring the capacity of English administration to impose law and justice. We were committed by an intense loyalty to the countryside, its beauty, the kindliness of its people. At the same time we were conscious of drunkenness, sloth, incompetence, of every sort of blackguardism that broke down boundaries, maimed cattle and burnt houses. For everything that was cultural we turned to England, and through England to Europe. Synge's characters might inveigh against the Boer War, the hanging judges, the poverty and distress in the West. That was the outcome of mismanagement, stupidity; but it was also — this Synge did not see clearly — the consequence of the wave of the economic depression of the last quarter of the Nineteenth Century, itself one of the many waves of the ground-swell of the two revolutions at the end of the Eighteenth.

He was not concerned with the politics of his Ireland. His protest on behalf of this peasant world is in part against the government, civil and ecclesiastical: but it is mainly a protest against the human situation. That in his view can be met in many ways; by stoicism, by laughter, by the 'nourishment of the imagination'. But behind it there is the oppression of humanity; by the cruelty of the sea, by the menace of the hill fogs; by the 'silent feet' of age; by the passing of all beauty. Behind it always there is the solitude, the quest for a love that it was his fate to find and to lose. Solitary, often morose, capable of being greatly moved to height and depth; loving passionately in the country of hill and wood and stream. And if (as I think) Yeats's image in "The Fisherman" and in "The Tower" is based on memories of Synge, I cannot do better (nor forge a stronger link with my own boyhood in Clare) than quote:

1. Lady Gregory to Yeats, 11 January 1912.

I leave both faith and pride
To young upstanding men
Climbing the mountain-side,
That under bursting dawn
They may drop a fly;
Being of that metal made
Before it was broken by
This sedentary trade.

XII
'THE BIG HOUSE'[1]
$i

This is a lecture, not an essay. Therefore I do not propose to document it as I go along; for that would be tedious, and, unless we were to do the reading together, would not be very profitable. And yet we should conjure up a long procession of writers whose work is germane to our subject, even if we do no more than name them. There would be much of Maria Edgeworth (some of you will have passed through Edgeworthstown on your road from Dublin): Banim, Lady Wilde, Lover, Lever; perhaps that most popular of Irish playwrights, Dion Boucicault; memoirs and letters beyond counting, from Sir Jonah Barrington in the Eighteenth Century to Sergeant Sullivan and *Anecdotes of the Connaught Circuit*. There would be Maxwell of *Wild Sports in the West*, W. R. LeFanu, the *Stories from Carleton* that Yeats edited, Lady Gregory's *Journals:*[2] and as we move into our own time there would be, among the most important, Joyce Cary of *Castle Corner*, Elizabeth Bowen, Cannon Hannay ('George Birmingham'), Lord Dunsany; and playwrights beyond number. We shall remember, too, the work of two of our friends who have lectured in Sligo, Edward Malins' *English Landscape and English Literature*,[3] Donald Torchiana's *Yeats and Georgian Ireland*. For "The Fall of the House" has been a dramatic subject from the Greek Theatre onwards; in miniature it is the fall of dynasties, of nations. It is a tragic wheel that turns incessantly. And just as Ireland's Renaissance, literary or political, may be seen as a kind of microcosm of larger movements in history, so the ending of a civilization (for my theme is nothing less) can, I think, be seen against what Sir Thomas Browne called 'the great mutations of the world'.

$ii

Go where you will throughout the length and breadth of Ireland, you will come at intervals, intervals which are seldom less than a couple of miles, and often a great deal more, on the traces of some large demesne. It will be apparent first, long before you come to its entrance, by a stone wall, sometimes of considerable height, in good, or, likelier, in bad repair. There are many things that do not love walls. This, is in fact, the 'compass of a pale', as Shakespeare would have called it, the park enclosure of Tudor England: designed to keep the deer (which were such an important item of the household economy) from wandering, and to keep poachers, like Shakespeare, out. Behind the wall there may well

---

1. Sligo, 1967.
2. And her newly-rediscovered autobiography, *Seventy Years.*
3. And his book now in preparation on the same theme in Ireland.

be screens of timber, now often untended, broken, 'hacked and wracked'; for firewood or rafters or malice. Some distance along the wall or paling will curve inwards, in a sort of funnel. There may be ornamental gates or their pillars, and there is certain to be a gate lodge. The design of that lodge will be Gothic or perhaps debased Georgian: for early in the Nineteenth Century competitions were set up for such 'ornaments to a gentleman's estate'.

The avenue that leads off the main road will be long, winding, perhaps as much as a mile; and you may see signs that it had been carefully landscaped when it was laid out. You will also see refractions at least of the theories of the Romantic Picturesque, of William Gilpin, 'Capability' Brown, Robert Adam.

The very title of the estate, sometimes of the locality, may seek to embody a Greek or Roman memory, for its owners would have been brought up with the Classics. There·may be bridges over a river, or an ornamental water, the curving track designed to reveal new 'beauties' as the traveller progressed. That avenue will probably be 'all grass today', though the hoof-beats of a ghostly rider may still be heard upon it (are not all ancient and disused roads subject to this haunting?) as in Yeats's *Purgatory*. This play is indeed in some sense my 'norm', perhaps text, for this essay.

Before you come to the house, or where it once was, the avenue will fork: one branch will lead to the stables and coach-houses, with all their ancillary buildings; hay barns, oat-lofts, all kinds of sheds, set in ordered structure round a big courtyard; for this was a horse-drawn economy. There will be outhouses and sheds for vast quantities of turf drawn in by horses, each September, from the bogs; a timber-shed, a saw-pit where the fallen trees of the woods are cut up for winter fuel. But the timber used for palings, gates, will not be oak, for this work is not planned, as in England, to outlast the generations. Look closely, and you will see other signs of improvisation.

Round another and smaller courtyard there will be rooms for coachmen, grooms, maids; a dairy and a laundry; a servants' hall where a dozen or more came to eat every day. It is, indeed, Elizabethan or Jacobean, on a greater or smaller scale: modified by Georgian or Regency wealth or taste or pride. We are aware of a self-contained economy such as that of Knole, Blenheim, Audley End, Madingley Hall in Cambridge, though the scale will be much smaller, the planning less precise and wise, the casual additions more eccentric. The buildings will be mainly lime-stone, perhaps covered with stucco. The warmth of brick, an alien mat-erial, will be rare, so that the dominant impression is one of grey tones. The generously-proportioned rooms may be Regency or late Adam, often with exquisite plaster-work in the cornices and mouldings. One is aware, too, that Victorian fashion and acquisitiveness had often overlaid the nobler ethos of the Eighteenth Century.

The Library we should have seen as the fruits of book-collecting tastes which ranged from say 1750 to 1880, and which probably reached its cultural peak round the turn of the century. There would be layers of the 'standard' authors, well-bound, solid: a good deal of history and biography: some theology (but this mainly earlier, of the great contemporaries of Bishop Berkeley). There would be family portraits, and perhaps some good copies, from France or Italy, of Old Masters. There might be a portrait by Hone, a landscape by Jack Yeats, a mystical painting by A.E. Yeats's description, though idealized, and founded on Lissadell, Markree, Roxborough, Coole, Tillyra, as they were in their prime, is not too far out:

> . . . Beloved books that famous hands have bound,
> Old marble heads, old pictures everywhere;
> Great rooms where travelled men and children found
> Content or joy; a last inheritor
> Where none has reigned that lacked a name and fame
> Or out of folly into folly came.

> A spot whereon the founders lived and died
> Seemed once more dear than life; ancestral trees,
> Or gardens rich in memory glorified
> Marriages, alliances and families,
> And every bride's ambition satisfied . . . [1]

One could go on quoting, for Yeats returns again and again to the dream that had taken so much of his 'heart and love'. From his 'Prayer for my Daughter' —

> And may her bridegroom bring her to a house
> Where all's accustomed, ceremonious . . .

The vision of an idealized Lissadell, Coole, Markree, is everywhere:

> Some violent bitter man, some powerful man
> Called architect and artist in, that they,
> Bitter and violent men, might rear in stone
> The sweetness that all longed for night and day,
> The gentleness none there had ever known . . . [2]

And on a smaller scale we remember that Robert Gregory (that epitome, in his eyes, of Renaissance man) had advised him and his bride over the restoration of The Tower:

> What other could so well have counselled us
> In all lovely intricacies of a house
> As he that practised or that understood
> All work in metal or in wood,
> In moulded plaster or in carven stone? [3]

1. 'Coole Park and Ballylee, 1931'.
2. 'Meditations in Time of Civil War'.
3. 'In Memory of Major Robert Gregory'.

Is there some memory — made ironical by history — of Psalm 74: 'A
man was famous according as he had lifted up axes upon the thick trees.
But now they break down the carved work thereof with axes and
hammers.'

$iii

And now it is essential to quote the famous passage from *Purgatory:*

Great people lived and died in this house;
Magistrates, colonels, members of Parliament,
Captains and Governors, and long ago
Men that had fought at Aughrim and the Boyne.
Some that had gone on Government work
To London or to India came home to die,
Or came from London every spring
To look at the may-blossom in the park.
They had loved the trees that he cut down
To pay what he had lost at cards
Or spent on horses, drink and women;
Had loved the house, had loved all
The intricate passages of the house,
But he killed the house; to kill a house
Where great men grew up, married, died,
I here declare a capital offence.

Yeats is thinking mainly of Coole; Sir William Gregory had been
Governor of Ceylon, and the founder of the family fortunes had been
a Director of the East India Company. But indeed one could
verify such a pattern from very many sources: the *Visitations of Ireland,*
the *Country Histories,* the older editions of *Burke's Landed Gentry
of Ireland,* from family vaults, from the tablets of Sligo or Mayo
churches.

How did people live in The Big House before it was killed, and what
manner of people were they? Because of their diversity, in time and race,
it is clearly impossible to give an answer that would be generally valid.
I shall try to keep, in the first place, to what is within my own experience,
and secondly what might be thought to be within the same compass
for the period of Yeats's own life. And even then we shall omit and
distort. First, some tentative generalizations.

The master of The Big House was, typically, either a landowner
living on the income of his land; or a servant of the state whose salary
or pension supplemented his income from property. Less frequently,
he had married an heiress; the fertile influx of American blood and
wealth that had given so much to England in the second half of the
Nineteenth Century had hardly touched Ireland. (We may think of a
time-lag of half a century or so, as in so many aspects of life). Many of
the big properties were hereditary; grants going back to the Tudors and
beyond, estates forfeited, for treason or rebellion, or as payment for the

hungry wars. Other landed properties had been built up by marriage: in Yeats's complacent words:

> Marriages, alliances and families,
> And every bride's ambition satisfied.

Yet other estates, land held by small farmers and often far removed from the seat of The Big House, had been acquired as a 'safe' investment, like the Irish Railway shares on which so many fortunes were lost. It was a form of capital investment that with all its disadvantages was widely accepted; perhaps in emulation of the English tradition, perhaps as giving a sense of 'belonging', sometimes to retain the sporting rights, often because the term 'landed gentry' still had a social significance.

It was a time of big families on the Victorian pattern; and we perceive a complicated and interesting train of cause and effect. The girls of the family were educated at home by a succession of governesses, themselves of no great academic achievement, in the lady-like virtues of music, needlework, French and amateur painting. Until 1914 it was rarely that they were sent away to school. A profession was nearly (but not quite) unthinkable. It was almost essential to see that they were married — we are back to Jane Austen's world — and they were most unlikely to get married without a 'fortune', dowry or jointure or some form of settlement. If the daughter ran away with a groom or tinker (as in *Purgatory*) that would put an end to ambition; but failing marriage, all that offered itself was a gradual acceptance of the status of family aunts, and perhaps a sort of terminal existence in a dower house. So it came about that many estates became encumbered with complicated marriage settlements, trusts of all kinds, and the raising of first or second mortgages on the 'property'. Such things were of little weight in Jane Austen's day, when death-duties were negligible and income tax did not exist. They mattered a great deal by 1912.

As regards the boys in the family there was an even more important consideration. When we read through the biographies of Irishmen of the Eighteenth and early Nineteenth Centuries, we are aware that they were usually educated at schools in Ireland; and these schools were clearly small but good. To these the sons of the gentry were often sent. Sometimes they were based on some local rectory; we remember that College livings, often remote, were presented to Fellows of Oxford and Cambridge Colleges when they vacated their Fellowships by marriage, and gave their learning to their pupils.

But by the mid-Nineteenth Century there is a striking change. The English Public Schools were developing rapidly. The new railways and steamships had brought them within reach even of the West. It seemed clear that they now provided the best preparation for entry into the Services, the Law, the Church, though I do not know what logic sent my great-grandfather and grandfather to Winchester, for that would have gone back far beyond our period. But I imagine that it was for some such reason that my uncles went to Sherborne and my father to Radley: even though there was a well-beaten track that returned to Trinity College, and back again to one of the English Inns of Court, before the traditional practice at the Irish Bar.

We may assess the gains and losses. No doubt some of the provincialisms were rubbed off the Irish schoolboy; and at Eton or Winchester or Westminster a whole new world was opened up. Perhaps there was some advantage for him in pitting his wits against the proverbially bovine Anglo-Saxon mind. It is also certain that his energies and his athletic powers found wider scope. The record of the services of Irishmen to many aspects of English life during the Nineteenth Century is impressive. As we should expect, for reasons of tradition and temperament, it is predominantly with the Army, the Navy, administration overseas and, to a lesser extent, with the Law.

It is, I believe, at this point that a characteristic schizophrenia was produced, or at least reinforced. Perhaps the watershed is the Act of Union of 1800; in which the Irish Parliament, through a mixture of corruption and folly, killed itself and with it the independence of Ireland. Much of the brilliance of English letters in the Eighteenth Century is due to the Irish element in English Society; even though the uncouth Irish nobleman, trying to cut a figure in London or Bath, had long been a theatrical figure of fun. All the opportunities in England were infinitely greater; Shaw's justification of himself in going to London is lucid and cogent. But it is the Irish schoolboy in England whom I have in mind: and his position (here I speak from experience) was interesting and sometimes painful.

For he was in a strange sense an alien, proud of his background and tradition, adjusting of necessity to a strange world. He was, like Yeats in 'the obscene bullying place' at Hammersmith, torn by nostalgia for the countryside and its people that he knew. He did not have, at least at first, the qualities that make for easy acceptance, for the establishment of identity, in an English school, He might be a fine horseman, a good shot and fisherman, handy with a boat; it was unlikely that he would be good at organized games, unless, indeed, he came from the society that centred round Dublin. In the holidays he moved into an entirely different world. To illustrate this we may quote an episode from Kipling's *Stalky & Co.* McTurk is "the mad Irishman" of the famous trio. The three boys have been trespassing, out of bounds, and are going through a tunnel in the furze of a Devonshire combe. A keeper fires at a fox that brushes past them. McTurk insists on going to the house to confront the angry owner, Colonel Dabney, who promptly accuses him of disturbing his pheasants.

'He choked with emotion. McTurk's heel tapped the lawn

and he stuttered a little – two sure signs that he was losing his temper. But why should he, the offender, be angry?

'Lo-look here, sir. Do-do you shoot foxes? Because if you don't, your keeper does. We've seen him! I do-don't care what you call us – but it's an awful thing. It's the ruin of good feelin' among neighbours. A ma-man ought to say once and for all how he stands about preservin'. It's worse than murder, because there's no legal remedy.' McTurk was quoting confusedly from his father, while the old gentleman made noises in his throat.

'Do you known who I am?' he gurgled at last; Stalky and Beetle quaking.

'No, Sorr, nor do I care if ye belonged to the Castle itself. Answer me now, as one gentleman to another. Do ye shoot foxes or do ye not?:

And four years before Stalky and Beetle had carefully kicked McTurk out of his Irish dialect! Assuredly he had gone mad or taken a sunstroke, and as assuredly he would be slain – once by the old gentleman and once by the Head. A public licking for the three was the least they could expect. Yet – if their eyes and ears were to be trusted – the old gentleman had collapsed. It might be a lull before the storm, but–

'I do not' He was still gurgling.

'Then you must sack your keeper. He's not fit to live in the same county with a God-fearin' fox. An' a vixen too – at this time o' year!'

'Did ye come up on purpose to tell me this?'

'Of course I did, ye silly man,' with a stamp of the foot. 'Would ye not have done as much for me if you'd seen that thing happen on my land, now?'

Forgotten – forgotten was the College and the decency due to elders! McTurk was treading again the barren purple mountains of the rainy West Coast, where in his holidays he was viceroy of four thousand naked acres, only son of a three-hundred-year-old house, lord of a crazy fishing-boat, and the idol of his father's shiftless tenantry. It was the landed man speaking to his equal – deep calling to deep – and the old man acknowledged the cry.

'I apologise,' said he. 'I apologise unreservedly – to you, and to the Old Country. Now, will you be good enough to tell me your story?'

For a second illustration we may quote from an admirable but forgotten novel, Lord Dunsany's *The Curse of the Wise Woman*. The son is a schoolboy home for the holidays from Eton. The family is a Catholic one: on the drawing-room table there is a fragment of the True Cross embedded in crystal. A raiding-party comes to shoot his father, who slips out, just in front of them, by a secret passage-way.

The raiders make the boy swear on the Cross that his father is not in
the house. He does so, and in his own sight damns his soul irrevocably.
Then they hear horse-hoofs on the avenue — that ominous and dramatic
sound[1]; his father has escaped. The raiders then turn friendly. The
geese are coming in at night to a certain bog: he ought to come up and
have a shot. As they turn to go the leader of the raiding-party gives him
a priceless piece of advice:

"And if it ever comes to it — and God knows the world's full
of trouble — *aim a foot in front of a man walking, at a hundred
yards.*"

I give you this story because it corresponds almost exactly with
my own boyhood experience; and the ballistics are accurate.

$iv

Violence there was in plenty, and that long before the Easter Rising
and its aftermath. And long before the Twenties it was a standard jest,
hearing a shot on a summer's evening, to say, 'There goes another
landlord.' Three known murderers lived within a few miles of my home.
I used as a boy to go snipe-shooting with one of them.

$v

It is now fashionable to talk and write as if The Big House were a
gloomy place, because of its Protestant-Puritan ethic. The protagonists
of this view often adduce the example of Synge's boyhood. But for
him the reasons were clear, and not least of them poor health and
religious conflicts. In its normal family life I do not think the House
differed from comparable family houses in England; that is, it depended
for its gaiety and vitality on the presence of young people. I know
of no evidence to the contrary. As I knew it the 'Protestant ethic' showed
itself chiefly in the practice of brief family prayers before breakfast, and,
if the weather was too bad to take the horses and coachman on the
long drive to church, the Master would read a brief service instead.

The household, as I have said, was semi-feudal. There was ample
domestic service. Wildish girls from the village would be brought in to
graduate upwards from scullery to parlour-maid, and eventually would
marry some worker on the estate, and settle down: having learnt at
least something of domestic economy from the Mistress of the House.
They provided excitement, comedy, an element of picturesqueness of
speech and behaviour: and all these with an intense loyalty.

I am going to quote from Somerville and Ross, *Experiences
of an Irish R.M.* for an admirable account of a party given by an old
lady, the famous Mrs. Knox:

Old Mrs. Knox received us in the library, where she was

1. as in *Macbeth* IV i. 139.

seated by a roaring turf fire, which lit the room a good deal
more effectively than the pair of candles that stood beside her
in tall silver candlesticks. Ceaseless and implacable growls
from under her chair indicated the presence of the woolly
dog. She talked with confounding culture of the books that
rose all around her to the ceiling; her evening dress was
accomplished by means of an additional white shawl, rather
dirtier than its congeners; as I took her into dinner she
quoted Virgil to me, and in the same breath screeched an
objurgation at a being whose matted head rose suddenly into
view from behind an ancient Chinese screen, as I have seen the
head of a Zulu woman peer over a bush.

Dinner was as incongruous as everything else. Detestable
soup in a splendid old silver tureen that was nearly as dark as
Robinson Crusoe's thumb; a perfect salmon, perfectly cooked
on a chipped kitchen dish; such cut glass as it is not easy to
find nowadays; sherry that, as Flurry subsequently remarked,
would burn the shell off an egg; and a bottle of port, draped
in immemorial cobwebs, and probably priceless.

Much of the comedy of Somerville and Ross, 'George Birmingham',
Dorothea Conyers, comes from this source. We need not question or be
self-righteous about it: the comedy of servants is as old as Terence and
Plautus, and Shakespeare makes much of it. There were gardeners,
coachmen, yard-boys; woodmen, gamekeepers, cattlemen and so
forth. George Moore relates that he spent much of his boyhood among
the people of Moore Hall, and comments on the excellence of their
spoken English. There were many indeterminate hangers-on. One of the
most picturesque I know of is described in that wild household of
Maxwell's cousin at Ballycroy in Erris;[1] then, in the 1840s, about as
wild and isolated a Big House as one could find. The establishment included a professional otter-hunter, with the emblems of otter and trident
embroidered on his smock. But indeed it was a flexible organization
of many-skilled people. In our local village the Big House provided
'trade' for the smith, harness-maker, carpenter (who was also the under-
taker), general store, possibly a stone-mason; these in addition to the
string of public-houses which we were strongly forbidden to visit. If there
were what in England would be called a 'home farm', at some distance
from the house, it made little or no money but produced oats
and hay for the horses, pigs for home-cured bacon, milk and
butter, poultry and eggs. If times were good the cattle and sheep might
go some way towards paying the wages of the men. But it was seldom
that farming of this sort paid. And you will find today the owner of the
Big House struggling, with inadequate help, to 'keep the place going',
precisely as Lady Gregory struggled vainly to keep Coole Park intact

1. *Wild Sports of the West.*

for her grandchildren. The events set out in her *Journals* of the late 1920s are a type-history of what happened so often: the slow erosion of the estate. The tactics go back to the agrarian troubles of the last century. Walls and fences would be torn down at night: cattle and horses turned loose or maimed. Haystacks and ricks would be burnt, young plantations felled. With them went the traditional warnings, the coffin badly drawn in red ink, the week's grace to leave under threat of shooting. And departure was often followed by burning: those who could afford to leave were well advised to do so. So often you read in *Burke's Landed Gentry* " — formerly of — ". And the ex-Irish landlord, lacking a title or some special achievement, would cut a very small figure in his new setting.

§vi
"But he killed the house . . . "

I have in my possession an edition of John Lloyd's *A Short Tour, Or an Impartial and Accurate Description of the County of Clare,* 1793. Lloyd was a 'hedge-schoolmaster' of the time. His book contains descriptions of all the 'gentlemens' seats' that he visited. There is a long and rather bad poem in 'heroick' couplets on the death of my great-grandfather, William Henn. We could follow Lloyd's tour today and point out the ruins of these houses. In more recent times there were in 1914 twenty-eight such houses in the County. By 1922 four were left standing. And this holocaust had no connection with the burning of the houses of the Irish Free State Senators in 1921-22; among them that of Oliver St. John Gogarty at Renvyle. The low white house at Duras where Yeats, Lady Gregory and Synge first projected the Abbey Theatre in the house of that picaresque eccentric, the Count de Basterot, is now a Youth Hostel; but The Big House, left standing, may suffer all sorts of more or less dramatic translations: monasteries, convalescent homes, mental hospitals.

'But he killed the house . . .'

Often, yes. Sometimes he killed it by his own spendthrift life, and there were many ways to do it. Lavish hospitality; emulation of his neighbours (particularly in the additions and improvements to his 'castle' as in Hogarth's *Marriage à la Mode*); carelessness over all kinds of business obligations. The ubiquitous presence of the agent who might or might not be honest, but whose essential function was to remit money to the landlord; who might well, because of choice or service, be an absentee. But more insidiously there was the tradition that business and money affairs were beneath the notice of a gentleman, as Tolstoi makes plain. That, too, is Elizabethan. Yeats made claims about his ancestry that could hardly be supported, James Joyce did the same, and lied even more flagrantly. But perhaps Shakespeare did so too when he claimed his coat of arms.

This attitude was in itself another cause of decay. The great brewing and distilling families had not yet acquired acceptance into the 'landed gentry'. Michell Henry had built Kylemore Castle on Manchester cotton, but lost his fortune as rapidly as he had poured it into Connemara. A certain healthy profligacy, which had brought fresh blood to the English aristocracy either by the bend sinister or by marriage with an actress or dairymaid, had seldom re-vivified the Irish families. But there were even subtler seeds of decay. Yeats recognized them:

> And what if my descendants lose the flower
> Through natural declension of the soul,
> Through too much business with the passing hour,
> Through too much play, or marriage with a fool?[1]

The soul might decline through sheer inertia; easy living, servants in abundance, much hospitality; women, horses and drink, the classic triad.[2] And the greater the integration of the people of the Big House into its purely Irish setting, and the less the contact with England, Europe, America, the more likely was this decay. Perhaps there are many analogies to be found with the American South. Again we can turn to Yeats and here he is, I think, writing of the decade after the turn of the century when, for a period, stability seemed to be in sight:

> . . . Public opinion ripening for so long
> We thought it would outlive all future days.
> O what fine thoughts we had because we thought
> That the worst rogues and rascals had died out.[3]

Or the Big House might decline by 'going native', by jettisoning all standards, by selling off the 'outside' land or woods, by sinking into the life of the small farmer: maybe driven 'quare', like Synge's Patch Darcy, by the soft rainy climate, the easy drink, the land on which the lowest standard of farming in Europe could provide a subsistence level. Round my home in Co. Clare there was evidence of what had once been prosperous arable farming, with big stone warehouses on the creeks, and quays to serve them. No doubt they passed with the Repeal of the Corn Laws: giving place to cattle for which — then as now — the erratic market depended on England; a food supply often too costly for the farmer to use for himself and his family.

§vii

And now, even at the risk of appearing cynical or bitter, I am going to tell you what I believe to be the truth; though I, more than perhaps anyone in this room, have reason to be nostalgic over the past:

> Nous n'irons plus aux bois,
> Les lauriers sont coupes . . .

1. 'Meditations in Time of Civil War', IV.
2. See, in general, the various Memoirs: and, in particular, Carleton's *Irish Tales*.
3. 'Nineteen Hundred and Nineteen'.

Yeats saw the Big House through rose-coloured, perhaps mystic glasses. He had drawn from Coole and from Lady Gregory what were for him the poet's essentials of leisure, comfort, friendship; and what seemed a stability that had grown out of past ages. Again and again he sought to align Coole Park with Urbino, Lady Gregory with the Countess of Montefeltro. When Coole was killed he sought something of its security and friendship with Lady Dorothy Wellesley. It gave him one of his favourite (and fruitful) myths; of 'gravelled walks', the 'many ingenious lovely things', the 'gardens where the peacock strays'. All these existed, and I remember the peacocks that screamed under my window in the early morning, and the sound of the gravel drive being raked. I am aware, in memory, of

A trance-like glory that those walls begot.

But let us look at it dispassionately. With every conceivable advantage, with wealth, leisure, security, the Big House contributed singularly little to the literary and artistic production of the last hundred years. It gave greatly to the Services, to the Law, though mainly outside Ireland. But the eminent names in literature came of humble or middle-class origins (as were Swift, Goldsmith, Sheridan): among them Shaw, O'Casey, Joyce, Beckett, James Stephens, A.E. Against them we can only set Synge in the first rank: Lady Gregory, and perhaps Lord Dunsany in the second, taking place with Martyn, George Moore (should we put him higher?). One can argue endlessly about the seating in the Hall of Fame.

Perhaps it was no more than the decay of blood and tradition that had served its turn. Perhaps it was because the landed gentry had lost the best of their youth—as elsewhere—in the 1914-18 war; and being a small community could not recover from that loss. It is probably just to say that the decline began, slowly, with the Act of Union in 1800. It gathered momentum through the second half of the century, as some of the consequences of the industrial revolution penetrated slowly into Ireland, and a new commercial class arose.

$viii

In this spider's web, this strange dichotomy, Yeats found himself entrapped. To foster Irish nationalism, both in art and in battle; to climb on the bandwagon of the early Movement even more blatantly than did George Moore; to dream of an Ireland re-united by its mythologies, its folklore, a strong peasant imagination; these involved him in a situation which the banality and ineptitude of much nationalist literature of the preceding century, and of the formidable and vulgar attacks of contemporary journalism on himself and his circle, appeared to discredit. How was 'Romantic Ireland' to be revived? How valid was the folklore that he and Lady Gregory had collected among the hills of Galway and North Clare? Was it true that the new mechanistic age, the world that (as

he thought) had been ushered in by Locke and Newton, could find its
anti-types in a kind of Irish enclave of sanctity, in which great writers
drew from heroic legends, from 'the book of the people'? He tried to
have it both ways, and he failed; just as the Anglo-Irish Ascendancy, for all
their virtues, all the opportunities for spreading 'sweetness and light' that
wealth and leisure should give, failed. And it failed because it looked
backwards to a House that, by the time of the Easter Rising, had already
fallen. On that problem I would quote part of a noble poem by A.E.:

> "We are less children of this clime
> Than of some nation yet unborn
> Or empire in the womb of time.
> We hold the Ireland in the heart
> More than the land our eyes have seen,
> And love the goal for which we start
> More than the tale of what has been".
> The generations as they rise
> May live the life men lived before,
> Still hold the thought once held as wise,
> Go in and out by the same door.
> We leave the easy peace it brings:
> The few we are shall still unite
> In fealty to unseen kings
> Or unimaginable light.
> We would no Irish sign efface,
> But yet our lips would gladlier hail
> The first-born of the Coming Race
> Than the last splendour of the Gael.
> No blazoned banner we unfold —
> One charge alone we give to youth,
> Against the sceptred myth to hold
> The golden heresy of truth.[1]

$ix

And so the curtain falls. I think that it has been moving, downwards, for a long time: perhaps, jerkily, for a hundred years and more. For
me it fell for the last time on 6 October 1970 when my house which had
been our home since the late Seventeenth Century (though for a decade
past in alien hands) was burned to the ground, a few weeks after I had
given this lecture in Sligo. In theory the Irish Aristocracy, in touch with
the peasantry and the soil, produced 'beautiful lofty things'. We may
quote:

> Aristocracies have made beautiful manners, because their
> place in the world puts them above the fear of life, and the
> countrymen have made beautiful stories and beliefs, because
> they have nothing to lose and so do not fear, and the artists

---

1. 'On Behalf of Some Irishmen not Followers of Tradition'.

have made all the rest, because Providence has filled them with
recklessness. All these look backward to a long tradition, for,
being without fear, they have held to whatever pleased them.[1]
Even for the Eighteenth Century it was, I fear, a dream world. It is
founded on an idealized vision of Urbino ('that grammar school of
courtesies') and of Versailles, transported to Coole Park. Lady Gregory
might collect her Visions and Beliefs from the hills of North Clare,
from the Workhouse at Gort; Synge might let down the roots of his
poetry into 'the clay and the worms'; even George Moore could write
movingly of his return to Moore Hall.

> It was a dream: now
> nettles wave above a broken stone.

It was, perhaps, in the nature of things. I believe (as I have written
elsewhere[2]) that this civilization had served its turn.

> How should their luck run high enough to reach
> The gifts that govern men, and after these
> To gradual Time's last gift, a written speech
> Wrought of high laughter, loveliness and ease?[3]

EPILOGUE TO CHAPTER XII

*At the Summer School at which this lecture was given an American
Professor was present. He has since written a book called* Happy Rural
Seat (The English Country House and the Literary Imagination)[4] *which
places us all deeply in his debt. In particular his chapter called Setting
the House in Order deals with Yeats, Elizabeth Bowen, Graham Greene,
Virginia Woolf, Joyce Cary and Evelyn Waugh. It carries my own
speculations a great deal farther, and covers the reading to which I
referred at the outset of my talk. In particular, there are most illuminating comparisons between 'Ancestral Houses' and the work of Henry
James; and a development of what Professor Gill calls 'this ambiguous
compound of eulogy and satire'. He draws attention, very properly, to
Padraic Colum's* Castle Conquer *(1923), Lennox Robinson's* The Big
House *(1928), Elizabeth Bowen's* Bowen's Court *(1942). The critical
balance which Professor Gill mentions seems to me just and wise:
as does the historical perspective which reaches back to the Seventeenth
Century.*

1. *Essays and Introductions*, p.251.
2. *The Lonely Tower*. Ch. I.
3. 'Upon a House Shaken by the Land Agitation'.
4. Richard Gill, (New Haven and London), 1972.

XIII
'THE PROPERTY OF THE DEAD'[1]

"Many have taken voluminous pains to determine the state of the Soul upon disunion . . . " (Sir Thomas Browne)

The title of this lecture is, as you will have realized, taken from a line in the fourth movement of the poem called 'Blood and the Moon'. Yeats is meditating on The Tower and its symbols. It is, unusually for him, cast in the formal structure of a Petrarchan sonnet. Such form is, by tradition, an intense and tightly-knit meditation on some subject, usually one of the 'great thoughts', as 'Longinus' calls them; such, for example, are Shakespeare's Sonnets on Love, Time, Death, Mutability, Friendship. In this particular poem what we might call the 'polar extremities', between which the poems so often move, are the Tower and the Moon: the Tower of which the winding stair images the ascent to heaven, the progress of the purified soul, but which is itself set, blood-stained, in history, passion, war. Around its windows come moths and butterflies, which may be emblems, as in Dante, of the souls of the dead. The stares or starlings have once built a nest in the crumbling masonry. They are noisy and quarrelsome. Now honey-bees, (emblems of amity, co-operation, sweetness, perhaps of sexual desire) are invoked to come to the tower in opposition to the civil war and bloodshed that stained it.[2] One part of his theme — the emblems, always, become more complex the more we perceive them in depth — is the 'purity of the unclouded moon', and the inability of history to detract from its permanence and brilliance. But here we had better quote from the poem:

No matter what I said,
For wisdom is the property of the dead,
A something incompatible with life; and power,
Like everything that has the stain of blood,
A property of the living; but no stain
Can come upon the visage of the moon
When it has looked in glory from a cloud.

My purpose is to invite you to explore with me some of Yeats's beliefs and attitudes to death, and the wisdom of the dead. There is nothing unusual in a poet's concern with such matters. Dante, whom he calls 'the chief imagination of Christendom',[3] had written of the great triad of subjects for poetry, Love, War and Death, in their many combinations: Love and War, War and Death, and the Return of the

1. Sligo, 1971.
2. 'The Stare's Nest by My Window'.
3. 'Ego Dominus Tuus'.

Dead, as in the Scottish Ballads. We may remember T. S. Eliot's less
graceful formulation in *Sweeney Agonistes,* and Beckett's in *Waiting
for Godot.* We could if we so wished conjure up a long procession of
poets for whom death has been a major theme, and among whom indeed,
it has produced much of our most powerful poetry. It does not need
Shelley to remind us that

> Our sweetest songs are those that tell of saddest thought.

In such a procession we should recognize Dunbar in his 'Lament for the
Makaris', François Villon's Ballade of dead ladies, and of his fellow -
thieves hanging blackened on the gallows: much of Shakespeare: more
of Donne, Herrick, Milton, Marvell. We know those pious Moralizers of the
Grave in the Eighteenth Century — Blair's *The Grave,* Young's *Night
Thoughts* — which moved so powerfully Blake's imagination when he
drew his visions for and from them. We know that with the Romantics
Love and Death begin to twine inextricably, like the roses planted on the
graves of lovers, or the apple and the yew — with all their depth-
symbolism — that mingled above the tomb of Baile and Aillinn. Keats
listens, 'darkling', to the song of the nightingale:

> Darkling I listen; and, for many a time
> I have been half in love with easeful Death,
> Call'd him soft names in many a musèd rhyme,
> To take into the air my quiet breath . . .

So Poe, Rossetti, Swinburne: many of Yeats's fellow-poets in the Nineties: Hardy, Housman, Eliot, Webster, who

> saw the skull beneath the skin

as did John Synge when the already tenanted grave was opened in the
island funeral on Aran. And through the valley of the shadows we
should take as our guides Sir Thomas Browne's *Urne-Buriall,* as well as
St. Paul's great lesson for the Burial of the Dead.[1]

§ii

I make no apology, then, for the subject. Not many poets have been
concerned to guide us into the underworld, the undiscovered country. I
can think only of four. They are Virgil and Dante, Blake and Yeats.
Yeats's theories, systems if you like, of the progress of the soul, are
contained in that exasperating and mysterious book — still mysterious,
for all the recent mass of commentary on it — and, in particular, in the
final chapter called *The Gates of Pluto.* That title, he tells us, he took
from Orpheus, who took it from Cornelius Agrippa:

> The Gates of Pluto cannot be unlocked; within is a people of
> dreams.[2]

A Vision is full of inconsistencies; it draws, typically, on many

1. I *Corinthians* XV
2. *A Vision* (A) p.220.

heterogeneous sources. But we cannot neglect it in its bearing on much of the important work. Among the poems are 'A Dialogue of Self and Soul', 'All Souls' Night', 'Cuchulain Comforted', 'The Black Tower'; among the plays, *Purgatory, The Words Upon the Window Pane, Calvary, The Only Jealously of Emer, The Death of Cuchulain*. I do not propose to go into the sources of his beliefs, or half-beliefs (I think of Browning);[1] but I would draw your attention only to my own views. I am certain that, wherever possible, Yeats tried to discover several lines, experiences, modes of thought, that seemed to converge upon a single point; and was prepared if need be to bend or distort them to manifest such a convergence that should be 'more philosophical than history'. Thus his theosophical studies, his early discipleship under Madame Blavatsky, his work for the Order of the Golden Dawn, seemed to establish points in common with the Vedic writers and the uneasy ghosts of the Japanese Noh plays; with folk-lore that he had accumulated with Lady Gregory in Clare and Galway; Cornelius Agrippa; Swedenborg, Blake. Overlying all is the tradition and the traditional imagery of Christianity which none of us can escape (even if we would), and which he uses whenever it serves his poetic occasion.

§iii

From the beginnings of recorded religion men have speculated on the nature, constitution, texture, and progress of the Soul; on the circumstances of its departure from the body, on its conduct in the after-life, and on the clues which might be found, by whatever means, as to the nature of that undiscovered country. There are perhaps seven main sources for the possibility:

1. Orthodox Christian doctrine.
2. Psychical research, in many forms, including the séance, and even white and black magic.
3. Classical sources: mainly Homer and Virgil.
4. The Egyptian Book of the Dead.
5. Hindu theology.
6. Buddhist teaching.
7. Comparative mythology and folklore: specifically from Ireland.

To these, in 1971, we should add an eighth; the possibility of electronically-recorded communication with the dead, as in Raudive's book, *Breakthrough*. In my view Yeats uses all seven. It is pertinent to examine first what we might call the body of inconography that seeks to symbolize the soul.

As we should expect, the commonest emblem is that of a bird: for obvious reasons. It is released after death into the air; it is free from

---

1. 'Bishop Blougram's Apology'.

the traditional mixture or 'gross' elements, earth and water, from 'all complexities of mire and blood'. It is at home (as waterfowl) on land, sea and in the air. White birds in particular are used to gesture towards the nature of Soul: swan — seagull — dove — albatross — goose — heron. 'Swan and Dove' is the title of a chapter in *A Vision,* being the vehicles by which spirit meets mortal in the two traditional kinds of annunciation or transmission of godhead. Wild geese, their mystery accentuated by their hound-like cry, have long been associated with the supranatural.[1] Yeats and Roy Campbell both use the image of a snipe: for the latter

> The dead like weary snipe, rising on high,
> Whined through the dusky pallor of the sky.

And indeed I known of no bird more mysterious, more moving in its twilight cry.

The soul may be thought to sing in its aerial blessedness: hence Shelley's 'Skylark'. Jeremy Taylor uses the emblem of the ascending lark to illustrate an accepted prayer. Once only in his mythology there is resurrection in the fourth element, fire; the phoenix, which adds piety and self-sacrifice to its other qualities. So, in another context the pelican, a type of Christian charity; though mistaken ornithology. The call of the curlew suggests the 'sweet crystalline cry' of a soul. The lark is a spirit of exaltation, of praise; the nightingale of the permanence of beauty. There are all kinds of human to bird transformations; Hylas to a nightingale, Procne to a swallow.

These soul-emblems are mainly, but by no means all, the white birds. Conversely, and obeying the normal white-black antinomy, the black birds are most commonly associated with ill-omen; originally, perhaps, through the forebodings of the battlefield and carrion. They are crows, ravens, vultures, from the raven of Macbeth's battlements to Cuchulain's Morrigu. Both Synge and Yeats noted the belief in the West that large flocks of black birds at sea suggested some supernatural congregation. To Synge they can be mourning birds: so of the drifting body in *Riders*

> . . . with no one to keen him but the black hags that do be
> flying on the sea.

In Homer the souls of the dead go 'squeaking like bats down to Hades', since the kingdom of Pluto and Persephone is dark. They come under the conjuration of Odysseus to drink the sacrificial blood poured into a pit: and, being naturally diaphanous, assume colour and form as they do so. Ghosts may haunt their slayers, but are not very intelligent, especially in Homer, and may be deceived by various means, such as the *simulacrae* of their slayers. The irrational behaviour of domestic ghosts, and especially of poltergeists, is notorious.

1. See *passim* E.A. Armstrong; *The Folk-lore of Birds.*

$iv

After the emblems of the Soul, we may glance at some of the beliefs about its destinations; both generally, and as Yeats appears to see them.

In very many religions there is a trial or ordeal in its first progress. Perhaps the most famous example is the ballad called *'The Lyke-Wake Dirge'*, where the soul must pass over a tract of moor covered with gorse, and cross a bridge − The Dreadful Bridge − over an abyss. (This is also found in Scandinavian and Muslim belief.) At some point it may undergo judgement, whether it be the three judges of the dead − Minos, Rhadamanthus, Aeacus − that Yeats takes from Porphyry (in Mackenna's translation) and uses in 'The Delphic Oracle Upon Plotinus'.[1] Or it may be the Last Judgement, with the hierarchy of Heaven and its recording angels: as seen by, say, Michelangelo or Blake.

Between death, and heaven or hell, there is a place of purification through suffering called Purgatory.

There is a place of bliss: of which the feature common to all religions is the achievement in it of the perfect union with, and knowledge of, God, the One, the Ineffable.

There is Hell: primarily a place of separation from God, but having for its condition torment (which may be mental) symbolized in some form of fire. Here, in orthodox Roman Catholic theology, there are two 'pains'; one of loss or separation, the other of fire.

There is a place called Limbo, to which go (again in Catholic orthodoxy) the souls of children who die unbaptised: as also, according to some beliefs, the souls of the 'virtuous heathen' who died *before* the promise of Christian Salvation. So Sir Thomas Browne:

> Meanwhile Epicurus lies deep in Dante's Hell, wherein we meet with tombs enclosing souls that denied their immortalities. But whether the virtuous heathen, who lived better than he spake, or erring in the principles of himself, yet lived above philosophers of more specious maxims lie so deep as he is placed . . . were a query too sad to insist on.[2]

We may mention briefly two other heavens. One is Tir-na-n'Og, the country of the ever young, the magic islands beyond the sunset, the land of eternal youth. This is the Land of Faery, in *The Land of Heart's Desire*:

> . . . Where nobody gets old and godly and grave,
> Where nobody gets old and crafty and wise,
> Where nobody gets old and bitter of tongue
> And she is still there, busied with a dance
> Deep in the dewy shadow of a wood,
> (Or where stars walk upon a mountain top).

1. Stephen Mackenna: Plotinus, *The Enneads* (Porphyry) p.17.
2. *Urne Buriall*, IV

It is clear that a number of beliefs unite in considering Heaven as a place in which music and song become a parable of unity and of harmony: based of course on the great passage in the *Revelation of St. John the Divine*.[1]

In Yeats's mythology the dance is super-added to the heavenly choir:

> Where her soul flies to the predestined dancing-place
> (I have no speech but symbol, the pagan speech I made
> Amid the dreams of youth) let her come face to face,
> Amid that first astonishment, with Grania's shade,
> All but the terrors of the woodland flight forgot
> That made her Diarmuid dear . . .[2]

Music, song, dance are all emblems of the resolution of conflict, the entry into harmony with the One through ordered ritual: hence the 'marbles of the dancing-floor', with their intricate maze-patterns that you can see on certain Cretan vases. Or heaven may be a place of meadows, as Tennyson's

> . . . the island valley of Avilion;
> Where falls not hail, or rain, or any snow,
> Nor ever wind blows loudly; but it lies
> Deep-meadow'd, happy, fair with orchard lawns
> And bowery hollows crown'd with summer sea . . .

Or, more powerfully, Shakespeare's vision:

> — Stay for me,
> Where souls do couch on flowers, we'll hand in hand,
> And with our spritely port make the ghosts gaze;
> Dido and her Aeneas shall want troops,
> And all the haunt be ours.

And Synge in *The Playboy* makes Christy Mahon speak of The Meadows of Ease: remembering, no doubt, the green pastures of the Psalm.

The 'song in heaven' is very relevant to Yeats, as we shall see later. For the moment I remind you of Donne's most noble poem, 'Hymne to God my God in my Sickness':

> Since I am coming to that Holy room
> Where with thy Choir of Saints for evermore,
> I shall be made thy Music. As I come
> I tune the instrument here at the door
> And what I must do then, think here before.

We can now consider Yeats's account of the progress of the Soul and relate certain poems and plays to the various stages. In so doing we shall have to simplify a little. We may start by recalling the conversation reported by Dorothy Wellesley:

> '"What do you believe happens to us immediately after death?"
> "After a person dies he does not realize that he is dead."
> "In what state is he?"

1. 19: 1-6.
2. 'Upon a Dying Lady'.

"In some half-conscious state."
"Like the period between waking and sleeping?"
"Yes."
"How long does this state last?"
"Perhaps twenty years."
"And after that what happens next?"
"Again a period which is Purgatory. The length of that phase
depends upon the sins of the man when upon this earth."
"And after that?"
I do not remember his actual words, but he spoke of the return
of the soul to God.'

Now it is always unwise to rely on reports of conversations. There
seems to me little in the account, if it is accurate, that is heterodox
from a Christian point of view. What Yeats wrote in *A Vision* is
different, much more specific, and more pertinent to the works.
We may attempt a summary:

(a) At death the man passes into what seems to him afterwards
a state of darkness and sleep ...

(So Hamlet's 'To sleep, perchance to dream . . . ' and maybe the changing refrains in 'The Black Tower'. For

There in the tomb drops the faint moonlight

— the light filtering through the stones of the empty dolmen?—
and

There in the tomb the dark grows blacker

— as perceived by the newly-dead.
and the classic 'Nox est perpetua una dormienda'.
Two other glosses here. There is a period, sometimes fraught with difficulty, in which the Soul as it were disengages from the body. Some
believe that this is the loosening of the Silver Cord,[1] a sort of
umbilical connection between the two, and that guardian spirits may
be brought in to help in the separation. There may be a period of confusion: as in 'The Cold Heaven':

Ah, when the ghost begins to quicken,
Confusion of the death-bed over . . .

We may remember other things: Bishop Berkeley's injunction to let
his body lie untouched for just this purpose; and the Shan States in
North Burma where the body is left in a hut with a hole in the roof
so that the spirit may go forth unimpeded.

(b) But the Spirit does not *sleep* — Hamlet's father again — unless
it recognizes that it is dead. Until it does it may well go on performing
its accustomed tasks. In *A Vision* Yeats quotes the little poem by W.H.
Davies:

---

1. As in *Ecclesiastes XI*: but there seems to be a somewhat similar experience in
states of trance.

> The first night she was in her grave,
> As I looked in the glass
> I saw her sit upright in bed;
> Without a sound it was;
> I saw her hand feel in the cloth
> To fetch a box of powder forth.
>
> She sat and watched me all the while,
> For fear I looked her way;
> I saw her powder cheek and chin,
> Her fast corrupting clay;
> Then down my lady lay and smiled,
> She thought her beauty saved, poor child.

Any strong passion, or violence, or sense of wrong, may produce, now or subsequently, this restlessness of the ghost. Here again the ghost in *Hamlet* is an archetypal but far from unique example. So Crazy Jane's love for Jack the Journeyman — we shall have occasion to return to the poem later —

> But were I left to lie alone
> In an empty bed,
> The skein so bound us ghost to ghost
> When he turned his head
> Passing on the road that night,
> Mine must walk when dead.[1]

If the individual, for any one of many possible reasons, does not realize that he is dead, the enactment may go on, at this stage or another. Christian exorcists report instances of having to convince 'perturbed spirits', even after many years, that they *are* really dead. Cuchulain is surprised when he sees the shape that his soul will take:

> There floats out there
> The shape that I shall take when I am dead,
> My soul's first shape, a soft feathery shape,
> And is not that a strange shape for the soul
> Of a great fighting man?[2]

And, a story of which Yeats is fond,

> "How did you know you were dead?"
> "I saw my thoughts going past me like blazing ships."

(c) 'During the darkness he is surrounded by his kindred, present in their simulacrae, or in their Spirits when they are between lives, the more recent dead being the more visable. Because of their presence it is called the *Vision of the Blood Kindred.*' This corresponds, roughly, to the phantasms of the living or dead which F.W.H. Myers records as occurring immediately before and after the moment of death.[3]

---

1. 'Crazy Jane and Jack the Journeyman'
2. *The Death of Cuchulain.*
3. See, generally, his *Human Personality and its Survival in Bodily Death.* (London, 1903), a book which Yeats knew.

This is followed by a period of *meditation* which ends with burial. 'The *Spirit* may appear to the living during this meditation' (instances of this are innumerable) 'but it it does appear it will show in the likeness of the body *as that body was before death'*.

The *meditation* may be moved and shaped by the *Burial Ritual*, for the Body has become a symbol, as thoughts inspired by the *Ritual* can affect the 'dreaming' spirit.

Here we may make certain comments arising out of modern psychical research; and commend, if that ever were needed, the practice of prayers for the dead. We might also reflect again on the ghost of Hamlet's father, one of whose complaints was that he had been interred 'in hugger mugger'; and regret — I have written of this in *The Harvest of Tragedy*[1] — the tendency of modern civilization to abandon the traditional rituals of death; perhaps because of our own unwillingness to confront the fact, which may well be one aspect of our psychological malaise.

In all these states Soul is attempting to free itself of what are called in 'Byzantium' the 'unpurged images', the impressions that are proper only to sense. This I believe to be the point of the poem 'Ribh Considers Christian Love Insufficient', for the unpurged images include those of man's imperfect apprehension of God:

> Then my delivered soul herself shall learn
> A darker knowledge and in hatred turn
> From every thought of God mankind has had.
> Thought is a garment, and the soul's a bride
> That cannot in that trash and tinsel hide:
> Hatred of God may bring the soul to God.

§vi

The next stage is of great *poetic* importance. I am admittedly simplifying Yeats's doctrine, which is made highly complicated by its relationship to the Phases of the Moon and the Gyres.

The spirit dreams through his past life, he 'dreams the events of his life backwards through time':

> If the thought of the past life permit, he will now perceive all those persons as they now live or as they have lived, who have influenced him, or whom he has influenced, and so caused the action, but if he has belonged to some faith that has not known rebirth he may explore sources that require symbolical expression."[2]

Two comments here. The elegiac poems, such as 'All Souls' Night' and 'The Municipal Gallery Revisited', perhaps also 'The Fisherman', may be considered in some sense as rehearsals for this 'review' by the

1. Methuen, 1956: Chapter 22, (2nd Ed. 1961).
2. *A Vision* (A) p.225

Spirit of its friends and enemies, its hopes and its frustrations. Perhaps this is common to all elegies, which are at once laments, celebrations, and, like 'Lycidas'., self-searchings by the poet.

Secondly — and this is utterly against Christian doctrine — Yeats appears to be committed to the Buddhist and Neo-Platonic ideas of reincarnation.

This is the point of the last stanza of 'Sailing to Byzantium':

> Once out of nature I shall never take
> My bodily form from any *natural* thing . . .

That is, he is at liberty — perhaps in view of the quality of the previous life — to select within limits the 'Body' into which he is to be re-incarnated: in this case it is not the animal or vegetable creation but the mechanized artefact of the golden bird in the third stanza of *Byzantium.*

We may liken this all-important *Dreaming Back* to the act of running a rope through our hands; at the end, or beginning, is a state of complete innocence, when the Soul has exhausted its survey of its own actions in life. But if in the process it encounters (to continue the image) a knot or tangle at any point, it may pause as it were at that point and be compelled to re-enact the violence of thought or passion (such as a murder) which may have taken place at some point in the past. The classic instances are in the plays: *Purgatory,* where a man and a woman re-enact as ghosts their marriage night in the skeleton of the burnt house (which itself becomes a kind of ghost for the purpose of the play, and as a background to it); and *The Dreaming of the Bones* where the ghosts of Diarmuid and Dervorgilla can never kiss as lovers, or gain their rest, until they have found someone to forgive them for having brought the Normans to Ireland in order to further their own selfish love. In a wholly different manner, *The Words Upon the Window-Pane* makes use of the spirit of Swift who breaks through the rather ordinary and slightly comic Dublin séance with his terrifying presence. In this the motivating passion is Swift's love for Stella, and his own political ambitions and frustrations.

This concept of the ghost is a normal one both in folk-lore and in psychical research. Any event of great intensity appears to generate some kind of waves which inhere in, or adhere to, many kinds of physical environment: a house, a wood, a sacred hill, a prehistoric burial place, a tomb of a saint or hero. How long this vibration-impression lasts is not clear; it seems that exceptionally strong events may impress themselves for perhaps three hundred years or so, but that the majority endure for not more than two life-spans, and often less. The appearance or manifestation may take place on some anniversary, at some spot such as a tomb or ruin, or merely if someone happens to be present who has the right 'apparatus' for receiving these particular vibrations.

I have written elsewhere of Yeats's desire to find confirmation of his beliefs from as many different sources or contexts as possible. In this instance he found, and used, several distinct sources which appeared to him to confirm one another. These were the classical sources in Homer and Virgil and Ovid. There was the normal mechanism of the séance: for which there was Biblical warrant in the story of the 'Witch' of En-Dor, and the 'raising' of the ghosts of the kings. There seems to have been a particular interest in Spiritualism in London and Dublin in the first three decades of this century: intensified by the great number of dead in the First World War, and confirmed by such books as Sir Oliver Lodge's *Raymond* and the work of Sir Arthur Conan Doyle. For a time in the late 1920s, it must have seemed as if physics, philosophy, and psychical research were on the point of breaking through the curtains of the invisible world, and of giving it — in spite of the mass of fraud, trickery,[1] self-hypnosis — some kind of scientific respectability.

Next, and perhaps most important, there was the fact that much of Irish folk-lore and mythology seemed to converge to give a broadly similar answer. To Lady Gregory's edition of *Visions and Beliefs of the West of Ireland* he appended his own essay called *Swedenborg, Mediums, and the Desolate Places.* His work on Blake had driven him back to Swedenborg, the Kabala, Cornelius Agrippa, Henry More. The *Plotinus* of his friend Stephen Mackenna is also of great importance. The details are far too long, and too complex, to summarize here: but in the essay we find constantly passages that are relevant. The philosophy of the ghost appears to link up at several points with faery lore.

Various forms of restlessness, or purgatorial wandering, are involved. There can be love affairs between mortals and the people of the Sidhe, as in the Scottish Ballads: notably in 'Thomas the Rhymer', 'The Wife of Usher's Well.' And we should remember that Yeats's great friend, the Theosophist 'A.E.', saw and painted his visions of the faery world.

§vii

We must return to the unravelling of the knot in the Dreaming Back. At the end of the progress the Soul is thought of as recovering what he calls 'radical innocence': that is that state in which all action, all impurities, have been exhausted. This state is sometimes symbolized by cherubs riding on dolphins (so common in Renaissance iconography) as in 'News for the Delphic Oracle.' They are then ready, after some unspecified time, for reincarnation. Here Yeats is following Porphyry. The innocent souls are incarnated by generation through water; hence the line in 'Coole Park and Ballylee':

What's water but the generated soul?

1. See Browning's 'Mr Sludge the Medium'.

and Porphyry's image of honey is used in 'Among Schoolchildren' for the act of generation:

> What youthful mother, a shape upon her lap
> Honey of generation has betrayed . . .

For the general imagery of honey — I have written of this elsewhere — we may remember both *Romeo and Juliet* and Kranach's picture of Cupid presenting Venus with the honey-comb. Honey is indeed a symbol with many aspects, according to Thomas Taylor's Commentary on Porphyry. It possesses a purging and preserving quality; it keeps dead bodies from putrefaction. In religious rites it is poured on the hands instead of water, to show that their hands are to be pure 'from all sorrowful, obnoxious and abominable concern'. By honey the tongue is purified from defilement. "But the theological poet intimates . . . that the divine essences are, as it were, bound, and drawn ·down by delight into the fluctuating empire of generation; and that when resolved in pleasure, they produce certain powers by their seminal virtue . . . Hence, since honey is assumed in purgations, and as an antidote to putrefaction, and aptly represents the pleasure and delight of descending into the fascinating realms of generation, it is accounted a symbol well adapted to nymphs, the divinities of waters; signifying the nature of the waters over which they preside free from putrefaction: intimating likewise the purgative qualities of the waters and their co-operating in the business of generation."[1]

This is of course the point at which Yeats throws in his lot with Buddhism, the Pythagoreans, and many others, against Christian thought. Christianity has no dealings with reincarnation, however attractive that theory may be in explaining what appear to be reminiscences of previous lives. For it commits us to a terrible circle of determinism, cycle after cycle, moving upwards and downwards in the scale according to the virtue that we have shown in our lives. We are bound inexorably on the Wheel. Yeats recognizes this, and postulates a factory which he calls The Thirteenth Cone, which is something like Divine Intervention. The explanation is complex, difficult, and to my mind unsatisfactory.

$viii

Finally, let us pass from these speculations to a brief consideration of their bearing on certain poems, simplifying a little in the interests of clarity.

It is clear from Homer, Virgil, Ovid and above all Dante that you must have a guide when you go down to the underworld: otherwise

---

1. *Thomas Taylor the Platonist,* ed. Kathleen Raine and George Mills Harper. Princeton, 1969. 'Concerning the Cave of the Nymphs': 306-7.

there may be no return. This may be another wise ghost — such as Dante's Virgil — or it may be the clue of thread in the labyrinth. That thread may be — symbolically — unravelled from mummy-cloth; that is, from the woven wisdom of the ancients in dealing with these matters. So —

> Hades' bobbin bound in mummy-cloth

of 'Byzantium', a similar thought in 'All Souls' Night', and the explorations of the tomb referred to in 'The Gyres':

> For painted forms or boxes of make-up
> In ancient tombs I sighed, but not again . . .

(Does this suggest the abandonment of Spiritualism, or Egyptian theurgy?)

So in the second stanza of 'Byzantium' the spirit-guide is invoked. The spirits of the dead have crossed the sea, borne on the backs of dolphins, to the stone quays of the city. This is clear from the early drafts. The guide, who is of course a spirit, the

> — mouth that has no moisture and no breath

is summoned by the breathless mouths of the newly-arrived spirits.[1] The third stanza, the description of the golden bird, becomes almost an interpolation, a throw-forward from the previous poem. In this case the form, though it is not a 'natural' form (that is, of a lower scale for the sinful, a higher for the virtuous), but to the golden bird, the artefact which is to become the symbolic environment of the poet in its permanence, and its virility; though there is much debatable matter in depth and complexity of reference. The poet himself does not appear to be among the 'innocent' souls, who are to be finally purified by the ritual dance. In the conclusion the smithies with their artefacts, the marbles with their mazes which stand for immutable order, may 'break the flood'; which is, as always, life, torn by the two forces of religion and love.

§ ix

Only in one poem do we find a fully developed account of the progress of the dead, and this is not wholly typical of Yeats's theories, for the location of the underworld is neither purgatory nor hell, but a kind of pagan limbo of its own. It is *Cuchulain Comforted*, dictated at 3 a.m. on January 7th 1939.[2] In the first draft it was called 'The Valley of the Dead.'

The hero Cuchulain is the most striking of Yeats's masks. It is the only one that he retains to the end. He is inextricably blended, through Pearse and his followers and Oliver Sheppard's statue, with The Easter Rising. We know that in Yeats's mind he stands for heroic

1. See in general Kathleen Raine, *Death-in-Life and Life-in-Death* and *News of the Delphic Orach*, Dolmen Press, 1974.
2. Not 13th, as stated in *Collected Poems*.

violence, in love and in war. and for the archetypal conflict between mistress and wife.[1]

This is by far the most Dantesque poem that he wrote. Nowhere else does he use Dante's *terza rima*. There are direct references to *Purgatorio* 6 and 7: and, I believe, to Blake's illustrations to that poem. We remember that in Tir-na-n'Og the spirits are perceived as birds, calling out to one another with human voices as they fly 'to unimaginable happiness'.[2]

In Dante there is only one Valley of the Dead, that of the Negligent Rulers in Purgatory 'where kings and rulers who have neglected their higher functions for selfishness and selfish war' are placed. Their spirits are outside the true Purgatory. Their punishment consists in the desire for active purgation, after they have humbled themselves, and learnt to cooperate with others: In Dante the spirits sing the hymn 'Te lucis ante sidere' in unison, to Heaven:

"so devoutly proceeded from the leading spirit's mouth,
and with such sweet music, that it rapt me from my sense of
self."

And in *Inferno* XV Dante and his guide Virgil meet a throng of souls who watch them.

'Come 'l vecchio sartor fa nella cruna.'

'Puckering at us their eyelids in such wise
As does the old tailor at his needle's eye'.

We can now comment on the poem. The spirit of Cuchulain arrives in the underworld. The spirits shrink away in terror from the aura of blood and violence. He leans against a tree: just as in the statue in the Post Office. The other spirits, white and diaphanous, watch him, in hiding, like wild creatures in the woods. Yeats calls these spirits 'Shrouds', which is another word for what he calls the 'Celestial Body'. Blake shows his spirits − and often other figures[3] − in shroud-like garments: perhaps because his master Busire had set him to copy the tombs in Westminster Abbey.

Cuchulain stands motionless in meditation. The shrouds creep forth: their leader advances 'because the man was still', carrying a bundle of linen. They have been terrified by the noise of battle that he has brought with him. But now

Your life can grow much sweeter if you will,
Obey our ancient rule and make a shroud.

The making of a shroud is, I take it, an image for his preparation for purgatory, perhaps for heaven. To make it involves humility, co-operation, difficulty (the threading of the needle's eye): before he can

1. *The Only Jealousy of Emer.*
2. *The Shadowy Waters.*

3. e.g.'Famine', 'Hunger'; and the illustrations, to Blair and Young.

join the spirits in the heavenly music, which may be the sign of their purification, the prelude to their acceptance. Perhaps there is some analogy with the phrase Yeats has used of 'making one's soul'. And of the making of his own verse he has the image of 'stitching and unstitching'.

Two more glosses, from Yeats's own statements:

> It (the Spirit) may stay in the *Purification* for centuries — become, if it died amidst some primitive community, the guardian of well or temple or be called by the *Thirteenth Cone* to the care of the newly dead.
>
> I think of those phantoms in ancient costumes seen by some peasant exercising such authority. 'We have no power' said an inhabitant of the state, 'except to purify our intention', and when I asked 'Of what?', replied 'Of complexity'."[1]

> "In piecing together detached statements, I remember that some spirit once said to me: 'We do nothing singly, every act is done by a number at the same time. Their perfection is a shared purpose of idea."[2]

Seen from this point of view the 'moral' of the poem is that Cuchulain must learn co-operation, humility, unity with a band of spirits whose characteristics are the direct opposite of his own: 'convicted cowards', exiles. Only then can they 'change their throats', so that they can sing. And this is the sign, the birds' throats of their new power to praise as a preliminary to the divine union. At the end of Emer's dance before the head of Cuchulain we have this stage-direction:

There is silence, and in the silence a few faint bird notes.

Up to this point Yeats's account of the after-life seems to be reasonably consistent with the poems and plays, and, broadly, in line with the Neo-Platonic tradition. I think particularly of two seminal works: Jung's *Memories, Dreams and Reflections* (which is startlingly close to much of Yeats's thought) and Kathleen Raine's *Defending Ancient Springs*. Nor is it, as I think, discordant with the main aspects of Christian tradition, and with the findings of modern psychologists who think in such terms.

There is a review of the spirit's past life in the 'Dreaming Back', which may be prolonged almost indefinitely. 'Teaching Spirits' (another age might have called them Tutelary Guardians) may assist the dreamer in his progress towards innocence; not wholly alien, perhaps, to the 'cloud of witnesses', or to the Communion of Saints. But in Section VI of *A Vision*[3] Yeats introduces some difficult and I think misleading terms. The first is that of the Covens: 'beings which have personality,

---

1. A Vision (B) p.233.
2. *Ibid.*, p. 234.
3. I have used both the 1926 and the 1937 versions: keeping to the nomenclature ('A' and 'B') which I used in *The Lonely Tower*.

though their lives consist of a number of minds held together by a stream of thought or an event'. Possibly this is the clue to the lines from *The Statues:*

> When Pearse summoned Cuchulain to his side,
> What stalked through the Post office? . . .[1]

– the spirits forming into a combined force excited by the notions of the Easter Rising and its violence. It may be yet another instance of the attempt to unify all national mythologies into a single force, in terms of history and the revolutions of the gyres.

When the Dreaming Back has been as it were exhausted there is a further attempt to align the progress of the spirit with the progress of the gyres. The cone begins to revolve in an opposite direction, and is associated with phases 23, 24, 25. There is no further capacity for pleasure and pain, and in this state or phase, which he calls the *Shiftings*, it is freed from Good and Evil, and again 'lives' through a life which is in all respects an antithesis of the Dreaming Back; the negative, as it were, of the film which has been unrolled, reviewed, assessed, in the previous state. Here Good becomes Evil, Evil becomes Good. Is there some debt here to Blake's *Marriage of Heaven and Hell,* as well as to Yeats's own motto of DEDI (Daemon est Deus Inversus) in the Order of the Golden Dawn? We remember the gnomon from *The Everlasting Gospel:*

> Both read the Bible day and night,
> But thou read'st black where I read white.

and 'This Angel, who is now become a Devil, is my particular friend. We often read the Bible together in its infernal or diabolical sense, which the world shall have if they behave well.'

In this state of the *Shiftings* there is no suffering, unlike the purgatorial condition of the Dreaming Back; for the soul cannot undergo any further sensation. Men and women now seek complete knowledge of one another in order to separate, in each other, what is *primary* (objective) from what is *antithetical* (subjective). "The man would know the woman utterly and so he must relive his love in all things whereof he was ignorant, turning good fortune into complete tragedy, or tragedy into good fortune, that he may test his love in every fire:[2] and if the woman be dead and in like condition she will be present in reality, but if not, in similitude alone."[3] 'Light' loves appear to be passed over casually, as it were, "but strong love given in ignorance" (I am not sure

---

1. Note the ghost-word, *stalked:* as Shakespeare, Collins 'Ode on the Popular Superstitions of the Scottish Highlands'.

2. This seems to be linked to 'the intercourse of angels', as in 'Ribh at the Tomb of Baile and Aillinn'. But the love-flame imagery is ancient and archetypal.

3. *A Vision* (A) p.230.

that I understand this) "may be relived again and again, though not with suffering."

Finally, the *Shiftings* appear as a state in which "though the soul is taught, there is no teaching, and there is no teacher but the *Celestial Body*, for it is a form of life: the soul is as it were folding up into itself". It now appears to be merged into a single unity, which is in contact with the mysterious beings of the Thirteenth Cone. But Yeats's visions, or those of the Instructors, are growing so complex that we can do no more than gesture towards the possibility that the Thirteenth Cone or Sphere seems to suggest time only rather than space, and such a speculation on the nature of eternity is perhaps not wholly discordant with Christian theology.

It is clear that these last speculations are confused, and to me, rather unfortunate in their language. The *Covens* seem to have unfortunate associations with witchcraft; the *Shiftings* an unhappy term for what is in effect a reversal of the panoramic Dreaming Back. The conversion into a sort of *Anima Mundi*, a collective celestial consciousness, seems to me to have no authority either in Christianity, Theosophy or Spirtualism.

§x

I have given this lecture for no other purpose but to invite your attention to an aspect of Yeats's beliefs, or half-beliefs, that receive too little serious notice. That it is, or should be, a serious concern seems to me entirely proper. Christian belief rests on the doctrine of the immortality of the soul. Many of Yeats's beliefs I find discordant with Christianity, as he himself admits:

I - though heart might find relief
Did I become a Christian man and choose for my belief
What seems most welcome in the tomb — play a predestined
    part.
Homer is my example and his unchristened heart.

On the other hand there are aspects of his beliefs which I do not find inimical either to my own 'temper' — I use Sir Thomas Browne's word — or to Christianity as I understand it. Among them is the Communion of Spirits or Saints, and the certainty that we are 'encompassed about with so great a cloud of witnesses'. Biologically as well as spiritually we know that we inherit ancestral characteristics. These are one aspect of what he calls 'The Great Memory'. I believe in the importance, of ritual, and prayer, and in the ceremonies of death. My experience leads me to be certain of the existence of evil, which we ourselves may on occasion generate and project: I do not think that anyone who has seen five wars, and cruelty beyond imagining, can believe otherwise. To speak of spirits of evil, or of good, is, in fact, no more and no less than a feeble gesture towards the incomprehensible. I am also certain that spirit, whether good or evil, can inhere in, and modify, localities, houses, churches: this being what we recognize as the numinous in such contexts. That there is much in the writings that we are tempted to dismiss as nonsense, I could concede: yet I would save somewhat for the flashes of imaginative insight which seem to me to arise.As a Christian,and with scriptural authority,I reject the spiritualistic séance: yet it provides the framework for one of the most remarkable plays, and for a statement about the endurance in time of the deeds and thoughts of a great man. If a ghost were to come to a table, in the candlelight, at midnight (as in 'All Souls' Night') it seems to me imaginatively true to assert that

> It is a ghost's right,
> His element is so fine
> Being sharpened by his death,
> To drink of the wine-breath
> While our gross palates drink from the whole wine.

— in precisely the same way as I accept Donne's 'The Apparition'

> When by thy scorn, O murderess, I am dead,
> And that thou think'st thee free
> From all solicitation from me,
> Then shall my ghost come to thy bed . . .

The question of the nature of the soul is, like all mysteries, something towards which our words and images can do no more than gesture: I do not find it un-Christian to think of it as a white bird. We have been given few descriptions of Heaven; yet it seems not improper to assert that it is a union with divinity, and that that union can be imaged in terms of musical harmony.

These things seem to me central in our lives, and I quote the great anthropologist Malinowski:

> "Nothing really matters except the answer to the burning question — 'Am I going to live, or shall I vanish like a bubble? What is the aim of all this strife and suffering?"

For those who demand 'proofs' there is a familiar text from the New Testament: for others there is a philosophical statement about all paranormal phenomena which is worth remembering:

> Single facts can never be 'proved' except by their coherence in a system. But, as all facts come singly, anyone who dismisses them one by one is destroying the conditions under which the conviction of truth could arise in the mind.[1]

The facts about 'the property of the dead' would seem to be of this nature. We have warrant for believing that life and death lie close to

1. Professor F.C.S. Schiller.

us in the world invisible. 'All imaginable relationships may arise between a man and his God'[1]. It is possible that we may live and die the better for some faith in the future.

1. *A Vision* (B), p.240.

XIV

TOWARDS THE VALUES[1]

$i

I am going to try to put before you (and maybe a wider audience) a series of issues which seem to me of central importance. And the title which I have chosen is the same as that which I have chosen for the last chapter of a book on the Bible. For there must come a stage at which we must confront the values of our work: "It is time I wrote my will." It is time, I think, that you and I confronted the values here, in the ninth year of the International Summer School and in the last year of my Directorship. At such conjunctions one dare not be less than honest. I will try to put the matter briefly.

$ii

Yeats as a writer is making certain statements, often of great complexity, in poetry, prose, drama, politics, propaganda. Over ten years we have been considering the nature of many of these assertions or statements, at many different levels. I do not doubt that we have, as Flecker said of Verrall the Greek scholar,

> — Found out old gardens, where the wise
> May pluck a Spartan flower.

But the central statements remain, and even if the involved and autonomous character of literature makes it difficult to do more than gesture towards their meaning, we must (in the last resort) admit that they have value, or that they have not. It is clear that these values will in any event be diverse, and that it is the task of the critic to separate and order them. But if, on balance, the values are not of central importance, in terms of what I take to be the tradition of Irish, English and European civilization — then (I borrow from St. Paul), *then* is our faith vain. And if it is vain, this great School or gathering is vain also. There are many enemies against us. It is time to face them. Are the values which this mass of literature appears to transmit significant in the modern world? Do we secretly believe — as so many have done — that

> 'Poetry is nothing else than a rhetorical fiction
> musically arranged'.[2]

$iii

I do not want to minimize the importance and weight of that mass of adverse or derogatory criticism. Clearly, it falls into two halves. There is, historically, the great and perpetual attack on all imaginative

---

1. Sligo, 1968; Printed in *The Southern Review*.
2. Dante, *De Vulgari Eloquio,* 11.IV.19.

literature. Plato (or at least one part of him), Aristophanes, Stubbes, Gosson, Peacock, Buchanan, perhaps Tolstoi. The long roll-call of the apologists or protagonists is familiar too: Sidney, Bacon, Johnson; Wordsworth, Shelley, Keats, and Coleridge; from whom, with Matthew Arnold, much of our modern apologetic derives. The attack is perennial; the defence shifts a little through the years, changing its direction from time to time against the mortars and napalm of the Philistines. But one result both in England and in Ireland, is the terribly small percentage of people who read poetry, and the only slightly larger proportion of those who read any serious literature at all. Yeats did not, in his lifetime, receive any great acclaim in Ireland; in this respect we may contrast him significantly with a most popular Irish poet of the third rank, Tom Moore, whose very name is unknown to most of you, but who was once a household word in Dublin, fêted and honoured wherever he went. Little of Yeats's work, and still less of his best work, lends itself readily to that great source of popular endorsement, the school text-books of this country. But current school-anthologies and selections are of profound interest as indicating what might be thought acceptable and 'safe': nationally, religiously, politically. Here as in England much second-rate verse has proved mcre acceptable — more easily taught, and more easily examined on — than the very greatest. We may, indeed, recall the conversation reported by Kate O'Brien at Yeats's funeral at Drumcliffe:

"Did ye ever read any of his poetry, now?"

"I did not; but I'd think the most of it is great coddin"

But apart from the Philistines there are powerful attacks within our own ranks. I would not deny or seek to evade the mass of criticism already formidable in bulk, which would denigrate Yeats and all his work. Some of it goes back to the preceding century. There is also what we might think of as an enveloping flank movement, which seeks to smother, with a quiet or ironical contempt, the whole Celtic Twilight; as well as that most misleading of Matthew Arnold's essays, *The Celtic Spirit in Literature*. Under this banner there is the attack on the faery world and all its imaginative values; the sentimentality of early love; on the unreality of much of the dream-world (we may think of Yeats's Indian Idylls, or O'Shaughnessy's "We are the music-makers . . .", or 'A.E.' and his cult of the Elder Gods, or James Stephens's fairy-tales). Yeats is also of that condemnation. Some of this we can ascribe to jealousy, or that wit which can only be embodied in malice (such as that of George Moore): to what G.K. Chesterton wrote of as

> . . . The little worm of laughter
> That eats the Irish heart.[1]

More specifically, Yeats has been attacked, in our time, by wise and

---

1. 'The Ballad of the White Horse'.

important. critics, as a magician, a ghost-monger, and astrologer.[1] For
these and other reasons his religious views were, like those of his
great contemporary, A.E., more than suspect; and we might remember the valued iconoclasms of Dublin's contemporary major poet,
who is no stranger to Sligo. His enemies have refused to allow to Yeats
any claim to be called a Christian; though in my view few of them
were or are wholly competent to adjudicate with impartiality or
authority on that traditional and complex quality of life and thought.
To the younger generation he is often 'a purveyor of antiquated
romantic stuff'.[2] More immediately, we remember the attacks by such
witty and sophisticated figures as Max Beerbohm and Susan Mitchell.[3]
Last Poems was attacked — largely I think on the strength of one
misread quatrain — as 'an old man's frenzy' a book which signalized
Yeats's loss of poetic talent in old age.[4] To Auden, Yeats was
'not conspicuously intelligent'.[5] To Ezra Pound (this was in 1936)
Yeats was 'dead', 'clinging to the habit of being a writer'. Shaw
decided, in 1888, that Gilbert and Sullivan's character of the aesthete
Bunthorne in *Patience*, produced seven years earlier and popularly
supposed to caricature Oscar Wilde, had really anticipated Yeats.[6] Irishmen are not, in general, too fond of one another. It was George Moore
who wrote
　　　　'A literary movement consists of five or six people who
　　　live in the same town and hate each other cordially.'[7]
and we also remember Dr. Johnson:
　　　　'The Irish are a fair-minded people: they never speak well
　　　of one another'.
Shaw had little good to say of Yeats, and indeed the two men, in one
sense of common stock, were antipathetic in every conceivable way. We
remember that Yeats turned down O'Casey's plays for the Abbey, and
saw no merit in that astringent and penetrating classic, Shaw's *John
Bull's Other Island*. We recall, too, that James Joyce attacked Yeats
for his insularity, his Irishness, his support for the Irish language.[8] It
was only to be expected that a host of other critics, including such
representatives as Professor Daniel Corkery (supported by a number of
people who write letters to the Irish papers before, during or after

1. See *passim*, Ellmann's *W.B. Yeats, Magician:* as also Yvor Winter's attack.
2. *A General Introduction to my Work.*
3. See   Chapter VII.
4. This was a fairly common criticism of the book: related, I think, to the
　　verses that began 'You think it horrible that lust and rage . . .'
5. *cit.* Ellmann, *Man and the Masks,* p.108.
6. St. John Ervine, *Life of GBS,* p.189.
7. *Vale*, p. 165.
8. *cit.* Ellman, p.33. *cf.* also Joyce's *The Day of the Rabblement.*

each Sligo Summer School) attack him on precisely opposite grounds, for not writing in Irish, for urging Gaelic studies, for not urging Gaelic studies, for using or for not using the 'Celtic Heritage,' for having been concerned overmuch with European and Eastern cultures . . . the list is endless. It is necessary, as ever, to keep our sense of humour.

For I would return to my conviction, from which I have never stirred; that Yeats's greatness lies precisely in the achievement of combining what he found best in the Irish tradition with the capacity to draw freely if eclectically on the rest of the world. The list of his debts is a long one. Something of its literature from Greece, and a good deal from its sculpture: something from the Hebrew, and particularly from the Kabala, much from Egypt, and a little from Babylon (but this last mainly in a group of rather specialized symbols). Of the importance of his debt to France, and in particular to Balzac and Claudel, we have just heard from Daphne Fullwood. There is something from Germany: in drama from Gerhardt Hauptmann (we know little of that debt), Eckermann's *Conversations,* much at second-hand of Hegel and — above all — Nietzsche. There are, I think, (after the Nobel Prize) some cross-currents from Sweden, and suggestions of an interest in the new sculpture of Brancusi. There is a curious ring-like debt, at the beginning and returning at the end, to Indian literature, on which a new book is in preparation. There is the debt to Japan, through Fenollosa, and the most strange coincidences of Japanese and Irish archetypal myths[1] which gave us, not only the *Plays for Dancers,* but *The Words Upon the Window Pane* and *Purgatory.*

$iv

Perhaps at this point we need a word of caution, to ourselves and to those who are to come. It is wrong to complain of *immense range, eclecticism and arbitrariness* of Yeats's reading and interests. All poets have ransacked the past; not systematically, but as time, opportunity, and often the talk of friends suggested. Nor would I minimize that curious tendency of books to come forward at the right moment out of their shelves when they have something special to give; even, on occasion, to fall open at some significant passage. Many of the complaints against poets are founded on the false belief that their poetry should be, but is not, a consistent and logical whole: that there is, in fact, derivable from it a 'philosophy', a total 'conspectus'. That is not the poet's job; it is the philosopher's. I would rather use — translating Aristotle's Φιλοσοφώτερον[2] — the word *philosophical* for the various attitudes

---

1. Here the publications of The Yeats Society of Japan (which is affiliated to Sligo) are of great interest: as also Shotaro Oshima's work, *W.B. Yeats & Japan* (Tokyo 1965).

2. *Poetics,* IX, 3.

transmitted in the poetry, keeping 'philosophy' for its own professional task of a systematic ordered whole. Here in passing we may note two things about the history of literary criticism. Most of its quarrels, apparent reversals, or 'revolutions' are concerned mainly with the meanings of the terms used, and (in our time) with the dress of fashion – that 'deformed thief' – as to its jargon. As a second proposition, I would hold that a great deal of literary and indeed of all art criticism is concerned with blaming the artists for not doing what they never intended to do, and were never equipped to do, by training, temperament or tradition.

We may glance at the fashionable exercise of *Quellenforschung,* the search for an artist's sources. I would admit most happily the thrill that the scholar experiences when he is suddenly able to gesture towards some source which the artist *beyond all reasonable doubt* made use of. It is one of the many small rewards in the life of that uneasy soul, the Researcher. But in his search for that fabulous animal 'the panther of our quest', the inmost meaning of the work, it is often irrelevant. It may, on occasion, dazzle, even blind us. Yet in the great PhD. factories of the world it is the commonest prize that induces young men and women,

'To scorn delights and live laborious days'

and to waste some of the best years of their lives in reaching for the doctorate which has become, to our sorrow, the second rung on the academic ladder, the faintly-coloured rubber stamp that purports to guarantee an ability to understand and to teach. We may indeed be grateful to Pound and Joyce who have provided the students of the next two decades with large fields to glean among so many varieties of alien corn. But I would invite your attention to what Kathleen Raine has written:

"At a time when nearly all criticism takes the form of analysis, parts have come to seem more important than wholes and are studied as if they were themselves the units of poetry. Myth, if it is discussed at all, is in general regarded, not as the most complete and comprehensive of poetic figures but as something superadded; whereas the myth, in any work, is the principle of orientation within which all the parts are related."[1]

I want later to enlarge a little on the use of myth. For the moment I suggest that we try to examine together what Yeats did *not* do.

§ vi

From one point of view, and the least important, it is possible to make a case for Yeats's relative failure to achieve his objectives. In the poems 'The Gyres' and 'Under Ben Bulben', and in the prose of *On the Boiler,* he seems to look forward to a new social and cultural

1. Kathleen Raine, *Defending Ancient Springs,* p. 133. (Oxford, 1967).

age for Ireland: a hierarchical traditional society, of the 'workman, noble and saint', to replace, perhaps, that ancient and ordered Ireland that had vanished in the decade after 1916, that was never—completely— noble or saintly, and can never return. (I have argued elsewhere that the Ireland of which he speaks had, since 1900 or so, outlived its vitality and its usefulness; yet he himself believed that he had assisted in its de- struction.) The great public undertaking in which he was implicated, Lutyens' Gallery to house the Lane Pictures, was still-born. His attempt in the Senate to achieve some reform of the Divorce Laws got nowhere. On a larger scale, his vision of an Ireland rendered conscious of her nationhood through imagery, scenery, and her ancient holy places - 'the unity that marries us to rock and hill' – had, I believe, no more effect than A.E.'s equally noble vision. I cannot trace any public effect of his satire, though 'To a Rich Man who Promised a Second Subscription' . . ., and 'To a Shade', are among the bitterest poems of our time. Nor did he, I think, have any large effect on the Rising or the Civil War. Critic after critic has pointed approvingly to the lines

'Did that play of mine send out
Certain men the English shot?'

and to his feeling of responsibility – his ultimate responsibility – for the Rising of 1916; but I doubt whether it was more than wistful desire, that of the Saint for the Swordsman that he could not be. I do not think we can point to any concrete evidence for success, during his lifetime, in his wish to follow Swift, 'to serve human liberty'. And he, for all his love of what is noble in the pastoral tradition, for the godlike places in Palmer and Calvert, did less than A.E. in making two blades of grass grow where only one grew before. Nor does the advice in *On the Boiler* – "Desire some just war" – seem to me to show any insight into the nature of modern war, or of any contribution which Ireland was, or is, likely to make, as a nation, to the modern profession of arms. I am not clear how any war that we can imagine can ever again be just. It is a lamentable fact of modern times that those who most frequently advocate the violence of war are those who have had least experience of it.

§vii

Few aspects of his poetry have been mocked at more than Yeats's vision of the 'faery' world; as having about it something effeminate, decorative, insincere, fin-de-siècle. Is there not a general odium attaching to all decorative supernaturalism that is felt to be written from the teeth outward? a long distrust that goes back through Christina Rossetti to Collins and the mechanics of the Gothick novel? that extends even to the fairy world of *A Midsummer Night's Dream?* Among the poets of this century my friend Walter de la Mare was the only one who seemed

to me to have been, modestly and unpretentiously, in full alignment
with that world. But I do not think that it is just to sneer at the early
poetry. It has, I think, two dominant values. The first rests on the
proposition that the life of the imagination is of central importance,
and has been from the beginnings. Thus all modern discussion of the
value of myth as nourishing, not only the imagination but the deep soils
of the unconscious, appears to me valid. We do wrong to bar fairy tales
from our children on the grounds that they minister to the desires for
power, for violence of action in adventure and warfare, for worlds in
which good and evil are seen in white and black. Should we not look at
The Wanderings of Oisin in the same light as Tolkien's *Lord of the Rings,*
and speculate whether the immense vogue of this last (which C.S.
Lewis once called 'the greatest achievement of the human imagination
since Spenser's *Faerie Queene')* is not because the modern consciousness
clutches at such tales to feed its starved soul?

> Mere dreams, mere dreams! Yet Homer had not sung
> Had he not found it certain beyond dreams
> That out of life's own self-delight had sprung
> The abounding glittering jet ... [1]

I am convinced that these are perennial aspects of the human psyche,
and that we disregard them at our peril.

But I would argue that out of them, as Yeats handles them, come
certain other values of importance. Much of the early poetry is
concerned with young love; its yearnings, its adoration of the eternal
woman — *das Ewigweibliche* — embodied in the Beloved. Much of it
deals with the delighted senses of youth in that whole context, and
sadness when that delight is seen to be evanescent. These are facts: we
mock them at our peril. And I would think further, that the ceremonies of love and courtship that these poems nourish are love's
integral parts, perhaps a training for that ceremony which was once,
and may be again, an essential preparation for married love and life, and
on which Yeats insists, repeatedly, directly or by implication, in the
mature poems. Perhaps I should develop this point. One aspect of love
is its inherent ambivalence. The greatest love-poetry, Shakespeare's
and Donne's, is intensely aware of this, and has the courage to state it:

> 'Two loves have I of comfort and despair.'

Within the whole range of Yeats's work we can trace a growing complexity, a closer approach to observed truth, in these attitudes. Love
may have

> ... spider's eye
> To find out some appropriate pain —
> Aye, though all passion's in the glance —
> For every nerve, and tests a lover

1. 'Ancestral Houses'

> With cruelties of Choice and Chance;
> And when at last that murder's over
> Maybe the bride-bed brings despair,
> For each an imagined image brings
> And finds a real image there . . .[1]

Against that we may set the ending of that too-little-considered poem,
'The Gift of Harun Al-Rashid':

> A woman's beauty is a storm-tossed banner;
> Under it wisdom stands, and I alone —
> Of all Arabia's lovers I alone —
> Nor dazzled by the embroidery, nor lost
> In the confusion of its night-dark folds,
> Can hear the armed man speak.

$viii

But out of this comes another value, which seems to me important.
It is not easy to pick up a book of poetry, or short stories, or criticism
of the last few years, which does not employ, as standard English, the
four-letter words which, up to 1939, no civilized writer would have
thought of using. Nor would one have found the constant and I think
tedious references to the functions of the body. Here I complain, not
on moral grounds, but on those of taste and breeding; even more on their
ineffectiveness because they short-circuit (as it were) much of the
traditional imagery of the nobility of the body's temple that rever-
berates below the surface. In the passage I have just quoted the images
of

> nor lost
> In the confusion of its night-dark folds. . .

are as rich and ambiguous as those in Spenser's *Epithalamion* and
Prothalamion, or certain poems of Blake; or in that ultimate source
of so much Western love-poetry, *The Song of Solomon.* In this reticence,
reliance on traditional imagery I find, not only that 'high breeding that
is the essence of all style', but one reason for the energy and power of
this kind of poetry. And I find in it one aspect of the value of tradition;
so much vulgarity in literature seems to me provincial; designed to 'épater
le bourgeois imaginaire', who has long since ceased to read it.

$ix

'The stars move still, time runs, the clock will strike'.

For each of us is, perhaps, his own Faust. I do not think it wrong
to suggest to you that certain cardinal virtues and values still stand,
though some may have seemed to have tottered a little in the last two
decades. One is patriotism, which still seems to me important so long
as it does not become chauvinistic,. or when ill-judged emotion blinds

---

1. 'Solomon and the Witch'

men to what Sir Thomas Browne calls 'the great mutations of the world'. Another is courage, that is in part physical but far more mental: in particular, courage in defeat. We may quote (for it is not untypical of several others) the poem for Lady Gregory, 'To a Friend whose Work has Come to Nothing':

> Now all the truth is out,
> Be secret and take defeat
> From any brazen throat,
> For how can you compete,
> Being honour bred, with one
> Who, were it proved he lies,
> Were neither shamed in his own
> Nor in his neighbours' eyes?
> Bred to a harder thing
> Than Triumph, turn away
> And like a laughing string
> Whereon mad fingers play
> Amid a place of stone,
> Be secret and exult,
> Because of all things known
> That is most difficult.

We need not think that courage is wholly an aristocratic virtue, Yet part of the attack on Yeats is founded on his snobbishness, his concern with aristocracy. Snobbishness I would define as the desire for inclusion, for false reasons, in a particular social class; but manifestly a desire which is unsure of itself, or is attempting to attain a new social level, which is not certified by traditional achievements, and which is not moderated in its attempts by a sense of humour. It may easily be made to appear anti-democratic: and we remember Tolstoi's massive attack on Shakespeare on just those grounds. But the desire for the aristocratic virtues may be readily distorted into an authoritarianism; which in turn brings in the terrible 'loaded' emotive words, Fascism, Communism, Imperialism, Nazism, Racialism, in particular: perhaps there are now being hatched Black Power, Integration, and others of which I do not know.

It is well to remember Robert Bridges in *The Testament of Beauty* (that great book which is too little read):

> The thicket of the people will take furtive fire
> From irresponsible catchwords of live ideas . . .

I do not wish to cross swords with Professor Conor Cruise O'Brien over Yeats's 'Fascism', or with the recent book, Mr. John Harrison's *The Reactionaries;* noting only that Mr. Harrison places Wyndham Lewis, Pound, D.H. Lawrence in the same condemnation with Yeats. But what I would assert is, briefly, as follows:

The modern political dilemma is that of democracy, slow and cumbrous in time of trouble, hesitant, often wrong-headed in its findings: set against some form of leadership, whether single or collective, which has the equipment, mental or physical, to exercise swift and decisive intervention in national or supra-national crises.

This is the Swiftian problem of the One against the Many, which Yeats discusses in the Preface to *The Words upon the Window Pane*.

For in the last resort, responsibility for any great action returns always to one man. This is one of the points made in the poem 'Long-Legged Fly', and indeed in all the 'heroic' poems. It is confirmed, in every detail, by the history of warfare.

If the man at the top, exercising the power to command, succeeds, he becomes a hero. If not, a Dictator, Führer, what you like. We may note that in present day Europe the two ascriptions are not necessarily incompatible.

The Celtic mythology and history on which Yeats drew so largely is of its very nature, aristocratic, authoritarian, violent, often bad-tempered; in other words 'heroic' in its celebration of individuals. So the leaders of the Rising had their heroic cult of Cuchulain:

When Pearse summoned Cuchulain to his side,
What stalked through the Post Office?

So also the work of Yeats's friend William Morris, and his impassioned re-casting of the traditional epics and sagas of the North.

In estimating the situation in which 'Fascism' emerges we have to assess, as objectively as we can, its social, political and economic contexts. As regards Ireland, we have not yet had a definitive and unbiassed history of the events of violence and suppression of free speech which were part of the background of certain counties in Ireland over the period from, say, 1926 (the murder of Kevin O'Higgins) to 1933. When that has been written — and it will be an interesting piece of objective research — we shall be able to estimate more accurately the background in which bands of law-abiding citizens set themselves up to restore local law, order and the right of free speech, having found that legitimate governmental means had failed them; and that a rough justice of counter-violence was, in their view, necessary.

I can find no better words to express my own point of view than those of a recent reviewer of Harrison's *The Reactionaries,*

'It is quite true that these writers (Pound, Lawrence, Yeats, Eliot) often displayed "aristocratic", "authoritarian", or "élitist" tendencies. But so has every great writer in history. Art is a matter of quality not of quantity. Its production is an "authoritarian", "aristocratic", or "élitist" activity conducted by individuals for individuals (who do not, however numerous, constitute a "mass"), in which democratic concepts merely lack relevance.

'It is true, of course, that Yeats and Eliot were critical of those populist and pseudo-scientific notions, or ideologies which (as they saw it) were combining with the gross effects of plutocracy to destroy tradition, corrupt civilisation, make a farce of eduction, debase politics, abolish the sense of history, devalue language, flatter the worst in each of us, and, in effect, to promote moral, intellectual, and social anarchy. But is there one single indisputably "great" imaginative writer of the past century and a half (to go back no further) who has not, in one way or another, been so preoccupied? Surely it is an odd view of history which holds that such preoccupations have been responsible, even indirectly, for the oppressions, genocides, liquidations, and other maniacal torments of recent years . . .

'It is true that Eliot, Yeats, and the rest were critical of demagogic politicians whose idea of democratic statesmanship appeared to be no higher that the adman's technique of flattering, misguiding, and manipulating human "masses" increasingly vulnerable to new instruments of persuasion and deception; but is this proof that they rejected "a liberal, democratic, humanitarian society" in favour of a "cruel, authoritarian, bellicose society"?

'Mr. Harrison simplifies to absurdity, in short, the enormously complex connection between a "free" writer's "beliefs" and his work. He is unduly selective in his quotations. He buttresses his special pleading with references to commentaries of doubtful value. He does not define his terms. He makes no attempt to examine the general assumptions of the societies in which these writers lived. And in the end he dodges the real issues by planting full responsibility for the ills which these writers recognised (and which he acknowledges) on "science" and "the continual threat of mass destruction".

'This is a great deal too easy. The essential freedom of an imaginative writer, as Anthony Cronin recently put it, is that freedom demanded by Yeats's father when he told his son that "a poet, of all mortals, is, or should be, freest to declare his belief in God in the morning and his disbelief in the evening," or when he argued that "nobody could say what Shakespeare's beliefs were because he had so many." I do not think Mr. Harrison has much sympathy with this view. Nevertheless, the prime subject of Mr. Harrison's specimens was the human condition and the forces that diminish it: "the oppressor's wrong, the proud man's contumely. The insolence of office . . ." They stood, each in his own (often absurd) way, *contra mundum*; but that is precisely how any artist of genius and integrity must stand when the general assumptions of society cannot be shared by those free spirits whose function is to be the very consciousness of their nations. They meant what they said — but not, I think, in the way Mr. Harrison seems to take it.

'I learned the other day, from an article by Conor Cruise O'Brien, that Mao Tse-tung, asked whether Marxism did not destroy the creative mood, replied: "Yes, it does. It definitely destroys creative moods that are feudal, petty-bourgeois, liberalistic, individualist, nihilist, art for art's sake, aristocratic, decadent, or pessimistic, or every other creative mood that is alien to the masses of the people and to the proletariat." Which disposes smartly of every great writer the West has produced. Bring on the Red Guards.'[1]

§x

I do not find, then, that the term *Fascist* as applied to Yeats is in any way responsible as an indictment: it is, to use Bridges' phrase again, an instance of

'irresponsible catchwords' of live ideas

That Yeats, when consulted about the Blue Shirts, proclaimed that the movement must have a philosophy, and, in that naive belief, propounded a neo-Hegelianism to O'Duffy through a long night's talk: that neither had a clue as to what the other was talking about; that in the belief that it must have Songs, wrote four very bad semi-comic poems; these are matters of record.[2] That he approved an hierarchical system of order, of 'degree', as Shakespeare did, is also clear.[3] In his eyes it was only too clear that 'discord' had followed the breaking of 'degree' of authority, of political and moral discipline; believing indeed that with the new faces and the new policies of the early 1930s he and his friends were 'thrown upon this filthy modern tide'. As a philosophic defence there was, at the last, 'The Black Tower'.

§xi

I return to this matter of the values. I would maintain that all the greatest poetry, from the Bible and Homer onwards, is 'philosophical' in the sense that it embodies, and communicates by its characteristic energy of statements, special attitudes towards 'action', doing; this term 'action' being understood of mental events, and particularly the growth and freedom of the spirit, as well as of physical events such as politics, war, religion, charity, love. I use this term as an extension of Dr. Johnson's 'What should books teach but the art of living?' and of Matthew Arnold's narrower and more difficult (because containing a suggestion of stasis) 'criticism of life'. Yeats's poetry, prose and drama seem to me 'philosophical' in this sense. It is not possible to do more

1. From a review by Iain Hamilton, *Illustrated London News* 17 Sept, 1966.
2. I am indebted here to Capt. Dermott MacManus.
3. *cf. Troilus and Cressida.*

than to gesture towards some of the resultant attitudes; but I have tried to isolate some of them as propositions. Among them —

That our first knowledge of 'romantic' or adolescent love is a universal and ennobling experience;[1] and that the lament for its pain or its passing is both natural, and an essential factor in our growth as we come to terms with that loss.[2]

That love passes through various stages of experience, loss of innocence, self-knowledge,[3] to a balance or tension in which bodily love is set against spiritual love,[4] *amor* against *caritas*. But these two dichotomies are reconciled *only* in the poetic statement itself.[5]

That there are moral and ethical justifications for imagining that love endures beyond the grave.[6]

That the supranatural world, the 'cloud of witnesses', is about us; in the Great Memory; in the honour paid to our ancestors;[7] in the sense of the enduring *numen* of the holy places of Ireland;[8] in the poems of country and our debt to it, and our striving for a unity with that country.[9]

That the dead and their wisdom may provide clues (however tenuous the thread) to our own death and after life; and that we do wrong to neglect them. How we may sleep to dream,[10] what dolphins may carry us to the further shore,[11] whether we are to be embodied as Yeats believed, in some terrible circle of reincarnation, imposed or self-chosen[12] what company of saints may greet us — these have been traditional concerns of poetry from the Book of Job onwards. I do not defend Yeats as an orthodox Christian, in spite of his use of so much Christian imagery. I do maintain that he was religious.

That is a deep and controversial subject; and I would do no more this morning than quote two fragments from Jon Stallworthy's latest book, that reproduces and considers the drafts of 'Under Ben Bulben'. I give them without comment:

> God comes to us in all things — in our
> passing thoughts in the sun in the leaves
> he is all in all this morning . . .[13]

1 'Ephemera', 'The Falling of the Leaves'.
2 'The Lover Tells of the Rose in his Heart'.
3 'Solomon and Sheba'.
4 'The Three Bushes'.
5 Donne's 'Ecstasy' is one of the archetypes.
6 'Ribh at the Tomb of Baile and Aillinn'.
7 'Pardon, Old Fathers . . .' 'Easter, 1916'.
8 'Stream and Sun at Glendalough': 'The Dancer at Cruachan and on Crô-Patric'.
9 'Old Tom at Cruachan'.
10 'The Tower', III.
11 'Sailing to Byzantium'.
12 'Byzantium': to be broken by the Thirteenth Cone.
13 *Last Poem*. London, 1968, p.221.

> I declare that no evil
> can happen to the soul except
> from the soul — that death
> is a brief parting & a passing sickness
> What matter though the skies
> drop for — children take hands
> & dance.[1]

For all such imaginings there is 'no speech but symbol': which echo in their multiplicity and their divine power of infinite expansion, the 'depths and dream' of our desire.

There are two final propositions regarding Yeats's attitudes: those to Time and to Tragedy. For is not Time a central preoccupation of all great poets? The inexorability of the waves that Shakespeare saw making towards the pebbled beach; the decay of beauty (yet its permanence in our minds and memories); the decay of great civilisations (yet their glory and their monuments given to us). Time is friend, and enemy. His progress may be arrested, perhaps for a moment, perhaps eternally, by some perception, a sonnet or a symbol; a nightingale, a Grecian Urn, a long-dead city, a Quattrocento picture, the Sistine Chapel, an island in a lake, a mountain tomb, a girl dancing by the sea-shore.

The second is the awareness of Tragedy. In our century Yeats alone of all the great writers has written of it, and what philosophy we may deduce from its fact or experience, with full understanding. That his vision of Tragedy is achieved and maintained with dignity, courage, and a total lack of that most terrible of vices, self-pity: that it is focussed on its traditional objects of Pity and Fear: that Yeats brings to it a characteristic virtue of what he calls *gaiety*: these I would maintain.

Towards such things we may and should gesture in all that we discuss and learn. But in the last resort we are concerned with things — I use Wordsworth's phrase —

> embodied in the mystery of words.

Why should it be that these shadowy, complex, bright and terrible things, their music and their mystery of words, that are in the last resort beyond analysis or explanation — why should they have that power, to make us 'better' than we are? I return, as I do so often, to that Greek or Sicilian critic, 'Longinus' for a sentence of explanation. It is the suggestion that, in reading great poetry, we become full and strange participants, re-creators, even (for a moment) poets ourselves:

> "For our souls are somehow naturally exalted by the true
> sublime, and become as it were a horse prancing or
> rearing, are filled with joy and exultation *as if they themselves
> had produced what they hear.*"[2]

1. *Last poems*, p.225.
2. 'Longinus', *On the Sublime*, vii.